PETER UNDERWOOD'S
—GUIDE TO—
GHOSTS
& HAUNTED PLACES

PIATKUS

Also by Peter Underwood

Death in Hollywood: The Lives, Loves and Deaths of Hollywood's Brightest Stars
Nights in Haunted Houses
Irish Haunted Houses
A Ghost Hunter's Almanac
Ghosts – And How to See Them
This Haunted Isle
The Ghost Hunter's Guide
Queen Victoria's Other World
Dictionary of the Supernatural
The Ghost Hunters: Who They Are and What They Do
Haunted London
Into the Occult
Deeper Into the Occult
Gazetteer of British Ghosts (*re-issued as* The A – Z of British Ghosts)
Gazetteer of Scottish and Irish Ghosts
Hauntings: New Light on Ten Famous Cases
A Host of Hauntings
A Ghost Hunter's Handbook
Ghosts of Cornwall
Ghosts of Devon
Ghosts of Somerset
Ghosts of Dorset
Ghosts of Wiltshire
West Country Hauntings
Mysterious Places
Ghosts and Phantoms of the West
Ghostly Encounters
Ghosts of North West England
Ghosts of Wales
Ghosts of Kent
Ghosts of Hampshire and the Isle of Wight
The Ghosts of Borley: A critical history of 'the most haunted house in England' (*with Dr Paul Tabori*)
The Vampire's Bedside Companion
The Complete Book of Dowsing and Divining
Lives to Remember: A Casebook on Reincarnation (*with Leonard Wilder*)
Jack the Ripper: One Hundred Years of Mystery
No Common Task: The Autobiography of A Ghost Hunter
Horror Man – The Life of Boris Karloff
Life's a Drag – A Life of Danny la Rue
Thirteen Famous Ghost Stories (*Editor*)

© 1996 Peter Underwood

First published in 1996 by
Judy Piatkus (Publishers) Ltd
5 Windmill Street, London W1P 1HF

www.piatkus.co.uk

This paperback edition published in 1999

The right of Peter Underwood to be identified as Author of this Work has been asserted by him in accordance with the Copyright, Designs and Patents Act 1988

A catalogue record for this book is available from the British Library

ISBN 0–7499–1800–4 pbk

Edited by Carol Franklin
Designed by Neil Sayer

Printed and bound in Great Britain by Mackays of Chatham PLC

This book is for
our friends
SHEILA and PHIL MERRITT
of Santa Clara, California
with happy memories
and good wishes always

ACKNOWLEDGEMENTS

For help in many ways in the compilation of this book I acknowledge with gratitude the assistance I have received from many people and especially my wife Joyce, my son Chris, my daughter Pamela and also Matthew Adams, Marc Alexander, Dennis Bardens, the Duke and Duchess of Bedford, John Bellars, Professor Hans Bender, Chili Bouchier, Tom Brown, Adele Butler, Tonia Campbell, Dame Barbara Cartland, Arthur C. Clarke, Dame Catherine Cookson, Revd John C. Dening, Charles and Lorraine Doerrer of New York, Dan Farson, John Fuller, John Godl of Sydney, Australia, Walter Goldsmith, Dulcie Gray and Michael Denison, Sir John Gielgud, Angela Hallam, Kevin Harvey, Miss Hislett, George Hoare, Hans Holzer, Rex Keating, Trevor J. Kenward, Joanna Lumley, Sir Peter Mansfield, Dr Kenneth McAll, Patricia McCaldin, Mrs E. McEvoy, Ian G. McIntosh, Laurie McQuary, Sheila Merritt, Philip Moore, Andrew Murphy, Dr A.R.G. Owen, Sir Reresby Sitwell, Mrs E. Southgate, Mr and Mrs James Le Gendre Starkie, Graham and Vera Stringer, Stuart Walker, Jack Watling, J.W. Whyle, Lt. Col. Patrick Wootton, Mrs I.E. Will of Australia and Basil Wright.

CONTENTS

Introduction   1

1   Ghost Hunting – the Practicalities   8
2   Hauntings in Castles and Stately Homes   19
3   Ghosts in the Public Domain   35
4   Investigations in Haunted Houses   67
5   Haunted Battlefields   94
6   Haunted Trees   109
7   Ghosts and Famous People   121
8   Haunted Inanimate Objects   135
9   Aerial Phenomena   148
10   Ghosts and Animals   165
11   Time Slips and Cyclic Ghosts   177
12   Poltergeists   193
     Bibliography   212
     Index   213

INTRODUCTION

G hosts seem to have been experienced since biblical times and certainly Shakespeare talks of them quite naturally, as do other historical figures of stature.

The mystery of ghosts and haunted houses is a subject that has puzzled and fascinated people since the beginning of recorded history, and doubtless even longer. The younger Pliny (*c*.61 – *c*.113) was 'induced to believe' in ghosts because of two authentic cases that came to his attention. One was that of a house in Athens where the appearance of a ghost was accompanied by the sound of rattling chains, manifestations that caused the house to stand vacant until Athenodorus, a philosopher who knew the history and reputation of the house, took over the property.

One night the ghost appeared to Athenodorus as he sat working at his desk, and it seemed to beckon him. The philosopher took up a lamp and followed the apparition into the courtyard, where it vanished. Next morning Athenodorus informed the authorities and asked them to dig on the spot where he had seen the ghost vanish. They did so, and found the bones of a man loaded with chains. After the remains were given a decent burial there was no more trouble in the house.

In 1570 Lewes Lavater published *On Ghostes and Spirites Walking by Night* – a source book for the Elizabethans, including Shakespeare – and a curious work for the times in which it appeared. The author concluded, just like many modern psychical researchers, that while there are many impostures, there are also genuine ghostly appearances. In 1977 and 1978 a haunted council house at Enfield was the subject of exhaustive, continuous and detailed investigation; some of the most elaborate ever undertaken. This was the poltergeist infestation known as 'the Enfield case', a resumé of which appears in Chapter 12. These are just three examples of the wide scope of material available for consideration.

Stories of ghosts are an important tradition in Britain and indeed throughout the world. Thousands of books have been written about them, fictional and factual, frightening and funny, sceptical and serious. There have been films, plays, songs, cartoons and television shows devoted to ghosts and three of Shakespeare's greatest plays, *Macbeth*, *Hamlet* and *Julius Caesar*, revolve around ghostly appearances. It is hardly possible to talk to anyone these days without being told that they know someone who has had a ghostly experience; after all it is generally accepted that each of us has a one in ten chance of seeing a ghost during our lifetime. Whether we know when we have seen one is another matter for most contemporary ghosts appear to be solid and act naturally, so it may well be that the percentage of people who see ghosts is higher than we think.

Books purporting to detail true ghostly experiences appear almost daily, but this comprehensive work aims to show that authentic ghosts and hauntings are still being encountered in all parts of the world, in all sorts of conditions and they are being carefully investigated and explored by responsible people.

> ... *O'er all there hung the shadow of a fear,*
> *A sense of mystery the spirit daunted,*
> *And said, as plain as whisper in the ear,*
> *The place is Haunted!*

These last lines from 'The Haunted House', a famous poem by Thomas Hood, described by Edgar Allan Poe as 'one of the truest poems by one of the noblist poets', runs to 352 lines and was first published in 1845, before the Fox sisters brought about the birth of modern spiritualism, before the assassination of President Abraham Lincoln, and before the foundation at Cambridge University of The Ghost Society in 1851, the first organisation with a scientific outlook on matters that, if established, completely alter our prospect on life as we know it.

Members of that original and unique club included Edward White Benson, eventually to become Archbishop of Canterbury, and Arthur Balfour, later to be Prime Minister.

Through membership of The Ghost Club Society and other organisations concerned with the serious exploration and investigation of the paranormal including The Society for Psychical Research, The Metaphysical Society, The Psychic Research Organisation, The College of Psychic Studies, The International Ghost Society and The Unitarian

Society for Psychic Studies, I have been fortunate enough to meet and talk with many well-known people in the psychic world and in fact from many other walks of life, and I shall introduce some of them throughout the course of this book, people like Lord Dowding, Dennis Wheatley, Paul Getty and Robert Graves.

I became interested in ghosts and ghostly activity at a very early age. As a schoolboy I used to spend large parts of my summer holidays with my grandparents who had farmed at Rose Hall Farm at Sarratt in Hertfordshire, which had long been associated with a fascinating ghost story.

Catherine Crowe in her *Night Side of Nature* (1848) tells of a visitor to the farm and his first-hand experience of this apparition and the haunted house in Sarratt. I paraphrase Mrs Crowe's somewhat verbose account:

Falling asleep quickly after a tiring journey a visitor and stranger to the area awakened in the four-poster bedstead to hear dogs barking and he heard his host, in the adjoining bedroom, open his window and quieten them. He went back to sleep only to be soon awakened once again, this time by an extraordinary pressure upon his feet. As he opened his eyes he saw, by the light in the chimney-corner, the figure of a well-dressed man in the act of stooping and supporting himself on the bedstead.

The figure wore a blue coat with bright gilt buttons but the head was not visible because of the bed-curtains, looped back and concealing that part of his person. In his haste to get into bed the visitor had dropped his clothes at the foot of the bed and his first thought was that it must be his host picking them up, which rather surprised him, but he raised himself upright in the bed and was about to enquire the reason for the visit, when the figure was suddenly no longer there!

Realising that he had locked the door and becoming more and more puzzled, the house-guest jumped out of bed and carefully searched the room. He found the door still locked on the inside, the window closed and fastened and nothing under the bed or up the chimney, in fact no trace whatever of his mysterious visitor. He noticed that the time was ten minutes after two and he returned to bed hoping for some rest but he was unable to get back to sleep and he lay there until about seven o'clock, puzzling his brain as to how his visitor could have entered and left the room.

In the morning when his host asked how he had slept, he mentioned first that he had been awakened by the barking of the dogs. His host apologised and told him that two strange dogs had found their way into the yard and he had called to his own dogs. Then the visitor mentioned his curious experience fully expecting that this would be explained or laughed at, but to his surprise the story received serious attention and he was told that there was a tradition of such a spectre haunting that one room.

It seemed that many years before a gentleman so attired had been murdered in the room under 'frightful circumstances' and his head cut off. From time to time people occupying the room claimed to see the highly coloured figure, but the head was never seen. As proof of the story the visitor was invited to prolong his visit to be introduced to the rector of the parish who would furnish him with such evidence as to leave no doubt in his mind but that the room was haunted. But the thought of another night at Rose Hall was frightening to the traveller and he took his leave.

In the nineteenth century the ghost had been so troublesome that a prayer-meeting had been held at Rose Hall but, like many exorcisms, it was unsuccessful. I once took a party of friends to Rose Hall and without my giving any hints three of them immediately located the haunted room.

Staying with my grandparents as a boy of perhaps ten or eleven years of age it was not unusual for a stranger to appear at the door asking whether they might see the 'haunted room' and at a very early age I was delegated to lead the way to the room in question and then to relate the ghost story. At first I always recounted the story in a fairly light-hearted way, finding it difficult to accept that grown-up people could believe that there really were ghosts!

But soon the reactions of the visitors and their not infrequent comments when I had finished, often on the lines of 'Well, we're not surprised because we have a ghost . . .', caused me to think that perhaps there was more in this idea of ghosts than I had at first thought and before long I began keeping notes of the personal ghost stories people related to me.

In the years that followed I became more and more interested in ghosts and I not only collected a mass of first-hand experience of people who thought they had seen ghosts but I soon began to make a point of visiting allegedly haunted houses, and as I grew older, spending nights in haunted rooms, and learning everything I could from anyone who would help me. Eventually, this led to my carrying out investigations for and on behalf of The Ghost Club Society, The Society for Psychical Research, The College of Psychic Studies, The Psychic Research Organisation and other like-minded bodies.

It is indisputable, on the available evidence, that apparitions of dead people have formed a part of human experience through the centuries, not only in England, Scotland, Wales and Ireland, but also throughout the world. There can be no doubt that even in this prosaic age, men and women with sound minds and sound bodies do sometimes see ghosts of dead persons in circumstances that rule out illusion or deception.

It is odd how things turn out. Borley Rectory in Essex (built in 1863 and destroyed by fire in 1939) was long known as 'the most haunted house in England' and it is a fact that everyone who lived there, four successive rectors, their wives and families – not to mention scores of visitors – all asserted that they heard, saw and felt things they could not explain. A ghost nun reportedly haunted the garden and churchyard for more than 50 years and there was unexplained bell-ringing, footsteps, whisperings, cold spots, fires, materialisation and de-materialisation of physical objects, lights, written messages and noises of practically every description. On a personal note I have talked with nearly a hundred first-hand witnesses of apparently paranormal activity at Borley – and I still get reports of curious happenings in the church and churchyard just across the road from where the haunted rectory once stood.

When I visited Borley accompanied by my friend Tom Brown one spring day in 1947 the thought never occurred to me that in the years that followed I would contact and personally interview practically everyone who had ever had anything to do with 'the most haunted house in England' and that I would come to be regarded as one of the experts on that remarkable case of haunting: having visited the area many, many times for the purpose of investigation, exploration and delectation; having written the book that has been considered to be the best of a dozen written on the Borley haunting; and having advised the BBC and independent television companies here and abroad on Borley and other hauntings. Perhaps the time has come to re-examine some of the wonderful, remarkable and memorable experiences I have had, walking along the edge of the unknown.

For some lucky people ghosts undoubtedly exist; but is their evidence objective? Or are their 'ghosts' really nothing more than imagination with no objective reality outside the minds of those who see them or think they see them? I hope to explore this question and invite you to step with me into the realm of the unknown.

At the same time we have to be as careful in accepting all experiences as we have to be careful in accepting translations from other languages. There is a story concerning an investigator who took a simple phrase, 'Out of sight, out of mind', translated it into French, then into Chinese, then back into English and it came back, 'Invisible, insane'.

Having been President and Chief Investigator of the leading para-normal investigative organisation in Britain for over 30 years it may be that I owe it to the readers of my previous 40 books to take them behind the scenes, reveal some of the secrets, and express and explore some of my conclusions in this difficult but totally fascinating field.

I have repeatedly noticed in my many investigations that structural alterations to the allegedly haunted house often affect the haunting. Occasionally an old house is quiet and without any apparitions or reports of anything like a haunting and then, following structural alterations, paranormal activity begins, almost as though a lid has been opened. But more often when supernormal happenings have been continuing for some time and then structural alterations are carried out – the disturbances completely cease, almost as though a lid has been closed.

Algernon Blackwood used to say that adventures come to the adventurous. Perhaps he was right. At all events I have rarely missed the opportunity to spend a night in a really haunted house and I have had more than a few adventures!

In the following pages I shall explore the evidence, based on my personal experience, of traditional and historical ghosts, characteristically haunted places like rectories, churches, theatres, hospitals and inns, specific hauntings that I have investigated, how investigations are carried out, poltergeists, haunted trees, battlefields, inanimate objects, time slips, the relationship between animals and ghosts, aerial phenomena and some interesting stories about ghosts and famous people. Sometimes it really does seem that all houses 'wherein men live' are haunted, but let me say at once that I have long ago come to the conclusion that there is nothing to fear from ghosts who mostly seem to be in a different dimension. As Franklin D. Roosevelt used to say: 'The only thing we have to fear is fear itself', so let us see what we can discover about ghosts, poltergeists and spontaneous psychical activity in general.

Peter Underwood
Savage Club
1, Whitehall Place
London SW1A 2HD

CHAPTER ONE

GHOST HUNTING – THE PRACTICALITIES

I have long ago lost count of the allegedly haunted houses I have visited for the purpose of investigating the reported paranormal activity, to explore the unknown, to hunt the ghosts.

PSYCHICAL INVESTIGATIONS PAST AND PRESENT

Perhaps the first real psychical investigation or ghost hunt I took part in was at a gloomy house called Woodfield in Aspley Guise in Bedfordshire in 1947, while one of the more recent was at Old Battersea House in London in 1992, the English home of the fabulously wealthy Forbes family of America.

At Woodfield colleague Tom Brown and I did little more than watch and listen but we learned valuable lessons for future investigations, not least that to learn to listen carefully to what is related to you can tell you far more than the relator intends. Also, to observe as much as you can at all times is one of the chief functions and duties of an investigator, and here again he or she can learn a great deal about the house and its occupants.

Woodfield had once been an inn and there had long been stories of thwarted lovers, the daughter of the innkeeper and her sweetheart, being put to death – perhaps unintentionally – by the irate landlord and the bodies being inadvertently discovered by a highwayman who remained silent on condition that he could use the inn as a hiding place. The bodies of the young lovers were buried in the cellar of the house but soon their ghosts haunted the house and the garden; the ghost of the contrite innkeeper had been seen inside the house and a ghostly highwayman on horseback haunted the grounds, visually and audibly, repeatedly being seen and heard entering the grounds through a hedge where once there had been an authorised entrance.

In the company of H.W. Richards of Luton Area Assessment Board, mediums Florence Thompson and George Kenneth, Dr Donald J. West, then Research Officer of the Society for Psychical Research, and others we explored every inch of the house and garden, looked closely at the cellar where the bodies were buried and also examined the cupboard where the young couple were left to die, and listened to the evidence of the occupants, the owner of the property and various local inhabitants.

I have never forgotten arriving for the first time at the gaunt and gloomy house in gathering darkness; sitting in at the seances in a room cluttered with furniture, glass and ornaments accumulated over many years and listening to stories of loud flapping noises, of apparitions inside and outside the house, of disembodied arms and phantom hoofbeats and shadowy forms. We listened and we learned. We took nothing with us but a notepad, pen and torch.

This is a far cry from later haunted house investigations which have included several cameras, tripods and stands and two large suitcases of ghost hunting equipment containing a dozen thermometers of various kinds, sound recording apparatus, magnetometers (for measuring magnetic forces), movement sensitive alarms, ESP or Zener (for more on these see page 16) cards and word-association tests.

CONSCIOUS OR UNCONSCIOUS FRAUD

Before going about investigating a haunting these days it is necessary to establish to your own satisfaction that the case warrants serious consideration. This can usually be established during the course of a preliminary visit. There are a great many lonely people about and visits from enthusiastic people with interesting ideas and plans for all-night vigils brings some welcome attention and variation from routine; it is necessary to make quite sure that what is reported to be happening is, in all probability, really taking place, that it is objective and not subjective and existing only in the imagination or wishful thinking of the individual or individuals concerned.

Here are some instances from my personal experience of situations where things were not quite what they appeared to be. Some 'phantom music' was brought to my attention by a leading psychical research society, music that had been heard by several investigators from various organisations which were convinced that the music was paranormal. I made a preliminary visit and the occupant of the house on the south coast, a widower, sat in a chair with padded arms and told me about the music that was heard in all the rooms in the house and of the interesting people who had come to see him and had heard the music for themselves; music that might be heard at any time....

After a little while I thought I could hear faint music from an adjoining room and, accepting my host's smiling invitation to investigate, I found that the very next room when I opened the door was full of music. I then heard different music from another room and there too the music seemed to fill the air.

My new acquaintance suggested a cup of tea when I rejoined him and he left the room to prepare it. I took the opportunity to look all round the room but could find nothing suspicious. Finding myself beside my host's chair, which looked very comfortable with its padded seat, back and arms, I sat down in it and, putting an arm on the armrest, felt a number of bumps underneath the upholstery. I pressed one and the music came again from the adjoining room, I pressed another bump and different music came from another room! My new friend came running into the room, grinning and not in the least put out. 'Ah! you've found my little secret, have you?' he said. 'Well, it gave me a lot of pleasure fixing it all up and I've had a lot of fun meeting all sorts of interesting people... well, there's nothing you can do about it, you know, I've never claimed it was ghostly music; people came, heard the music and told me it was "paranormal"! Anyway, it will all be removed tomorrow and there won't be any proof of anything ... and no more music – what a pity!'

Some months later a psychical research society asked me whether I would like to explore a curious case of haunting, a ghost dog that barked in answer to questions. When they told me the name of the man who lived in the house of the barking dog, down on the south coast, I told them I wouldn't bother to visit!

I was once called to investigate apparent poltergeist activity that seemed to focus on the young teenage daughter of the house where she lived with her mother and stepfather. In particular a plant-pot seemed to attract the 'geist' and was mysteriously moved on many occasions during the hours of darkness to various parts of the house including the stepfather's room which was kept locked and into which the girl was forbidden to venture.

Having talked with the three inhabitants I was suspicious of the possibility that a human hand was responsible for much of what was happening, and with the permission of the husband and wife I spent some hours exploring the property and talking with the occupants separately. In the end I 'doctored' the plant-pot so that if it was moved it would leave a minute trail of fine sand. This was very simply accomplished by inserting a quantity of silver sand beneath the plant in the pot and drilling a small hole in the bottom of the pot. In addition, after the daughter had retired on the night I had chosen for my tests to be explored, I smeared substances around her bedroom door and doorway so that if she opened the door and left the room she would betray what she had done and where she had gone by purple dye on her hands, and by flour and soot on her feet.

Later that night the plant was found in the stepfather's locked room but I was able to trace a trail of sand back to the girl's bedroom from where she had ingeniously transported the plant-pot by climbing in and out of the windows, thus avoiding the locked door. An examination of the girl's hands and feet revealed traces of the marker material and I left shortly afterwards convinced – as were the girl's mother and stepfather – that here was one house *not* haunted by a poltergeist!

In fact fraud plays only a small part in reported paranormal activity, although a large percentage of ghost reports have a natural and mundane explanation. In the dead of night wails and whistlings that sound distinctly unearthly may be due to a central-heating boiler flue where slight damage turns it into a woodwind instrument when the wind is in the right direction; nocturnal footsteps may be the result of floorboards and furniture cooling; a shadowy figure may turn out to be a jacket or a dress hanging in a peculiar way on the end of the bed or on the back of a door; strange moving lights may be a trick of the moonlight; taps may be the branch of a tree blowing in the wind and sometimes touching the window. Animals moving in the darkness, paper or cloth fluttering in the wind, animal and bird cries, rattling tiles and guttering that may not be noticed in daylight; tricks of light and shade and self-deception in the form of waking dreams and wish-fulfilment – the strong but uncon- scious wish to experience something of a paranormal nature – all such possibilities and much more must be considered and examined. A cardinal rule in the investigation of hauntings is *always* look very carefully for a normal explanation before considering the possibility of a supernormal source. In my experience you will find a natural expla- nation nine times out of ten.

VIOLENCE AND HIGH EMOTION

In those cases where there does not seem to be a rational explanation for what is going on it will often be found that some violent or highly emotional event has taken place at the affected house. I talked to Professor Henry Habberley Price, Professor of Logic at New College, Oxford, on this very subject. He told me he was interested in the effect of electro-magnetism on the human body's system. Since it is known that naturally occurring materials such as stone and wood have very low but measurable magnetic fields it seemed reasonable, he felt, to assume that buildings constructed with these materials also produce such fields. Indeed, he suggested that a building's own magnetic field might be minimally altered because of some highly emotional event, which he called a 'psychic charge'. He believed that human beings, experiencing some violently stressful emotion such as suicide or murder, could become unwitting transmitters of a faint signal which endured in the building as a psychic charge and other human beings in the vicinity could become receivers. In receiving the signal from such a charge the percipient 'sees' an apparition of the person who first transmitted the charge.

CARRYING OUT AN INVESTIGATION

Should your preliminary visit convince you that there may be something worth investigating there is much you can and should do before you attempt to carry out any practical investigation. Maps and early documents devoted to the area can often be of interest and a visit to the local museum or contact with any local archaeological society can produce basic knowledge of the area and its buildings. It can also provide information about earthquakes, landslides and the where-abouts of rivers and streams, pools and lakes and underground water. There is a theory that water running underground through streams, old sewers and so on beneath or close to the foundations of a house, may subject that property to spasmodic thrusts as the water builds up and such jolts might cause objects in the house to move, while the general strain on the house may produce creaks, cracks and groans that sound eerie at night. Such possibilities have to be taken into account depend-ing on the reported supernormal activity. At all events knowledge of previous buildings in the area may produce a clue to any apparitions seen and/or the phenomena reported, while unobtrusive personal enquiry in the immediate area may provide a background to the people concerned and local knowledge and opinion.

It is always necessary to hear the story of the alleged haunting from the people immediately concerned, fully and as comprehensively as possible. Where a couple of people are involved it is a good idea to hear the stories independently if possible. This is where an assistant, associate or colleague comes in useful and they should seek to separate the couple while the initial interview takes place, perhaps on the pretext of seeing another part of the house or garden or being shown the exact site of some manifestation. Afterwards that person may be asked to give his or her story, fully and in their own words, and it is quite surprising how many little discrepancies will become apparent. Dates, times, witnesses – all sorts of things may conflict and need to be ironed out later. It is vital to listen, observe, listen some more and make copious notes all the time.

The precise time of day or night of the actual investigation will depend on what has been learned of the case: whether the manifes-tations occur mainly during the hours of darkness or daylight, whether they occur in any particular part of the house, at any particular time or period, such as when the moon is full, and whether any member of the household is absent or present and so on. The whole purpose, apart from helping to reassure and comfort the people most affected, is to establish that what is happening is objective and not subjective. A simple personal test, incidentally, should anything of an apparently paranormal nature be seen, is to depress one eyeball with one's finger. If the sighting appears to be double, it is objective; if it remains a clear single shape, then it is subjective and has no objective reality outside the head of the person perceiving it.

There is at least one prominent investigator who thinks ghostly activity depends on the moon and it is certainly true that many ghostly demonstrations occur only on nights when the moon is visible. So it may be that moonlit nights are more favourable for ghostly appearances than other nights. In common with so many other aspects of ghosts and ghost investigation this possibility needs looking into and more evidence is needed before any decision can be reached.

GHOST HUNTING APPARATUS

The apparatus taken on any investigative visit will again depend on what has been experienced but on a typical ghost hunt one would expect to take such obvious aids as cameras (together with slow, regular, fast and infra-red films), at least one camera equipped with time exposure facilities and another of the polaroid instant type; notebooks, graph paper (for rough maps and plans), writing implements of various colours; sound recording apparatus (including normal, miniature and very sensitive) with extending leads, thermometers (regular, maximum/minimum and thermographs) and torches of various kinds with spare batteries and bulbs.

Other items in the serious ghost hunter's bag will be several measuring tapes, black cotton and thread, coloured adhesive tape, gummed labels, thin wire and self-adhesive labels and impact adhesive which should enable the investigator to seal rooms, passages, doorways and windows in such a fashion that he knows immediately whether they are opened or used without his knowledge.

Other simple equipment that can be extremely useful on investigations includes tie-on luggage labels; a couple of mirrors, one that can be swivelled in any direction such as an old car rear-view mirror; candles and matches; an assortment of small screws, nails, tin tacks and panel pins, together with a small hammer, screwdriver, bradawl, pliers; also useful is luminous paint and a strain gauge (for measuring the force necessary to close or open a door or drawer), a spring balance (for measuring the weight of any article apparently moved by paranormal means), while each member of the team should have a reliable watch, preferably with luminous dial, and watches should of course be synchronised at the commencement of each investigation; and various transparent envelopes and containers (useful for the preservation of questionable and dubious material).

More ambitious investigators will include in their equipment such items as fully automatic cameras, ciné and still, with remote control; apparatus for measuring atmospheric pressure, wind force and humidity, while such instruments as metal-detectors, walkie-talkie sets, sound-scanners, magnetometers and electric field measuring devices, even closed circuit television, capacity charge recorders, infra-red telescopes and voltmeters are valuable in their way. However I believe that accurate and careful investigation by serious and honest researchers far outweighs such interesting scientific evidence. In fact some of the more sophisticated instruments are too delicate and accurate, so much so that they will even detect the presence and movement of small insects, which can be disconcerting.

I remember one investigation at haunted Borley Church which involved Professor John Taylor, at that time Professor of Mathematics at London University, when equipment employed included a magnetometer for measuring magnetic fields and electric field measuring devices that would indicate television-type waves and those of long-wave radio. Although everyone present was satisfied that the equipment was performing perfectly, nothing unusual was recorded, although more than once the investigators felt 'strange sensations' including a definite coldness and 'a feeling of strength' that seemed to emanate from one spot. Later, at the tower end of the church, the area farthest away from the equipment, one of those present experienced a feeling of distinct unease that he was totally unable to account for.

The sum total of scientifically recorded evidence on that occasion amounted to some slight movements in the area of the font, at the tower end of the church, and one or two blips in the electric field and it could not be certain that these were paranormal in origin, for it was established that at least one bat was inside the church and a number of moths – at least the elaborate equipment proved that much! So it is small wonder that I tend to rely on the more simple equipment and the most reliable of fellow investigators.

PROCEDURES DURING THE INVESTIGATION

Simple gadgets and procedures can often be organised at the scene of the haunting that might be especially applicable in particular cases. Objects that might be evocative, such as a small bell, a simple toy, a photograph, a dagger, a Bible, a crucifix, can be scattered where objects have been moved and each carefully ringed by chalk so that any movement can be measured. Other gadgets include simple electric bells triggered by trip wires; a bowl of mercury that detects tremors; spirit levels that establish or disprove slight movement; a sealed tin full of fine dry sand with a small hole in the base that leaves an almost invisible trail if it is moved. A balanced rod connected to a bell or buzzer reveals the movement of an object placed on one end of the rod; a floor-covered sheet of newspaper reveals footsteps; and spread sugar quickly reveals the presence of someone or possibly some 'thing' by the unmistakable crunch – both substances often exposing a ghost's earthly agent!

It is often useful to establish the telepathic or extra-sensory perception of the human occupants and a pack or two of Zener cards* can provide this information and interest everyone present. Zener cards are packaged in bundles of 25, each bundle comprising 5 cards bearing a simple design: a circle, a star, a cross, a square and a set of wavy lines. The cards are shuffled and the investigator's assistant (the agent) turns the cards over one at a time and the person being tested (the percipient) records his guess as to the identity of the card, while out of sight of the agent and the cards. Such experiments are thought to establish the presence of extra-sensory perception, after taking into account chance expectation.

I have also found routine and specially written intelligence and word-association tests very interesting and often revealing. During one investigation such a test showed without the shadow of a doubt that a little girl was jealous of her baby sister and that her parents were more concerned about the girl's baby sister than about the little girl who

---

* Zener cards are obtainable from the Society for Psychical Research, 49 Marloes Road, London W8 6LA and the Foundation for Research on the Nature of Man, Box 6847, College Station, Durham, NC 27708, USA.

revealed her unconscious – and occasionally conscious – sympathy with the 'poltergeist'.

During any actual investigation rotas will be organised and arranged in which those taking part are regularly employed in checking equipment, making half-hourly patrols and generally ensuring that any happening that may occur is explored, verified, investigated and recorded immediately. It may well be that information obtained at an initial investigation will point the way towards a second investigative visit, when specific areas might be explored in the light of the initial investigation.

John Cutten, one-time Hon. Secretary at the Society for Psychical Research, who spent many nights with me in haunted houses, devised and built a ghost detecting unit that consisted of a camera linked to a tape-recorder, linked to photo-electric cells, linked to a noise and vibration detector, an electric bulb, a sensitive wire circuit and a buzzer. Any noise in the vicinity would result in the automatic exposure of a photograph from the camera, a significant drop in temperature would also cause the camera to operate and in both instances the tape-recorder would be set in motion, and the light and alarm buzzer would operate. There was also a draught detector which would operate the equipment but the trouble was the necessary sensitivity of the equipment; for example someone sneezing in an adjoining room could set the equipment in motion, as could a heavy lorry passing by and causing vibration.

While I am convinced that in all circumstances there is a good argument for simple equipment being just as effective as the most sophisticated apparatus in the investigation of ghostly phenomena, it must be admitted that some of the ingenious instruments that have been devised are interesting and thought-provoking and perhaps valuable to those who consider instruments infallible. In particular, there is the 'spectre detector', designed and built by Dr Alan Gauld and Tony Cornell, which reflects the computer age we live in.

This computer-controlled ghost hunting kit records interference with any one of various senses (temperature, infra-red, ultrasonic etc.), triggers cameras, video-cameras and tape-recorders, and is followed by a detailed print-out of the readings on all the instruments.

In spite of all this it should always be remembered that the value of any report is only as good as the investigators concerned and not really dependent upon the equipment used. A lot of ghost hunting and serious psychical investigation is quietly waiting for ghostly activity that never occurs, but just occasionally, very occasionally, something happens, usually at the least expected moment, that is quite inexplicable in our current knowledge and then all the waiting, all the preparation, all the work and worry is quickly forgiven and forgotten.

CHAPTER TWO

HAUNTINGS IN CASTLES AND STATELY HOMES

In this chapter we look at the many stories of haunted castles and stately homes, and consider whether or not they are anything more than unsubstantiated stories, embroidered with each telling and having no foundation in fact. Indeed, when the average person thinks of a haunted house, it is usually an ancient pile in a lonely area haunted by a ghostly historical figure from the past. In this book I seek to show that there are many other authentic haunted places, people, objects and animals including properties of every age and description but of course there is a tradition of ghosts in castles and stately houses.

If there is anything in the recording stone theory – that on occasions traumatic events are in some way preserved in the very stone of buildings, recordings that rerun spasmodically – then it seems reasonable to accept that the ruins of some buildings may be haunted and certainly there is well-established evidence that some ruins have been the scene of a variety of unexplained happenings. One immediately thinks of Bramber in Sussex; Berry Pomeroy in Devon; Porchester Castle in Hampshire; the Abbey at Bury St Edmunds, Suffolk; Minsden in Hertfordshire; the old palace at Richmond, Surrey; Corfe Castle in Dorset; Bayham Abbey in Sussex; Odiham in Hampshire; the Chateau Gratot near Coutances in France; Gurre Castle north of Copenhagen in Denmark; Ayers Rock, Alice Springs, Australia; Schwarzenberg Fortress near Regensberg, Bavaria; and Bontida Castle, Translyvania.

The stone-tape theory does seem to have quite a lot going for it. The idea that scenes or events from a place's history become trapped in one spot and that years later those snatches from the past are spontaneously rerun, like a video-tape, and can be heard and/or seen by witnesses, is at the very least a plausible and convenient idea that answers such questions as why the same incident is repeatedly reported by generations of witnesses, often people with no knowledge that what they have seen has been previously seen by other people. Two big questions remain: what causes the tape to be recorded in the first place and what decides when it should play? In both cases the answer may lie in the atmospheric conditions and in the human beings present. It may be that certain sympathetic and dominant individuals taking part in a traumatic event under certain conditions may cause the event to be recorded and it may be that similar climatic conditions, and the presence of a sympathetic and commanding influence, may trigger the play button and that once started anyone present may witness the recorded event; *may*, but not necessarily *will*.

GLAMIS CASTLE

Never shall I forget my first view of Glamis Castle, Angus, Scotland's house of mysteries, or my tours of that atmospheric building. The ghost stories of Glamis are numerous, varied and doubtless exaggerated over the centuries, but there is good evidence for ghosts there including 'Earl Beardie', Alexander, fourth Earl of Crawford from the days of James II of Scotland – a ghost seen by, among others, a former Lord Halifax and a relation of Sir Shane Leslie. A ghostly black boy sits by the door of the Queen Mother's Sitting Room and the Queen Mother has herself encountered this phantom on two occasions. A female figure sometimes seen in the vicinity of tower clock is surrounded by a reddish glow; she is thought to be a Lady Glamis who was burned to death on Castle Hill, Edinburgh, charged with witchcraft. And there have been reports of a tall male figure in a dark cloak seen by a Provost of Perth; a woman with mournful eyes and a pale face who peers out of an upper window; a tongueless woman who runs across the park; and a strange, thin man who races up the long drive to the castle and disappears at the doorway. One of the better-authenticated ghosts at Glamis is a Grey Lady seen in recent years by a score of people in exactly the same place in the chapel, as I was told by Lord Strathmore who had seen her himself, as has the Dowager Countess Granville. Glamis is a haunted castle if ever there was one, although as castle factor James Kemp told me, 'the ghostly associations are a feature that is not stressed at the castle ...'.

It seems to me that ghosts and ghostly happenings *have* probably been experienced at Glamis Castle, but not nearly as often or in such spectacular detail as generally related. In actual fact the more recent manifestations of the Grey Lady appear to be well authenticated and more substantial (if that is the word) than many of the older stories.

ODIHAM CASTLE

Odiham Castle, still known locally as King John's Castle, is romantically situated on the banks of Basingstoke Canal in Hampshire. From here King John set out on a summer's day in 1215 for the meadows at Runnymead where, says Arthur Mee, 'he threw himself on the ground in his rage and gnashed his teeth and gnawed chips of straw before he sealed Magna Carta.' Doubtless he returned to Odiham Castle in a worse temper than he had set out. Here too the young Scottish king David, son of Robert the Bruce, spent the greater part of his 11 years' captivity in England. And here came Henry I and Princess Eleanor and Earl Simon de Montfort, all making merry with lavish hospitality and entertainments – but it is none of these luminaries who have left behind a phantom form, but the ghost of a long-forgotten wandering minstrel.

On still, moonlit autumn evenings the clear notes of some piping instrument have been heard, a snatch of some vigorous tune left hanging in the quiet air for a moment and, more rarely, the shadowy form of a wandering minstrel, that 'thing of shreds and patches', has been glimpsed among the age-old stones. Alasdair Alpin MacGregor and his wife are among those who have heard music near these old castle ruins.

In 1980 I talked with many of the local inhabitants and not a few of them had heard the piping music, and one or two claimed to have seen the colourful phantom form. One elderly man who had lived thereabouts for all of his 80 years told me that during his youth there were frequent tales of the ghostly forms of the unfortunate prisoners at Odiham Castle in years long past being seen among the ruins on quiet nights. He well remembered that friends of his had seen figures silently emerging out of the ruins, dressed in clothes of a bygone age, and as silently and mysteriously disappearing.

PORTCHESTER CASTLE

I discussed ghosts on many occasions with actor Sebastian Shaw, a long-standing member of several organisations devoted to the study of psychic activity. Shaw told me that one of his most direct contacts with the supernatural had been through his wife, an actress who died in 1956.

The incident occurred when they were visiting Portchester Castle during a touring holiday on the south coast. A castle guide had warned the couple that there was supposed to be a ghost at a certain point on the steps of the castle keep, but neither Sebastian nor his wife sensed anything.

Later on in the tour, however, they went into one of the ruined rooms of the castle and as they walked through a stone archway Mrs Shaw went chalk white and started trembling. After a few seconds she turned tail and ran out of the castle.

Sebastian chased after her, and when he caught up with her and asked her what was wrong she told him that as she entered the room it felt as if she had been hit across the face with a wet flannel.

'She absolutely refused to return,' Sebastian told me. 'So I went back to see whether I could find out from the guide whether there was anything about the room that was peculiar. He told me that tradition had it that it was the room long occupied by Isabella of France, the wife of Edward II of England, one of history's most notoriously evil women, who had had her husband put to death in a terrible way.'

Sebastian Shaw was convinced that such experiences are linked by a form of telepathy and that the vibrations of things that happen continue in such a way that some people can pick them up. 'My wife was one of those people,' he said. 'Something very, very evil had happened in that room and she sensed whatever it was the moment she walked in.'

Portchester Castle was built by the Romans and, although it is now nothing but a shell, the air about the massive walls seems to breathe history, and it was a castle known to King John, Richard II, Henry I, Edward II and Edward III. Henry VIII and Anne Boleyn stayed there while hawking and it is even said that Pontius Pilate, when he was very old and troubled by his conscience, was brought to Portchester Castle in a Roman galley.

The ghost most frequently and fleetingly seen here is only described as 'a tall, whitish object' and a naval man I once knew said he had witnessed a very level-headed and cheerful person suddenly come to a halt half-way down the steps to the dungeons. She said she simply could not continue, 'there was such an unpleasant atmosphere there'. Did she detect something in the vicinity of the dungeons where once prisoners in the Napoleonic wars had been held in appalling conditions, or did she pick up her companions' feelings of fear and repulsion?

CAPESTHORNE

Among the well-known big houses long reputed to be haunted is massive Capesthorne, near Macclesfield in Cheshire, with its ghostly columns of figures, a Lady in Grey – and a severed arm!

Lt. Col. Sir Walter Bromley-Davenport took me on a tour of those parts of the house that had been the scene of apparently inexplicable happenings. On one occasion Sir Walter, a former army boxing champion, lieutenant colonel of the Cheshire Regiment and Member of Parliament, had seen a line of shadowy, spectre-like figures descending the steps into the family vault. Another time he had glimpsed a 'grey female form' gliding along the corridor leading from the drawing-room to the dining-room in the oldest part of the house. He noticed the figure's head was bowed and she wore voluminous grey skirts, although she moved briskly and was soon lost to sight. Sir Charles Taylor, another MP, saw a similar figure while visiting Capesthorne one weekend.

Sir Walter's son William had his singular experience in the East Wing, part of the Queen Anne structure, which he occupied before his marriage. On a still, windless night he was abruptly awakened by a rattling window and woke up to see 'an arm – with nothing attached to it – reaching out, as if from nowhere'. He assumed the head and body were outside the window, and leaping out of bed he rushed to investigate, throwing open the window. Outside there was nothing to be seen and there was a sheer 30-ft drop to the courtyard below. Since then the bedroom has been known as 'The Room with the Severed Arm'.

During the time I spent at Capesthorne my instruments showed no abnormality in any of the 'haunted' areas but, based on human testimony, I agree with what Dr George Owen (renowned psychical researcher) told me after his visit: 'In my view,' he said, 'there is no doubt that Capesthorne Hall is haunted, but the influence at work is mild and benign and quite possibly associated with former occupants.'

The ghosts at Capesthorne were not to be tempted to manifest for us on that or subsequent occasions and we accepted Sir Walter's wishes when he said, 'I do hope you will understand our reluctance to celebrate this matter and we feel the less we talk about them here the better.'

If pressed on the point I would probably say that as a genuine historical haunted house I find Capesthorne wanting. I would like to see more independent evidence, a wealth of varied witnesses, a scientifically inspired investigation and some concrete evidence of the phantoms long reputed to haunt this rambling, fascinating place. But wouldn't we all?

I have to say that one curious incident at Capesthorne has remained in my memory. We were being led towards one of several 'very haunted' rooms in this 98-room mansion when our guide, Sir Walter, was called away. We walked on and, after a few moments, as we were approaching the aforementioned 'very haunted' room we heard footsteps from inside the room, approaching us. They grew louder and more distinct and sounded quite heavy. We decided that our host had made his way ahead of us and was coming to meet us. As we reached the door, the footsteps on the other side also seemed to reach the door and as we hesitated, not wishing to open the door in his face – we were astonished when a familiar voice boomed out *behind* us! Sir Walter had returned. So who was on the other side of the door? We lost no time in opening the door; inside the room was deserted, not a soul to be seen (Sir Walter approved that expression I remember) and there was no way anyone could possibly have disappeared, silently, in the few seconds it took us to open the door after hearing the footsteps just the other side, it seemed. It was one of those moments you wish you had recorded and sent someone on ahead to enter the room by another door; now it was too late. We wondered, too, whether the whole episode could possibly be explained by some kind of echo of our own footsteps, but immediate experimentation proved this not to be the case. An echo of some past event? Some odd acoustic quirk? Some trick played on us (and on Sir Walter who also heard the footsteps)? Or a manifestation of something not of this world? You make your choice and I'll make mine.

THE 'MORTON GHOST'

A case that has been described as 'the best authenticated ghost story of all time' occurred in Cheltenham just over a hundred years ago. On the face of it the 'Morton Ghost', as it was known for many years, seemed plausible enough: a mysterious female figure seen many times in and about a house in Pittville Circus Road.

The chief witness was a 'lady of scientific training' who became a doctor in 1895 (10 years after the apparition had probably ceased to appear) and, although 7 other people are said to have seen the apparition and upwards of 20 more had heard noises attributed to the ghost, independent evidence is not well established. A wealth of contemporary evidence once existed, it is understood, in the form of letters written by the chief witness Rosina Despard to her friend Catherine M. Campbell (although Rosina did not mention the startling experience of seeing this apparitional form about half-a-dozen times in two years to *anyone* apart from this one pen-friend 'who did not speak of them to anyone'). These letters have never been in the possession of any independent investigator and they now appear to have disappeared without trace.

There is a story that the property was purchased when new by a Mr and Mrs Henry Swinhoe who lived there happily enough for a dozen years, until Mrs Swinhoe died suddenly. Her husband was inconsolable but remarried two years later, only to find his second marriage a battleground of quarrels, arguments and violence. The subject of most of the disputes was the management of the children of the first marriage and the possession of the first Mrs Swinhoe's jewellery. Unbeknown to his wife Mr Swinhoe hid this under some floorboards in the front sitting-room.

Within two years of his second marriage Mr Swinhoe was dead, his second wife having left him. When she died at Clifton in Bristol two years after that her body was brought back to Cheltenham and buried a few hundred yards from the house in which she lived in disharmony with Henry Swinhoe and his family.

Six years after the death of Henry Swinhoe, and following short occupancies of the house by an elderly couple and a single man who always maintained that he never saw anything unusual while he lived there, although by this time there were vague stories of a ghost in the house and garden, the property was leased by a Captain Despard and his family comprising his invalid wife, four unmarried daughters and two sons; however there was plenty of room in the 14-bedroomed, 3-storey house. Almost immediately Rosina (aged 18½) began to see the figure of a tall lady, dressed in black, on the landing of the top floor where Rosina's bedroom was situated. She described the figure she had only seen fleetingly in great detail with the added apothegm: 'the face was hidden in a handkerchief held in the right hand'.

Subsequently Rosina claimed to see the same figure 'about half-a-dozen times, at first at long intervals and afterwards at shorter', yet she still mentioned these strange appearances to no one, apart, apparently, from writing about them to one friend. Three other people also claimed to see the figure in black with a handkerchief to her face. There were also a few other reports of the 'ghost' being seen and of course there were 'inexplicable' footsteps; but already, to my mind, the probable answer was clear.

It should be added that *two years and two months* after Rosina had first claimed to see the figure, she told her father about the mysterious figure, describing what she and a few others claimed to have seen and heard. She had already decided that the figure must be that of the second Mrs Swinhoe. She found her father 'much astonished' at what she told him, for he declared he had never seen or heard anything untoward, nor had Rosina's mother although the latter point is dispensed with by Rosina who says her mother 'is slightly deaf and an invalid'. Although he made a number of enquiries her father was sceptical and at first he was unwilling to discuss the 'ghost', take the matter seriously or co-operate in any way and this is readily understandable if, for reasons of his own, he had installed someone inside the house.

It seems to me that everything points to the 'ghost' being a real, living person. A pet dog, on hearing the 'ghostly' footsteps, sprang up and sniffed at the door, wagging its tail and moving its back as dogs do when expecting to be caressed; the family cat never showed any signs of seeing the 'ghost'. The distinct figure was seen from many angles and close to; it 'almost' but never quite spoke and descriptions by those who say they saw the figure correspond to a remarkable degree. Could the vast majority of the alleged sightings and the 'mysterious noises' attributed to it be evidence of a real person living in the house with the willing connivance of Captain Despard (and possibly Mrs Despard), but unbeknown to the rest of the household; an illicit lodger, in fact?

After all Mrs Despard was repeatedly described as 'a great invalid' so it cannot be considered to be beyond the bounds of possibility that the Captain might seek consolation, companionship and an intimate relationship with another woman. Perhaps such a liaison had been easier before the Despards moved to Cheltenham when the obliging lady may have lived nearby. But with the move and the large and growing-up Victorian-minded family to consider, what was to be done? In a rambling, dark house, as the property was in those days, it would not have been too difficult to secrete a person in one of the many bedrooms, without the children and servants knowing. Any order given by Captain Despard would have been obeyed implicitly and without question, and the evident incapability of Mrs Despard would have made such a deception that much easier and it could well be that Captain Despard had his wife's tacit approval.

The natural reluctance to be seen and perhaps recognised could well account for the 'figure' always having a handkerchief to her face – a singular preoccupation for which no satisfactory explanation has ever been discovered – until now. We have to consider the initial reactions of Rosina and others who claim to have seen the 'ghost': that it was real and solid; the perpetual inability of Captain Despard (and his wife who may have been in on the secret) to see the figure; the reaction of the domestic animals; the really incredibly long period of time between when Rosina first saw the 'ghost' and when she spoke of the matter to her father – could she have known or guessed at the true explanation? And could this 'scandal' have been the 'private matter' so often alluded to in her personal correspondence which has so conveniently 'disappeared'? Could witness after witness have really seen a ghost when they saw a figure 'so lifelike that they took it for a real person'; a figure that made sounds when it moved and needed doors to be opened to enable it to enter a room! For years now I have believed that the 'Morton' case is one of the less convincing cases of haunting in the records of psychical research.

Since I threw a few practical and more than possible ideas into the story of the previously mysterious Cheltenham case, including the distinct possibility that the phantom figure in black with its 'extreme lifelike' appearance, a figure that invariably held a handkerchief to its face, presumably to prevent recognition or being seen plainly, was in fact a real person, many independent and impartial psychical researchers and scientists, including Arthur C. Clarke, have accepted this lucid and previously overlooked solution.

SALISBURY HALL

When the Goldsmiths lived at Salisbury Hall near St Albans – Walter, a talented painter and art restorer, and his wife and daughter – none of them had any doubt about the place being haunted and I was invited to visit them, to hear the long and fascinating history of ghostly activity there, and to spend a night in that historically haunted house.

During the seventeenth century the present house was built on the site of an earlier property and one Asgar the Steller, a Saxon noble, seems to be the first recorded inhabitant. William the Conqueror gave the manor to his friend Geoffrey de Manderville after the Norman Conquest and in 1380 Sir John Montagu, Earl of Salisbury, acquired it by marriage and the name was changed. During the Civil War Salisbury Hall was used by Charles I as a headquarters and armoury; in 1668 Charles II found another use for it. That year he became infatuated with the orange-seller Nell Gwynne, an affair that lasted until the king's death 16 years later. For Nell he purchased Salisbury Hall and here the Merry Monarch and 'pretty, witty Nell' lived and loved, secluded and not too far from London. Here Nell gave birth to a son who became Duke of St Albans. After Nell died in 1687 her ghost is said to have been seen on many occasions at Salisbury Hall where she had spent the happiest times of her life. Not all ghosts are unhappy or the results of unhappiness and it is not only dark deeds that bring them back to haunt, it seems.

The ghost of Nell Gwynne has been seen on the staircase, in the panelled hall and in her former bedroom – and seen by some reliable witnesses including Sir Winston Churchill's stepfather George Cornwallis-West, who tells of seeing the figure of a young and beautiful woman standing in the corner of the hall. She seemed to look at him intently, and then turned and vanished. Weeks later, looking at a portrait of Nell, Cornwallis-West realised just how much she was like the figure he had seen. Until he encountered the ghost at Salisbury Hall, Cornwallis-West had always been sceptical of ghosts. In the years that followed the same figure was to be encountered by Dame Nellie Melba, Eleanora Duse and King Edward VII, all visitors to Salisbury Hall.

Neither Walter Goldsmith nor his wife had ever seen the ghost of Nell Gwynne, they told me, but they had most certainly heard ghostly footsteps (as had their predecessor Sir Nigel Gresley) on several occasions, seemingly going down the stairs and into the Crown Chamber.

They had also on two occasions heard a disembodied laugh, while their daughter had heard similar sounds and seen the ghost of Nell in the bedroom Nell had once occupied.

During the long hours of darkness that I spent alone in that room I had, at one period, the overwhelming impression that 'someone' was in the room, someone who was happy and meant no harm to me, but was there as a right and questioned my presence. A few seconds after experiencing this overpowering and ungovernable impression, one of the Goldsmiths called out that there was a shadowy form or figure coming down the stairs, where they were stationed. One is tempted to postulate that Nell had succeeded in manifesting on the stairway after failing to do so in her bedroom. Or was it all imagination in that house of memories?

Two other ghosts have been reported at Salisbury Hall: a knight of the Middle Ages usually seen in the vicinity of the medieval bridge over the moat; and a cavalier who staggers through the Crown Chamber with a sword in his chest – could it sometimes be his footsteps heard on the stairs? But do Nell and the other ghosts still walk at Salisbury Hall I wonder, now that the property is used as the prestige offices of a Japanese company?

WOBURN ABBEY

Woburn Abbey was another historic and beautiful house I visited and there the Duke and Duchess of Bedford talked at length to me about their ghosts.

That historic pile, owned by the Russell family for over 400 years, is now the home of Henry, Marquess of Tavistock, the son and heir of the 13th Duke who now resides in France. Lord Tavistock, it has to be said, is dismissive about the ghosts.

After inexplicable footsteps, unexplained doors opening and closing is the most widely reported phenomenon in haunted houses and at Woburn I found an interesting variation. The Duke showed me a rather long and narrow apartment which he called 'the television room'. I learned the reason for the odd-shaped room was because when the room had been half the present size the family watching television were continually annoyed by the unexplained opening of the doors to the room. Time after time the doors at both ends of the room would be carefully closed, only to open again by themselves minutes later. New catches were fitted and still the doors repeatedly opened, night after night, just as though someone had opened the doors at one end, had walked silently and invisibly the length of the room, and then opened the doors at that end and had passed through, leaving the doors open. New locks were fitted to the doors again, but still they opened and closed by themselves and in the end the Duke had the wing reconstructed so that there is a completely open passageway where the self-opening doors once were. This cured the problem in the television room, 'but then the ghost turned his attention to other doors' I was told, and the Duke went on to recount how his son, his wife, servants and various visitors had all told him of their bedroom doors opening and closing by themselves – especially, it seemed, the Green Bedroom and the Rose Bedroom.

The Duke and Duchess showed me their bedroom where not only door-opening, but other unexplained incidents had occurred including unpleasant 'touchings' on their faces as they lay in bed, almost as though they were caressed by a wet hand; and there had been glimpses of shadowy figures that could have been the form of a monk.

Strangely enough both the 'touchings' and a monk-like figure have been reportedly experienced elsewhere in Woburn Abbey. Two workmen on different occasions saw a ghostly monk, and ten women on ten separate occasions have felt an invisible hand touching them, usually in the Sculpture Gallery. There was once a hopeless and despondent monk at Woburn; he was the last Abbot of Woburn who spoke out against marriage between Henry VIII and Anne Boleyn – and paid for his outspokenness with his life. He was hanged from the oak tree south of the house. In May 1971 and again in May 1991 a figure in a brown habit was seen standing between the pillars at the entrance to the Sculpture Gallery, a figure that suddenly vanished in both instances.

There is said to have been a murder at Woburn, perhaps 150 years ago, when a manservant to the then duke was killed and his body was hidden in a cupboard. Later the body was pushed out of the window, dragged to the lake and thrown in. The corridor outside the room where the murder took place is now haunted. Often the air is icy cold and dogs react to invisible presences as they do to something unseen and unheard by human beings that apparently lurks in part of the North Wing.

Dr George Owen, psychical researcher, after a thorough investigation at Woburn Abbey came to the conclusion: 'There is a good *prima facie* case for supposing that Woburn Abbey is "haunted" by an influence generating physical phenomena'.

GAWSWORTH HALL

Another lasting memory is when I visited Raymond and Monica Richards at their sixteenth-century half-timbered manor house called Gawsworth Hall. 'A dwelling cannot have occupied the same site for 900 years without acquiring some influences...' I was told as I viewed the tilting ground formed by the Fitton family, one of whom, the wayward Mary Fitton, may well be the 'dark lady' of Shakespeare's sonnets, a lady whose ghost walks at Gawsworth and elsewhere, a 'mysterious lady in ancient costume'. The nearby 500-year-old mansion known as the Old Rectory was once the home of Mary Fitton.

Raymond and Monica Richards said there had long been the paranormal smell of incense in the Hall, and among the ghosts and ghostly activity encountered both at the Hall and at Gawsworth Old Rectory we learned of the ghostly figures of a girl, an eccentric playwright, and a man with dark eyes and a little pointed beard. In addition there had been distinct sounds: of smashing glass; a woman's voice; raps, bangs and tappings that they were satisfied had no logical explanation. Indeed, while I was there with them in the library, Raymond and Monica suddenly looked at each other and told me to listen – could I hear those footsteps? I heard nothing but Raymond and Monica Richards could obviously hear something and I saw their eyes follow something invisible, and then they both gasped and seemed much distressed.

When they had recovered themselves they said a young female form in a cloak had materialised within the room we were occupying, a form that had moved the length of the library and then disappeared in the direction of the Oratory where a macabre discovery had once been made. When an old cupboard had been removed bones forming a human skeleton had come to light. No one ever discovered whose body had been hidden for so many years at Gawsworth Hall or what secrets it held. At all events I had, by all accounts, been present when an apparition put in an appearance.

BREDE PLACE

Soon after Winston Churchill was married someone asked him where he and Clementine were going for their honeymoon; he replied, to much laughter, they were going to Brede! He meant, of course, Brede Place, once described by architect Sir Edwin Lutyens as the most interesting haunted house in Sussex, a property then owned by the Frewens who were related to the Churchills.

More than 600 years ago one of Edward III's knights, helped by monks, erected this medieval manor house. Two hundred years later the Oxenbridge family added two wings and the following owners, the Frewens, restored the house, improved the garden and added some period furniture, tapestries and pictures. It was Roger Moreton Frewen who told me all about the hauntings associated with this historic house.

On the practical side the house was a favourite haunt of smugglers in the eighteenth century and it may well be that a horror story about a former owner, Sir Goddard Oxenbridge, was the invention of the smuggling fraternity to keep prying eyes away. Sir Goddard was presented as a giant ogre who devoured children and eventually, so the story goes, he was captured and sawn in half with a wooden saw at a spot long known as Groaning Bridge, and then the word spread that various portions of the luckless giant would continue to be seen in different parts of the house for ever!

I was shown the remarkable chapel and its adjoining rooms, all very haunted I was told, and when I learned that the bones of a priest had been found buried underneath the original altar during restoration in 1830, with a gilt cross round the neck, I could not help but think there may be some connection; if nothing else such an event could have provided the traumatic atmosphere that may be required to feel and fuel a ghostly presence. Certainly one owner was convinced that certain parts of that interesting house were haunted and some parts were clear: indeed she felt she could draw a line through the house to divide the part that was evil and the part that was not affected. In particular she singled out the rooms adjoining the chapel 'which used to have a room over it but which was so haunted that it had to be taken down, and the dungeons beneath are certainly haunted...'.

In 1936 Clare Sheridan, *née* Frewen, and her son Dick made their home in the house. After Dick's untimely death his mother was much drawn to the occult and she was always talking about the ghosts she encountered at Brede Place. There was Martha, a Tudor maid servant who was hanged in the garden; there was Father John, a priest who lived and died at Brede; a headless man who roamed through various parts of the house and a lady in Elizabethan costume who wandered about the house and grounds at dusk.

During the Second World War British and Commonwealth soldiers billeted at Brede complained of the occasional appearance of the ghosts and once more than a dozen hardened soldiers claimed that a phantom priest or monk had walked through a file of men in the so-called 'haunted corridor'. What I found specially interesting at Brede was the most peculiar influence at highly localised places. An odd sense of sadness and foreboding was to be encountered in the 'haunted' corridor, yet move a few yards away and all was well, move back to the previous spot and the overwhelming feeling returned.

Exactly the same 'sense of the supernatural', as it has been called, existed in the grounds, on the crest of a small hill behind the house, where the servant girl was said to have been hanged. It was very odd and may have been subjective, but I carried out a few tests which seemed to prove otherwise and those small localised regions, 'patches of the past' if you like, bring back to me vivid memories of historic Brede Place where, I feel sure, the remnants of ghosts still linger.

That there are haunted castles and stately homes cannot be denied, the evidence being quite overwhelming and some of my investigative visits to such properties remain real and lasting memories: night visits to the Jacobean mansion Bramshill in Hampshire; Glamis Castle that exudes mystery; Harlaxton Manor, Lincolnshire, a Victorian dream palace with echoes of past events; Blickling Hall in Norfolk with its heavy atmosphere of history; Hampton Court Palace, London, where some of the private apartments have long been haunted. The list is endless, but of course knowing much of the psychic history of a beautiful building before visiting it does mean you are half-way to accepting almost anything you may encounter as possibly representing paranormal activity. It is to be hoped that the experienced psychical researcher will be aware of this fact and consequently be that much more on guard.

It is not only castles and stately homes that are haunted. In Chapter 3 we look at some haunted public places where ghosts and ghostly activity have been experienced by people completely unaware that such activity has been reported before.

CHAPTER THREE

GHOSTS IN THE PUBLIC DOMAIN

B uildings in the public domain include churches, theatres, inns, prisons, hospitals and even a few roads. Why should such places be haunted? It may be that they see every type of humanity and/or have experienced every type of human emotion: are in fact a microcosm of everyman and everywoman.

Whole books have been written on haunted churches, haunted inns and haunted theatres and the available good evidence is quite astonishing. Time after time, for instance, I have come across clergy who are highly sceptical of reported paranormal activity anywhere, but when I ask about the ghost seen in *their* church or churchyard, then its 'Oh well, that was true. I know the people involved and in fact I thought I caught a glimpse myself; yes, that was certainly true . . .'. Human nature being what it is, we do not like to accept anything in the realm of the superphysical we have not experienced ourselves. And while this is a healthy attitude in some ways, it is an unscientific position, for evidence should be carefully examined in an impartial and unbiased fashion and a conclusion·reached based on the results so obtained. It has always seemed to me to be of the utmost importance to obtain good first-hand evidence of allegedly paranormal activity as soon as possible after the event, and preferably to visit the site and obtain corroborative evidence.

During the course of an extensive survey I carried out some years ago with the co-operation of psychical ·investigator Mollie Goldney, together with Dr Letitia Fairfield, sister of Dame Rebecca West, it was established that there are more reportedly haunted churches than any other type of building, and more reportedly haunted rectories and vicarages than any either type of inhabited building. It is interesting to speculate on why this should be. I have long been aware that concentrated thought may contribute to the atmosphere necessary for the production of 'psychic activity' and there is likely to be much concentrated thought in churches and rectories, and indeed in theatres, possibly in hostelries and prisons too!

HAUNTED CHURCHES

Stories of allegedly haunted churches are legion. I have to say that I am more than convinced by some of the evidence and by some of the odd experiences I have had in churches on many occasions; not to mention the experiences of all sorts of people at all sorts of times all over the world.

LANGENHOE
Perhaps the most haunted church I have subjected to scrutiny – so far – was at Langenhoe, on the Essex marshes. I investigated this remarkable case for ten years, on and off; spending many hours with the rector in charge, both at his home and at the church; locating and interviewing witnesses near and far; collecting evidence that included one incident almost unique in the annals of psychical research and organising scientific investigations, including spending a night in the deserted church. Sadly, after the living was combined with a neighbouring parish, the haunted church stood for some years alone with its ghosts and, when it eventually fell into decay, it was pulled down and now there is nothing to see of it. Phenomena reported by varied, reliable and first-hand witnesses at Langenhoe included the phantom form of a singing girl, both inside and outside the church; a man in modern dress inside the church; the sound of voices, music, bell-ringing, movement of objects, footsteps, bangs, raps and other noises, door locking and unlocking and the embrace of a naked young woman! On various visits to the haunted church I personally experienced most of these manifestations but not, I regret to say, the latter . . .

ST THOMAS'S CHURCH, REGENT STREET
Prebendary Clarence May was a priest at St Thomas's Church, Regent Street, London, when I knew him but his thirst for knowledge, his willingness to learn and his eagerness to serve others made him not only an unusual man of the cloth but a man who, as he might have explained

it, with one foot in this world and one in the next, lived an exceedingly full life.

After his death I asked Clarence May's widow about the ghost her husband saw at St Thomas's, Regent Street but she told me he never talked about it. The affair 'caused some publicity' when, as he had told me, he 'unmistakably saw a figure moving across the High Altar. Imagining it to be a priest, and knowing he must emerge at the sanctuary door,' he added, 'I went to meet him. There was no one there. After the service I mentioned having seen someone to the verger who declared that it might be the late Rector, Mr Bainbrigge, whose death had left the living unoccupied.' There was also the fact that Mr Bainbrigge had introduced the Reserved Sacrament in the church and the then vicar, Father Evitt, had wanted to remove it while Clarence May sympathised with Mr Bainbrigge and he told me 'it came as no surprise' that he saw the spirit form of Bainbrigge at the High Altar.

BORLEY CHURCH

The church at Borley in Essex, the village once famous as the locale of 'the most haunted house in England', seems to have been haunted at one time and may still be. I spent many hours, in daylight and in darkness, in the little church at Borley where so many people have experienced so many different incidents which seem to have no rational explanation.

I talked at length with the late Revd A.C. Henning, rector of Borley-cum-Liston; Ernest Ambrose (organist at Borley before the First World War); the Revd H.S. Cheales of Wyck Rissington; James Turner, poet and writer; John May of Bury St Edmunds; Norah Burke the novelist; Susanna Dudley of Stradishall Manor; the Revd Stanley C. Kipling of Barnoldswick; Mr and Mrs Wilson and daughter Vivienne from Long Melford; Steuart Kiernander of Buxton; Terry Bacon, a local man; St John Saunders, a publisher from Chelmsford; Grant Vallender, a psychical researcher; Jon Simons and Maria Matthews of London; Geoffrey Croom-Hollingsworth, a researcher from Harlow; Guy L'Estrange JP; Paul de Vos from the Society for Psychical Research; Professor John Taylor of London University; Charles Chilton, radio personality; comedian Michael Bentine and many, many more people: *all* are satisfied that they experienced paranormal activity in or around Borley Church.

Apparent phenomena experienced include tapping, banging and crashing sounds, voices and the sound of singing, footsteps, abnormal

coldness, movement of objects, the sound of doors opening and closing, organ music, shadowy or veiled figures, the smell of incense,
bell-ringing, a ghost nun, pinpoints of bright light, apparatus malfunc-
tioning, and a powerful and resolute but invisible resistance. Some of
these activities have been measured, recorded and scientifically established and my personal experiences at Borley Church, alone and in the
company of reliable companions, tend to persuade me that churches,
like rectories and vicarages and other buildings saturated with the
concentrated thought that accompanies religion, might well be conducive to psychic activity.

ST JAMES'S CHURCH, GARLICK HILL

An unusual haunting is associated with St James's Church in Garlick
Hill, London. For years the mummified body of a young man, locked in
a cupboard in the vestibule, was shown to the curious and 'Old Jimmy
Garlick', found during excavations in 1839, is a unique example of
medieval embalming. The unknown man may be London's first lord
mayor (six lord mayors were buried here), but whoever he is, he is
restless and I possess convincing evidence that 'Jimmy Garlick' or a
figure resembling him has been seen by English and foreign visitors,
young and old, by a visiting priest, by Sir John Betjeman and during a
solitary visit one midday I thought I glimpsed 'something' moving in
the balcony, something that could well have been the singular naked
ghost of Jimmy Garlick. I certainly established to my complete satisfaction that I was the only human being inside the church at that
particular time.

OTHER HAUNTED CHURCHES

Other well-established haunted churches include St Bartholomew's the
Great, where the ghost of its founder Rahere, a monk and a courtier to
Henry I, has been seen and heard on many occasions: by clergy, lay
visitors, cleaners and psychical researchers; Holy Trinity Church, York,
with its hooded ghosts, very similar, it would seem to the ghost haunting St Mary's Collegiate Church, Port Elizabeth, South Africa, recounted to me by a number of first-hand witnesses.

When the haunting of St Dunstan's church, East Acton, was at its
height I visited the church and talked at some length with the Revd
Hugh Anton-Stevens and his secretary. I knew that there were reports
of phantom monks being seen inside the church, built on land once

owned and occupied by friars, since the 1930s, but Mr Anton-Stevens told me with a matter-of-factness that took my breath away: 'About a dozen such monks can be seen on most evenings walking in procession up the central aisle and into the chancel...'. Later I stood where the vicar and others had stood when the monks were seen – and at the same time – and I stood in the place where the phantom monks had walked – and at the same time as they had been seen – but I saw nothing and I felt nothing. Later still I talked with Kenneth Mason, a former naval lieutenant who told me that one evening he saw six monks in grey hooded cloaks walking in procession inside the church with their heads bowed and he claimed that he purposely stood in their path – and they passed right through him, and he felt nothing.

Dr Oskar Goldberg, member of the Security Council of the United Nations, told me about his personal involvement in the Millvale Church, Pittsburgh, USA case where he had himself seen the 'man in black' apparition manifesting in his old church: a form that arrived unexpectedly, remained for a while and was seen by scores of responsible witnesses, and then departed in silence and was seen no more.

HAUNTED THEATRES

THEATRE ROYAL, DRURY LANE

One of the most haunted theatres must surely be the Theatre Royal, Drury Lane, London, with its daytime phantom of a Man in Grey, reportedly seen by literally scores of people; the ghost of Dan Leno; a mischievous ghost and other friendly and unfriendly phantoms. But the Man in Grey is perhaps the best-known of all theatre ghosts, and deservedly so.

The ghosts of the Theatre Royal have fascinated me since I first heard all about them from W.J. Macqueen Pope. 'Popie' was never happier than when he was recalling the sightings he had had of the famous ghost, for this down-to-earth theatre historian told me he had seen the ghost not once but several times. The ghost is that of a slim young man dressed in a white ruffed shirt, a grey riding cloak and a three-cornered hat of the eighteenth century; and he wears riding boots and sports a sword. What is especially interesting is that this well-attested phantom is a daytime ghost, seen between the hours of 10 a.m. and 6 p.m.;

consequently he is usually sighted at matinees or rehearsals, and when he is seen it is taken to be a good omen for his appearance has invariably preceded a success for the production.

In the 1870s, when the Drury Lane Theatre was being reconstructed, a hitherto unknown room was discovered behind the brickwork that covered a former doorway, and there they found some threads of grey clothing and the skeleton of a man with a dagger in his ribs. The victim was thought to be one of the young 'bloods' of David Garrick's time who had been stabbed to death because he was a nuisance to somebody in the theatre of the day. Popie was convinced that it was the ghost of this man that returned to those parts of the old theatre that he knew.

Certainly the ghost here walks, soundlessly, always following exactly the same route. Starting from a room now used as a bar, on one side of the upper circle, he walks across the auditorium, turns left, ascends the stairs, walks round the back of the upper circle, down the stairs on the other side and disappears through the wall on the opposite side of the theatre to that from which he appeared. He is always seen taking the same route, in the same direction, counter-clockwise. Occasionally he rests in a seat in the fourth row and he always moves in a leisurely and unhurried way, as though he is thoroughly accustomed to the theatre.

The evidence for the appearance of this ghost is impressive. In 1939 more than half the cast of *The Dancing Years*, who were on stage for a photo call, saw him cross the upper circle. Another time a theatre cleaner was in the theatre one morning just after 10 a.m. when a rehearsal was in progress. As she entered the upper circle she saw a man dressed in grey, sitting on the end seat of the fourth row, by the central gangway, apparently gazing down at the stage. Thinking it must be an actor she put down her cleaning apparatus and went to speak to the figure. As she drew near the figure seemed to melt and it quickly disappeared completely. A movement near the right hand side of the circle caught her eye and she saw the same figure, just as it vanished into a solid wall. She said afterwards she had never heard of the ghostly Man in Grey, although her description fitted other first-hand accounts, even to the sword and riding boots.

During a matinee one still summer afternoon a female member of the audience in the upper circle asked an attendant whether actors in the musical came out among the audience for she had noticed a man in a long grey cloak and a three-cornered hat pass through the entrance doors ahead of her. There was no living person in the theatre at that time, on the stage or off it, remotely resembling such a description.

The theatre was taken over by the Entertainment National Services Association (ENSA) during the Second World War and an ENSA official saw the ghost near the upper circle entrance as he was climbing the grand staircase. A year later a member of ENSA headquarters staff, a stranger to London who had never heard of the Man in Grey, saw the same figure and asked who it could be.

Over the years not only actors and performers at the Theatre Royal, but also firemen, theatre officials, producers, theatre-goers and visitors have all reported seeing a strikingly similar figure and a number of witnesses mention a peculiarity the Man in Grey shares with other spontaneous apparitions: when witnesses approach too closely the features of the phantom form become hazy, the outline blurs and the whole thing quickly vanishes.

Even experienced ghost hunters – who usually spend hours and hours in haunted places and see nothing – seem to have had better luck at the Theatre Royal. James Wentworth Day carried out a 'ghost hunt' at Drury Lane Theatre in the company of Popie and Harry Price, at that time the leading psychical researcher in Britain. James told me he saw 'a grey-blue, almost luminous light move across the dark void of the royal box'. A moment later the same form, 'moving with the uneven action of a man with a limp, appeared at the back of the upper circle . . .'. Apparently two members of the party of six saw this 'strange blue light'.

Other ghosts seen at the Theatre Royal, Drury Lane include the great clown Joey Grimaldi (seen, among others, by American actress Betty Jo Jones); the one and only Dan Leno (seen by, among others, Stanley Lupino, father of Ida); actor Charles Macklin who murdered another actor in the Green Room here in the eighteenth century; actor-manager Charles Kean who died in 1868; and theatre manager Arthur Collins – all benign and harmless spectres from the past who enrich the lives of the living.

MORE HAUNTED LONDON THEATRES

Other haunted theatres in London include The Adelphi in The Strand, scene of the murder in 1897 of actor-manager William Terriss whose daughter Ellaline Terriss (Lady Hicks) first told me about the ghost. She said her father's last words were, 'I will come back' and by all accounts he did, in the theatre, in nearby Maiden Lane and elsewhere in the immediate vicinity. The Coliseum in St Martin's Lane has a soldier ghost that dates from the 1914–18 war; a uniformed figure that walks down the dress circle gangway and turns into the second row, usually just before the lights are lowered for a performance to begin. The figure has been recognised as that of a soldier who spent his last evening on leave at the theatre and the ghost was first seen by impresario Harry Martin and his daughter on 3 October 1918, the date that the soldier was killed in action. There is also the London Palladium where a ghostly lady in a crinoline climbs the old Crimson Staircase which is a remnant from a previous building.

The Haymarket Theatre is haunted by the ghost of two past managers, David Morris and John Baldwin Buckstone; an unidentified elderly man; a figure dressed in eighteenth-century costume; and sundry other figures. The ghost of John Buckstone, who is said to have died of a broken heart during his tenancy of the theatre he loved to distraction, is one of the most enduring theatre phantoms, first reported as long ago as 1880, a year after his death in Queen Victoria's box. The last reported sighting I have is of Buckstone's ghost being seen in 1994 when the individual form was reported by two American visitors who asked about the oddly dressed gentleman they had just seen who seemed to walk through closed doors.

Still other haunted London theatres include The Albery Theatre in St Martin's Lane, harbouring the ghost of its originator Sir Charles Wyndham, while at Sadler's Wells the ghost of clown Joe Grimaldi has been seen at dead of night. The Old Vic has the spectre of an unrecognised but distraught woman, and in addition many of the vanished theatres of London, the Metropolitan, the Royalty, the Marlborough, Collins Music Hall and St James's all had their individual and in some cases very persistent ghosts.

HAUNTED PROVINCIAL THEATRES

London is not unique in possessing haunted theatres. In the provinces there is the historic Stamford Theatre in Lincolnshire where director Sue Cameron told me she and others working in the theatre had become convinced over a period that they had a phantom who shuffles about the place; the old Theatre Royal at Portsmouth boasts the ghost of the theatre's founder, Henry Rutley; the old Castle Theatre at Farnham in Surrey was long reputed to be haunted by the sounds of a

In Nottinghamshire an investigator seeks to tempt ghostly activity with powder, thermometers, a bell from a haunted church and various 'trigger' objects (see Chapter 1). © *Peter Underwood*

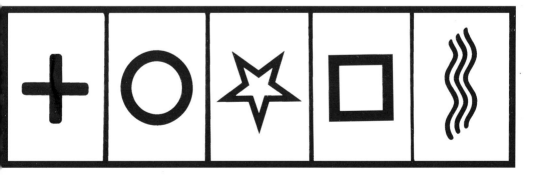

Zener cards are used to establish the presence of ESP - extra-sensory perception (see page 16). © *Mary Evans Picture Library*

Salisbury Hall, Hertfordshire, is reputedly haunted by the ghosts of Nell Gwynne, a knight of the Middle Ages and a cavalier who staggers through the Crown Chamber with a sword in his chest (see pages 28-9).
© *British Tourist Authority*

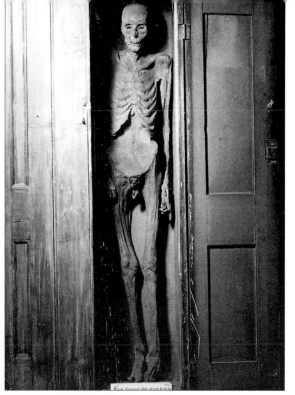

ABOVE
The Spaniards Inn, Hampste.
Heath, London. The inn has
many associations with
highwayman Dick Turpin ar
his ghost has long been said
haunt the hostelry and the
nearby heath (see page 52).
© *Chris Underwood*

LEFT
Sombre Bodmin Jail retains
ghostly remnants of its one-t
prisoners (see pages 53-4).
© *Peter Underwood*

murder that took place there, especially unaccountable footsteps that I can personally vouch for.

The Castle Theatre building, now an Italian restaurant, is built on the site of a property that once housed servants from nearby (and haunted) Farnham Castle; it is a haunting that may have continued for over 300 years. The story goes that a thespian of old reached Farnham and was given shelter by the castle servants before he died there. Soon there were tales of unexplained sightings and sounds attributed to the dead actor. About a hundred years ago a skating rink occupied the site and soon the occupiers of neighbouring properties were complaining about loud and frightening sounds emanating from the building long after it was closed for the night.

Soon a cinema replaced the skating rink, and still the footsteps and various unexplained sounds continued, and there was mysterious inter-ference with the film projector, both during the showing of films and when the cinema was, for all practical purposes, empty. In 1939 a group of travelling players discovered the now empty building, settled there and called it the Castle Theatre. Over the succeeding years inexplicable incidents continued to be reported and it was disclosed that a man had hanged himself from a curved beam in what became the foyer of the theatre.

Peter Gordon, when he was director of productions at the little theatre, told me of some of the many mysterious happenings he and others at the theatre had experienced: lights switched on at night when the theatre was deserted; records on the gramophone changed; foot-steps; whispering voices from deserted parts of the theatre; loud bang-ing sounds that echoed through the empty building; a clock that inexplicably stopped and started by itself; the sound of people moving about in a deserted room; movement of objects; 'shadowy forms' glimpsed by different people on different occasions; and an awful feeling of sadness and despair that would suddenly descend on the foyer and engulf everyone who was there at the time, and then as suddenly lift and be gone.

Another theatre director, Laurence Ray, complained of props disappearing at the most inappropriate time, of loud crashings and banging noises that had no explanation and the eternal footsteps. No matter how often he heard them they sounded so definite and real that he would go to see who was there but of course there was never anyone.

The old Theatre Royal at Margate, Kent, has long been haunted, as I had personally established after a number of visits during the hours of daylight and the longer and more interesting hours of darkness, and its haunted reputation continued as the theatre went through various existences as a cinema, a bingo hall, even a furniture storerooms and through it all the forceful influence of Sarah Thorne, its best-remembered manager, made her presence felt in no uncertain way; while another Theatre Royal, this one in Bath, also has a resident ghost. This is a Grey Lady who walks the Lower Circle corridors and boxes, a woman who committed suicide by throwing herself from the window of the room above the bar – a ghost reportedly seen by scores of actors, actresses and members of the staff and audiences. I have walked the route of this unnamed but restless phantom on several occasions, in daytime (once for the television cameras) and in darkness, but I have neither heard nor seen anything of this particular phantom – but I live in hope!

Britain's oldest playhouse is yet another Theatre Royal, this one at Bristol (it was opened in 1766). Actress Chili Bouchier had personal experience of the ghost here. Chili entered films in 1927 when she appeared in *Shooting Stars* and went on to play leading roles in scores of British films. When she was appearing at the Bristol theatre as Becky Sharpe in Thackeray's *Vanity Fair*, she believes she heard the ghostly sounds of an unhappy phantom.

The part required one quick costume change and for this Chili used a room which was situated on the opposite side of the stage to her own dressing room. During one evening performance she rushed off stage to make the change, only to find the dressing-room in darkness. She asked her dresser, a rather moody and sullen Irish girl, if she had switched off the lights which should have been on to assist the split-second change but the girl shook her head. Once the light was back on Chili found her carefully arranged clothes had also been disturbed and the jewellery required in the scene had also been rearranged. Then Chili discovered to her dismay that one important piece of jewellery was missing altogether and she sent the dresser out to look for it.

As the girl left the room the lights dimmed mysteriously and the atmosphere became overwhelmingly gloomy and suddenly very cold. As Chili was wondering what on earth was happening she heard, coming from a corner of the room, the sounds of someone sobbing and groaning and weeping piteously. Before Chili had time to investigate fully the girl came back, and the sounds ceased and the lights came back on. Questioned, the girl admitted she too had heard a voice moaning and the lights had dimmed for no apparent reason on two occasions. The room was not used after that night and the manager said afterwards that the theatre dog always refused to go into that old room used by Chili as a changing room. Mrs Sarah Siddons (1755–1831) was generally regarded as the finest tragedienne of the British stage and although for years she failed on the London stage she had tremendous success in the provinces and at Bristol; she was always best in tragic roles and perhaps something of the tragedy she portrayed so well on stage became impregnated in the place where she had known a kind of success.

The Lyric Theatre at Wellingborough, Northants, has a well-authenticated ghost whose identity is less well established. Barbara Mansfield, acting manager and theatre secretary, who described herself 'not by any means a spooky person' said she saw a figure twice, crossing the balcony in the foyer, and she noticed in particular the dead white face. Maintenance engineer Michael Lamb nearly resigned his job when he came face to face with the ghost one night when he was working backstage. The figure that frightened him seemed to be wearing a brown jacket and light-coloured trousers, and he saw the same figure a second time. The theatre snack-bar girl, Sheila Le Fevre, has said that she saw the ghost 'several times' in a downstairs kitchen and Violet West, a former bank clerk, was among seven people who held a vigil at the Lyric and saw the ghost they sought. 'It looked like a white shadow or a statue ... and it moved ... from one side of the foyer balcony to the other side and then it disappeared', they reported afterwards.

A group of researchers attempted to establish the authenticity of the haunting with movie cameras, temperature devices and recording apparatus, and one of the party, Elaine Futter, stated that she saw the ghost on the balcony: 'I can't really say what happened. Something made me look up and this image was there. It was gone as quickly as it appeared.'

During the course of a subsequent seance in which one or two raps as answers 'yes' or 'no' were obtained in reply to direct questions, it did seem to be established that the haunting entity was someone deceased; that 'it' wanted 'help' and later the words 'Daniel – help' were received. A few days after this visit some members of the local clergy did what they could to 'lay the unquiet spirit to rest' and messages subsequently obtained spelt out 'bless these bones' and 'bring back priest'. The intriguing affair continued until a sum of money went missing from the Lyric Theatre, whereupon the owners put a ban on all psychic investigations and so another possible ghost eluded the ghost seekers.

The Theatre Royal at Bradford is reputed to be haunted by the ghost of Sir Henry Irving (1838–1905), the greatest figure in the theatrical world of his day and the first actor to receive a knighthood. After an excellent performance in *Becket* he collapsed in the foyer of the Midland Hotel and died almost immediately, but it is at the theatre that his ghost has reportedly been seen, the theatre where he gave so many memorable performances and perhaps where he gave his true self and certainly where his last thoughts, his enduring love and his passion for living were centred. The theatre was his whole life and it is only to be expected that if his ghost is to appear anywhere it would be seen and felt in the theatre that always filled his mind and thoughts.

Watford's Palace Theatre, built in 1908 as a music hall, survived as a souvenir of Edwardian theatricals attracting many famous entertainers including Marie Lloyd (1870–1922), but the ghost here, known as Aggie, is thought to be something to do with a former stagehand. One former manager told me he often heard mysterious footsteps coming from the stage when there was no possibility of a natural explanation. One particular dressing-room also seemed to be psychically affected and there have been numerous reports of apparently inexplicable happenings, but invariably a pleasant, warm and friendly atmosphere persisted. Once, I was told, four theatre staff heard the mysterious footsteps simultaneously. Very late one night a new set was being erected and it was noticed that some curtains, covering a doorway into the gallery, billowed and parted as though someone had walked through them. As they watched, the onlookers clearly heard distinct footsteps cross the empty gallery and then saw the curtain on the opposite door billow out in the same way.

Theories concerning the possible identity of this ghost vary. Built on ground where French prisoners of the Napoleonic wars were buried, it is thought the 'restless spirit' may be one of the deceased soldiers. Secondly, it was thought it might be a former stagehand who never really left the theatre he loved; and thirdly it was wondered whether it might be a former theatre nightwatchman. Certainly many of the reported manifestations took place late at night when most if not all the staff would have gone home – on the other hand darkness has long been regarded as conducive to psychic activity. The former manager I talked to told me he had seen a figure that vanished in front of his eyes, late one night, when he had chanced to return to the theatre for something. As he was passing the 'haunted' dressing-room he heard a sound, as though a door had opened, and turning he saw a dark figure seemingly trying to enter the dressing-room. The manager shone his torch and for a moment he saw more distinctly a short, stumpy figure with its back to him, moving silently from side to side as though trying to open the dressing-room door. The manager went forward to see what was going on when suddenly there was nobody there! He found the dressing-room deserted and was entirely satisfied that the figure could not have passed along the passage, either way. He could not say whether the figure was that of a male or female.

OTHER HAUNTED THEATRES

England is not the only habitat of haunted theatres. The Theatre Royal in Glasgow, that became the headquarters of Scottish Television, has long been haunted and it is considered to be unlucky to talk about the ghost. The premises do seem to be haunted by poltergeistic phenomena, as I can personally testify, and also by ghostly forms, one of which has been recognised as that of a former manager whose hurrying form has been noticed – and probably more frequently *not* noticed – in the busy atmosphere that I encountered there.

The Olympia Theatre in Dublin may date from the eighteenth century, certainly it was known to such shining lights as Dan Leno, Little Tich, Vesta Tilley and Marie Lloyd, and more recently Charlie Chaplin, Laurel and Hardy, Harry Lauder, Noël Coward, Alec Guinness, Sir John Gielgud and Marcel Marceau. Among the tragic events that have taken place here are the collapse of the proscenium arch in 1974, destroying the whole stage and orchestra pit and the death of a chorus girl, killed by a jealous admirer during the Black and Tan troubles. The disturbances here include loud knockings, usually beginning around 10 p.m. and continuing for about 15 minutes, that centre on the theatre's Green Room. For years these sounds have been reported intermittently, although no set pattern has been discerned and no rational explanation has ever been discovered. Some researchers think the conscientious and hard-working manager-director Dan Lowry (who died in 1897) may be responsible, still worrying about his beloved theatre. Whatever the explanation, witnesses of the rhythmic knocking include Jessie Matthews, Dame Edith Evans, Michael Mac-Liammoir and many theatre staff over the years.

Among haunted European theatres there is the Comédie Française, the national theatre of France, where the dying cries of a wealthy admirer of Hippolyte Clarion, a noted French actress of her day, can be heard. The ghostly cries were reportedly heard by actors, staff and audience at the theatre for a period of over two-and-a-half years when they stopped completely. On his deathbed the admirer had said he would haunt Hippolyte Clarion for a period as long as they had known each other. Up to the time of his death they had known each other just over two-and-a-half years.

American haunted theatres include the palatial Tampa Theatre in the city of Tampa on the west coast of Florida, named after the Indian village which flourished there in the sixteenth century. The theatre, opened in 1926, embodies all the frills and embellishments of the best early twentieth century theatres. Today it is haunted by the benign presence of Foster Finley who went to the Tampa Theatre in 1930, four years after it opened, and spent 38 years projecting Hollywood films through the whole dazzling golden era of the cinema.

According to Michael Norman, Foster Finley loved the Tampa Theatre and practically lived there, arriving between 7 and 8 in the morning in the days when the place didn't open until 1 p.m. A neat, balding man who always wore a suit and tie, and invariably had a cigarette dangling from the corner of his mouth, everyone liked him and in all the years he was there he was never known to complain about anyone or anything. 'The nicest guy you'd ever want to meet' said one of his colleagues. Perhaps he loved the place so much that something of him remained long after he was taken ill and died in 1965.

Far above the auditorium, at the top of the balcony, small windows reveal the locality of the old projection room, always a dark and gloomy area, yet Foster Finley spent hours and hours up there, and today his ghost haunts this chamber in particular. Here there have been unexplained movement of objects, touchings, ice-cold draughts, doors opening and closing by themselves, the sound of dragging chains and the frightening feeling that something invisible was present ... and there are those who have glimpsed the form of a short, balding, neatly-dressed man, with a cigarette dangling from the corner of his mouth, standing in the shadows; a form or figure that disappears as suddenly and as inexplicably as it appears.

In 1984 a group of six interested people attempted an all-night vigil in the haunted theatre. Within minutes of settling on the stage in the dark theatre *all* the members of the group had the overwhelming impression that they were being watched by someone or something invisible – one woman became so scared she ran out to the entrance lobby and stayed there. Another member of the group saw something unexplained reflected in a mirror and a moment later in another mirror; another heard faint strains of old-fashioned music permeate the deserted theatre. One of the men felt something invisible sit on a seat next to him; another heard sounds of movement from the auditorium seating area. Yet another saw 'someone' walk in front of the stage. Soon the group gave up and left the theatre without completing their all-night vigil. The 'South's Most Beautiful Theatre' may also be the South's most haunted theatre if we consider the wealth of varied evidence from a variety of witnesses extending over thirty years.

Then there is the Orpheum Theatre in Memphis, Tennessee, built in 1928 to replace an earlier theatre destroyed in a fire. The story goes that a child named Mary was killed in a fall there in 1921 and her ghost haunted the theatre – and the later theatre built on the site. That the ghost of little Mary has been seen and heard for more than 70 years seems indisputable. She has been seen to occupy one particular seat, C5, and her vacant stare and odd appearance have repeatedly caused patrons to comment on the 'odd little girl in the quaint dress'.

Casts of various visiting companies have reported a feeling of unease in the empty theatre and a New York company in 1977 decided on a seance; afterwards some of the actors claimed to have seen the ghost child. Workmen, new to the theatre, have found the atmosphere 'weird', one finding his work inexplicably interrupted and another finding his tools mysteriously transported from one place to another. A night maintenance man saw a small girl running along an aisle in the deserted theatre; another heard a female voice singing – when he went towards the sounds they ceased, but as he left the theatre later, he heard the singing again coming from inside the deserted theatre.

Footsteps that have no human origin have been reported times without number at the theatre and witnesses include a project director, a sceptical organ restorer and a hardened cleaner. The ghost of little Mary was seen yet again one warm April evening in 1979, by three separate members of the audience; she was seen again ten years later and from time to time right up to the present day. We each dream of a different heaven, perhaps Mary had dreams of make-believe and illusion in the theatre she once knew, and when the conditions are right maybe she 'returns', in a manner of speaking, as a ghost.

Other haunted theatres include the original Metropolitan Opera House in New York where the ghost of Frances Alda, wife of director Giulio Gatti-Casazza, used to occupy her favourite seat in the stalls; the long-gone New Theatre on Broadway with its 'forbidding supernatural aura' where actor Charles O'Farrell saw the ghost of a murdered man and a beautiful woman; and Ford's Theatre in Washington, where Abraham Lincoln was assassinated in 1865, still haunted by the presence and by the footsteps of the murderer John Wilkes Booth.

Then there is the Princess Theatre, Melbourne, Australia, with its ghost of opera singer Frederick Baker (Frederici) which was the subject of a television documentary; and the site of an old theatre at Port Elizabeth, South Africa, with its heavy phantom footsteps.

HAUNTED INNS

Inns and hotels of every description, and in every part of the world, have stories of ghosts and hauntings; many, it has to be admitted, are best taken with a grain or two of salt, for the resulting publicity is sometimes a consideration. That there are authentic ghosts in actual haunted inns and hotels I have not the slightest doubt, however; indeed if human testimony can prove anything and personal experience means anything, then believe me there have been inexplicable experiences in such establishments that suggest beyond reasonable doubt ghosts and ghostly activity do exist.

THE BULL, LONG MELFORD

I remember a night at The Bull at Long Melford with fellow investigator Tom Brown. At The Bull there had been reports of phantom figures seen over a long period by different witnesses; mysterious happenings, especially unaccountable loud crashing sounds, and a wealth of phenomena of a poltergeist nature. We visited The Bull – as indeed I have done a score of times since – and we were satisfied that we did not experience anything of a paranormal nature during our initial visit. However, I am satisfied on the evidence I have that paranormal activity may well have taken place there in the past and who knows, it may well take place again in the future.

One of the features of the disturbances current at the time Tom and I spent a night there was the apparently paranormal opening of one particular door, a door that led into the entrance hall where a murder had taken place, long ago. However a simple exercise in experimentation resulted in a logical answer to this particular 'phenomenon'; an experiment I may say that resulted in my being invited to become a member of an exclusive investigating society of which I became president 13 years later.

THE GRENADIER AT HYDE PARK CORNER

I have spent more than one night at the haunted Grenadier public house at London's Hyde Park Corner. Here the ghostly form of a guards officer, flogged to death by fellow officers for cheating at cards, returns to the historic pub each autumn. As the date for the annual spectral appearance approaches the pub's dogs are seemingly aware of 'something' in the haunted area of the cellars, where the victim expired. The feeling of unease on the part of the animals gradually increases until the appearance of the annual apparition and then the dogs soon lose their unrest and return to normal – until the next autumn; or so it was a few years ago. I have personally witnessed this unease and reluctance to enter the cellar on the part of the dogs at The Grenadier and during a later visit, taking part in a BBC television film, I talked with six people who had personal knowledge of the haunting, both the ghostly grenadier and the animals' awareness.

OTHER INNS AND THEIR GHOSTS

Looking back I recall spending nights in many haunted rooms in hotels and inns all over the country: at The Wellington, Boscastle, Cornwall, with its haunted room and disappearing ghost; St Anne's Castle Inn at Great Leighs, Essex, with its long history of hauntings and a room that couldn't be slept in; The Bush at Farnham, Surrey, with its ghost of a girl who makes her presence known to prospective brides; The Bird Cage at Thame in Oxfordshire with its ghost from Napoleonic days, its leper spectre and phantom of a convicted criminal; The Dolphin, Penzance, Cornwall, with its appropriate ghost of an old sea-captain; The Eclipse at Winchester, Hampshire, with its ghost of Lady Alice Lisle who spent her last night on earth here and was executed outside the haunted bedroom; The Angel, Guildford, Surrey, with its ghostly Polish army officer; The Crown at Bildeston, Suffolk, with its four separate ghosts; The Old Silent Inn at Stanbury in Yorkshire with its tinkling bell and echoes of a murder long ago; The Bear at Woodstock in Oxfordshire with its room haunted by disembodied footsteps; The Old Inn at Widecombe-in-the-Moor with its daytime spectre of an unknown man and the sound of a crying child; Weston Manor, Weston on the Green, Oxfordshire, with its phantom coach-and-horses and ghost of Maude, a nun who loved a monk; The Blue Posts, Portsmouth, Hampshire, with its ghost of a murdered man not buried in consecrated ground; The Talbot, Oundle in Northamptonshire with its phantom Mary Queen of Scots, and many more.

I also spent a night, in fact several nights, at The Ferry Boat Inn in Cambridgeshire where a suicide has long been reputed to return on the anniversary of her death, 17 March. I can't claim ever to have seen Juliet but from personal experience I have no doubt that this delightful inn is, or was, haunted. And the last time I was at The Spaniards on Hampstead Heath, I actually heard the clatter of horses' hooves, just for a second, followed by complete and utter silence. I am satisfied that no actual horses were anywhere in the vicinity at the time. This inn has many associations with highwayman Dick Turpin and still possesses knives and forks said to have been used by him and his associates, and the curious will be shown Turpin's room with the tiny, foot-square window. The ghost of Turpin and the hoofbeats of his steed have long been said to haunt the inn and the nearby heath, especially in the stillness of a quiet night.

HAUNTED PRISONS

SHEPTON MALLET PRISON

Shepton Mallet Prison in Somerset is nearly 400 years old and was long a notorious army 'glasshouse' for criminal serving men and it has been reputed to be haunted by a seventeenth-century White Lady who was executed there.

I visited the prison following reports of inexplicable banging and breathing sounds, a chill atmosphere that was localised and a 'presence' in the night duty room. Such reports became so numerous that the prison governor at the time spent a night in the haunted room himself and sent a report to the Home Office saying he was 'unable to find any satisfactory explanation' for the happenings he and prison officers had experienced.

One prison officer I talked with said he had suddenly felt something icy-cold touch the back of his neck and something invisible pushed against a door of the haunted room that he was trying to shut. Another officer witnessed this incident and saw a vague white female form that vanished when he approached.

During the hours I spent in the haunted night duty room I found one of the doors exceedingly difficult to close on occasions; my instruments registered a singularly lower temperature in one corner of the room and I recorded the snatch of a sound something like heavy breathing that I was totally unable to explain.

One officer I talked with insisted he had found himself attacked by something invisible, he had been pinned down by the neck and although whatever had attacked him had then gone away, the paralysed feeling lasted for hours. Nothing would induce him to enter that room alone again. Another warder told me 'I wouldn't do another night duty alone in the duty room for £1000'. After my visit I contacted the Home Office for their conclusions and they told me, 'All is now quiet there'. Nevertheless stories continue to reach me of odd happenings and experiences at Shepton Mallet Prison.

BODMIN JAIL

Bodmin Jail in Cornwall was built in 1778, enlarged in 1820 and became the county jail in 1837. Later it was taken over by Naval authorities who continued to use it until after the First World War when it was put up for sale. During the Second World War it was used first as a Civil Defence base and then by the American forces as a barracks. Some of the nation's irreplaceable treasures were stored there for the duration of the Second World War.

There would appear to have been plenty of traumatic and eventful activity at Bodmin Jail that could have given rise to haunting phenomena, plus the fact that for well over 50 men and women those sombre surroundings were 'the last place on earth' that they saw. Hangings took place at Bodmin not only for murder but also for burglary, stealing sheep, forgery and even for setting fire to a corn rick. Murderers who met their end there included Matthew Weeks whose pathetic victim, his sweetheart Charlotte Dymond, was murdered on the green slopes below Roughtor on Bodmin Moor – where her ghost walks to this day.

Many of the buildings remain much as they were at Bodmin Jail and the reputed paranormal activity includes the rattle of keys in the vicinity of the old cells, a common enough sound years ago; heavy footsteps, another common occurrence surely; as would have been an over-whelming feeling of regret, remorse and sadness: all feelings that have been reported by a mass of visitors.

The towering old cell blocks are certainly atmospheric places. Here countless prisoners spent months and sometimes years picking oakum and tombstone engraving, and listening to the death knell that sounded on execution days from the centre of the jail.

When the premises were used as a dance hall and night club the proprietors collected a wealth of reports detailing odd happenings, strange events and curious experiences. Making enquiries they discovered that previous managers had complained of objects being moved and of dogs refusing to go anywhere near some parts of the old prison.

There were stories of people being followed by sounds of an invisible person, of voices, harsh and guttural, of the faint and faraway slow clanging of a bell and of footsteps, some slow and dragging, some light and running, some heavy and plodding.

GHOSTLY HOSPITALS

In a survey I conducted to discover the most haunted inhabited and uninhabited buildings hospitals came quite high on the list and it is a fact that in these places of hope and sadness, life and death, beauty and ugliness, there is a lot of belief in ghosts and ghostly activity.

Many hospital hauntings are interesting and convincing, and there seems hardly a hospital in the world that does not boast at least one ghost or has done so in the past.

CAMBRIDGE MILITARY HOSPITAL

A short history of Cambridge Military Hospital, written in 1974, reveals that the legend of a Grey Lady haunting the women's ward seems to stem from a nursing sister in the Queen Alexandra Imperial Nursing Service who inadvertently administered a fatal dose to a patient and afterwards, in her remorse, committed suicide by throwing herself over a hospital balcony to her death.

The Grey Lady ghost is said to have been seen and heard by patients and staff at the century-old hospital on many, many occasions, apparently making her rounds as she so often did during her lifetime. She was reliably reported in 1969 when she was seen by a night orderly sergeant and often, the hospital administration office told me in 1980, the ghost seems to appear when the staff are under pressure of some kind, extremely busy perhaps, or understaffed. Here we have a ghost that attempts to be benign and comforting and helpful, but can be very frightening for those who confront it.

Ward 13 used to have a balcony but the original hospital has been enclosed by subsequent buildings and various floors and corridors have been added but it is still most frequently in the vicinity of the ominously numbered Ward 13 that the ghostly Grey Lady walks.

ST THOMAS'S HOSPITAL, LONDON

When I heard that a Grey Lady ghost haunted St Thomas's Hospital, Lambeth, London, I lost no time in contacting the authorities, visiting the hospital and making exhaustive enquiries. The old building on the Albert Embankment was founded in the thirteenth century by the canons of St Mary Overy's Priory and dedicated to Thomas à Becket (c. 1118–70), saint, chancellor and Archbishop of Canterbury, murdered by four knights in his cathedral where his tomb is a shrine to this day. The hospital survived the Black Death, the Plague, the Great Fire of London and the Blitz of the Second World War and was the establishment that Florence Nightingale used as a base to revolutionise world nursing. Although the Grey Lady ghost appears to be kind and helpful, its appearance often heralds the death of the person who sees her.

I talked with people who claimed to have seen the ghost – and lived to tell the tale! They included doctors, nurses, patients and administrative staff. The ghost was usually described as appearing to be a very nice, middle-aged lady dressed in a grey nurse's uniform. The figure was reported to me as having appeared in various wards of a particular wing that used to specialise in the treatment of malignant disease, Block 8.

One cold November morning in 1943, Charles Bide, a member of the hospital staff, told me he was at the top of Block 8. The night before a German bomb had damaged the hospital. Windows had been blown in and there was dust and debris everywhere. Mr Bide looked after the 180 clocks at St Thomas's and he was wondering how many clocks and other articles had been lost in the bombing. He noticed an oil painting, hanging askew, and a large mirror, the glass miraculously undamaged. Having lifted down the picture, he turned the mirror and saw, reflected in the glass, a woman of about 35. 'She had a good head of hair and her dress was old-fashioned and grey in colour, it looked ruffled'; and Charles Bide thought to himself that she had probably been lying down, resting, after a busy night.

As he looked at the figure, he suddenly felt very cold – although he had the distinct impression that she meant no harm – but the coldness grew rapidly, becoming intense and penetrating, and Charles Bide felt frightened. The thought came to him that he was alone at the top of the building; at least he *should* be alone. Everything seemed quiet all of a sudden and he hurriedly left. He always regretted that moment of panic. He felt later that the ghost may have had some message for him. She seemed to be making an effort to communicate and he told me he thought that if he had stood his ground, she might have received help and he might have learned who she was and what she wanted.

Mrs Bide never forgot how shaken and subdued her husband was that day. She knew him as a sensible and down-to-earth man, not at all the type to have hallucinations or see something that was not really there. It was some time before he would tell her of his experience and years later she told me she believes that the expression he saw on the face of the ghost troubled him for the rest of his life.

A former superintendent at St Thomas's, Edwin Frewer, encoun-tered a similar figure soon after his arrival at the hospital. He was walking along the main corridor in the company of his chief, a Mr French, on their way to Block 9 when the new superintendent suddenly experienced a feeling of extreme coldness and he came to a sudden stop in the open section between Blocks 7 and 8, as he saw a nurse approach-ing him from the direction of Block 8. He saw, with some surprise, that she was dressed in an old-fashioned uniform with a long skirt. She looked very worried and after hurrying towards the two men she suddenly disappeared. The only places of exit from that particular part of the corridor were a door to a sleeping block (which was tried and found locked) and the ward devoted to male venereal disease, where female nurses were not allowed. Mr French was more than a little puzzled when Mr Frewer stopped dead in his tracks since he did not see the figure. Long afterwards Mr Frewer commented, 'The memory of her face, with its look of anguish, remains with me after all these years.'

Some years after his sighting of the Grey Lady, Edwin Frewer was approached by one of the hospital physicians, Dr Anwyl-Davis, who had had an almost identical experience one day. It was in the same corridor of the hospital and the figure seems to have disappeared at almost exactly the same spot. Dr Anwyl-Davis never forgot the encounter and often described the experience. As the lifelike apparition approached him, he raised his hat and bid her good morning. The figure made no reply but continued on her course, seemingly oblivious to the presence of Dr Anwyl-Davis. A moment later the figure had vanished.

Although the appearance of the ghost nurse frightened them, it did not presage the death of either Charles Bide, Edwin Frewer or Dr Anwyl-Davis, but there is evidence that the form was seen by five patients shortly before they died, and it was probably seen by many others.

One evening in September, a nurse was filling the water jugs in the ward at about 8.30 p.m. and when she came to the bedside of an elderly man suffering from cancer he told her there was no need to fill his water jug as he had already been given a glass of water. Since no other nurse was on the ward at the time, the night nurse was somewhat puzzled and asked the patient who had given him the water. He replied that the very nice lady dressed in grey who was standing at the foot of the bed had done so. The nurse looked in the direction of the old man's smiling gaze but she could see nothing and certainly there was no 'lady in grey' anywhere on the ward. Two days later the old man died.

Two months later another nurse in the same unit, but a different ward, was washing the back of a man of 70 who had widespread cancer, but who was currently expected to recover sufficiently for him to go home. Suddenly the patient asked the nurse whether she always worked with 'that other nurse'. No other nurse being present at the time, the patient was asked which other nurse he meant and he pointed in a certain direction where the nurse could see no real person. The patient said the 'other nurse' was dressed differently and she had been to see him several times in the last few days. He died shortly afterwards.

Thirteen months later the figure was seen again in the ward where the patient had been given a glass of water. During the night a man of 37, also suffering from cancer, asked the nurse about a lady warming her hands at a radiator. The nurse could see no one and when she asked the patient to describe the figure, he said, 'The person in the grey uniform.' He also died a couple of days later.

Two months later a similar figure was seen yet again in another ward in the same unit. This time the patient was a woman suffering from cancer. One morning she told the night nurse that during the night she had been visited by a lady dressed in grey who had been very kind to her and had given her a cup of tea. She died the next day.

A year later another female patient, a young pregnant woman of 28 with multiple myelomatosis, had a very similar experience in the same ward. During the night, she said, a nice woman, sympathetic and kind, stood at the foot of her bed. She did not find the figure at all frightening, but she too died a few days later.

These five witnessed examples of a 'grey lady' in one unit were collected by a doctor at the hospital who became interested in the long-standing legend that in the wards of that particular unit a lady in grey had sometimes been seen by patients who died shortly afterwards.

The fact that the figure was invariably described as being dressed in grey is extremely interesting in view of the fact that the present sisters' uniform of Oxford blue with white apron and collar came into use in the early 1920s. Previously a grey dress had been worn. In addition to these experiences, which were all written down and signed by the nurses concerned, a number of other reliable accounts of the Grey Lady appearing to patients who died soon afterwards were obtained by word of mouth but dates, times and other details are no longer available.

There is written evidence, however, for at least one other appearance that took place in a different ward of the same unit, vouched for by a state registered nurse. While she was on night duty she was called, as night sister, to supervise the administration of a dangerous drug to a patient known to be dying. She asked the patient whether she could make her more comfortable in bed, whereupon the patient replied that the other sister had just done so. There was no other sister on duty at the time and neither the night nurse nor any other nurse had recently attended to the patient; she died the following day.

The sceptical may point to the fact that patients in hospital wards specialising in the treatment of such diseases are likely to be under the influence of pain-killing drugs, and perhaps in a state of delirium and likely to experience hallucinations, and this is true to the extent that all the patients in the six accounts described would have had analgesic drugs at the ward sister's discretion; these drugs have opium derivatives or synthetic analogues of morphia, and the hallucinogenic properties of these drugs have not been fully explored, yet the fact that six quite separate reports are so similar would seem to outweigh objections on this score. It is extremely interesting to notice that more than a dozen dying patients in one unit of a massive hospital had almost identical 'hallucinations'. These 'hallucinations' had all the impressions of reality to the person concerned who was able to reconcile the apparition with specific articles and particular parts of the ward, and was able to describe, soberly and sensibly, the experience to nurses and others.

The chaplain at St Thomas's at the time of my visits, the Revd Kingsley R. Fleming, respected the integrity of those who saw the ghost. 'I'm convinced that it is possible to be aware of such manifestations,' he told me. 'Obviously there must always be in these cases a spiritual awareness in the person and a willingness to accept what is happening to them . . . Hospitals are places of constant crisis . . . There is a terrific supercharge of emotion and feeling and people who die are not always able to come to terms with their anguish or remorse.'

The legend of the Grey Lady of St Thomas's is known widely among the staff of the hospital, although it is obviously guarded from the patients and no factual basis has been established for the legend. There is a story that a nursing sister fell to her death down a lift shaft at the turn of the century; another story says the ghost is that of an administrative sister who committed suicide in her office on the top floor of the haunted unit; a third rumour tells of a nurse throwing herself off the balcony because she felt she was responsible for the death of a patient; and a fourth says the ghost is that of a nursing sister who died in Block 8 from smallpox. It has not been found possible to obtain confirmatory evidence for any of these deaths, I have been led to understand. Some of the nurses maintain that the Grey Lady is only visible on the floor level of the wards as they were before the present block was rebuilt. Among recent reports of sightings of the Grey Lady there were three in 1989, two in 1991, four in 1993 and one in 1994.

PRINCE ALFRED HOSPITAL, SYDNEY

The Prince Alfred Hospital at Sydney, Australia was and may still be haunted by a ghost nurse. The figure was seen on many occasions, as Alasdair Alpin MacGregor learned during the two years he spent in Australia. A former private secretary to the Chancellor of the Duchy of Lancaster, he heard about this hospital ghost from a journalist, David Barnes, and carefully checked out the story for himself. He found that far from being in the least frightening, the apparition was commonly referred to as the Good Ghost Sister.

One trainee nurse said, 'She is not a terrifying or nasty ghost. In fact she's quite beautiful and is always kind and helpful. She appears at the most unexpected times and usually when the staff are exceptionally busy. She seems to haunt one particular ward most of the time but she has been seen elsewhere including the operating theatres just prior to an operation. She appears to be so real and solid that sometimes the staff speak to her, thinking she is a new member, but she never replies. She has been known to draw attention by her presence to something important.'

'I saw her,' another nurse reported, 'and followed her into a room to ask a question thinking she was the Sister in Charge. When I looked round the room, it was deserted! There was no other door or anywhere she could have gone. I thought I must have been mistaken about the room, although I knew deep down that I hadn't. Three nights later the same thing happened again!'

Another nurse told Alasdair MacGregor that when she was at the hospital nearly all the girls had seen the Ghost Sister but they were afraid to say much for fear of ridicule. One of the older Sisters heard what was being said and told them they were not seeing things; she said there was nothing to worry about because the Ghost Sister was well known and had been doing the rounds for nearly 30 years.

Alasdair MacGregor talked with seven or eight nurses who had personal experience of the Ghost Sister including Sister Jacqueline Bull at her home in Elizabeth Bay, who had seen the ghost on about ten occasions. She too insisted that there was nothing sinister or frightening about it and although the figure did appear at the most unexpected times, nobody was scared. Twice she followed the figure into a room where the Ghost Sister disappeared. She appeared to be so real and natural that Sister Bull and others to her certain knowledge had mistaken her for a real nurse and had spoken to her. 'There are dozens of incidents that can be checked,' MacGregor was told, 'but there is simply no explanation for the appearance of the Good Ghost Sister.'

HAUNTED ROADS

FOUR SISTERS CROSSROADS

Among the haunted roads that have come to my attention is part of the A12 near Ipswich. Here, at a spot known as Four Sisters Crossroads, Stratford St Mary, more than a dozen people have had peculiar experiences, in particular Irene Heath who told me something of the unnerving and unpleasant encounters she had had – with 'something'.

Taking the incidents in chronological order, Irene Heath's first unexpected experience at the spot had been a few years earlier when a tyre on her car burst when she was travelling along the 'haunted' stretch of road. Not long afterwards, travelling alone in her car late at night in the area of the crossroads, she suddenly became aware that 'something was in the back of the car'; something evil and frightening. She turned on the interior lights of the car and turned round several times, convinced that she would see something awful, but nothing was visible; yet she still had an overwhelming impression that something malevolent and evil was in the car. The impression, vivid and very frightening, lasted for what seemed like a quarter of an hour, in fact until with considerable relief Mrs Heath turned into the gates of her home.

One morning, two weeks later, while she was travelling along the same stretch of road, her car suddenly and inexplicably went into a spin and crashed. The vehicle was a complete write-off but Mrs Heath stepped unharmed from the wreckage. The car was in a perfectly sound mechanical condition before the crash, having been serviced only days before. An accident assessor's inspection suggested that the brakes had suddenly 'grabbed', but there was no real explanation.

After this experience Mrs Heath made a determined effort to avoid that area, but one night, since it happened to be the most direct and quickest way home, she found that she had automatically taken the road that led to the crossroads. As she approached the area, again alone and late at night, she had the unalterable impression that 'something evil' was in the car behind her, and this time she felt a distinct prod in the back, as though something claw-like had prodded her. At the same time Mrs Heath became conscious of a pregnant and clammy coldness inside the car.

A few months later she again found herself driving along the same stretch of road. It was after midnight and she was alone. At first she merely noted that there was a clammy coldness inside the heated car, and then again she had the really frightening impression that something incredibly evil was in the car with her. The impression lasted for perhaps five seconds only and then there began an inexplicable and loud banging noise from the direction of the back of the car. This distinct and thunderous noise only intensified the terror Irene felt; now she was absolutely certain that 'there was something in the back of the car'. Mr Heath told me that he had thoroughly examined the car afterwards and tested it, but he was totally unable to discover any physical reason or cause for the noise. Certainly there were no marks of any kind nor any trace of mud which might be expected had the noise been the result of some mechanical fault.

Mrs Heath arrived home on this occasion in a terrible condition and indeed she did not fully recover for several days. She told us she felt the 'phantom passenger' might be trying to drive her to destruction or worse . . .

Is it possible that Mrs Heath's experiences stemmed from deep-rooted fear of attack, misfortune or molestation in this particular area, I wondered, resulting in the unconscious manifestation of the embodiment of evil?

It is interesting that the Four Sisters Crossroads, the traditional place for the burial of suicides and murderers, used to be an accident 'black spot', several fatalities having occurred in the immediate area. It may owe its name to four trees that once stood at the crossing or perhaps to the local tradition that four sisters met there to part and go their separate ways in life, long, long ago. There was another tradition too that years ago a ghostly group of four people were sometimes seen there and that a gallows stood at the spot. It is also interesting that the stretch of new road on which Mrs Heath had her uncanny experiences follows exactly the line of a very old road.

Mrs E. Southgate of Belstead in Essex has related to me an experience that befell her husband at this same place over 50 years ago. Then a young man in his twenties, he was returning home one dark night along this stretch of road when he sensed rather than saw someone walking towards him. As the form seemingly approached him, he thought it odd that he could see nothing, but he heard what sounded like a lady in a long silk gown rustle past him very quickly. A countryman, used to country sounds, he was always certain that this was something not of this world, and he was very frightened and never forgot the experience.

OTHER HAUNTED ROADS

The A75 between Dumfries and Annan in Scotland has a ghost car, according to the Ferguson brothers who came unexpectedly upon a large furniture van and realised to their horror that they could not avoid a collision – then they were upon the van and it had completely vanished! Other drivers on this stretch of road have also reported seeing an old-fashioned furniture van which inexplicably disappears.

Also, according to reports, there is a phantom car that travels at great speed along the road from Sligachan on the Isle of Skye. This is described by all those who claim to have seen it as an old Austin 7 that has its lights blazing but there is no driver. It makes no sound, travels at a speed that has been described as far too quick for a normal car and then suddenly it disappears. Witnesses include an officer of the Island Observer Corps, a postman and a doctor.

Phantom cars have also been reliably reported from Germany where the autobahn between Baden Baden and Frankfurt is regularly haunted by a small, dark phantom car, while on Highway 167 between Abbeville and Lafayette in Louisiana, USA a 1940 black car is sometimes reported, apparently occupied by a worried-looking woman and a child wearing nineteenth-century style clothes – a car that suddenly and inexplicably vanishes.

EMILY'S BRIDGE

There is a haunted bridge, commonly known as Emily's Bridge, at Stowe in Vermont, a New England state of the USA, if we are to accept the testimony of people like Edward Rhodes, vice-President of the respected Stowe Historical Society and a lifelong resident of Stowe.

Emily's Bridge, also known as Gold Brook Bridge since it is situated on Gold Brook Road, was built in 1844 by John Smith, a well-known builder of covered bridges in those days. It is only 50 ft long with unpainted board sides and a metal roof.

One wet night in the autumn of 1975 Edward Rhodes and a friend Jim Holden pulled up their car on Emily's Bridge to escape the pelting rain for a while. Suddenly Jim Holden became aware of human voices, although nothing was in sight or visible during the frequent flashes of lightning. He didn't like it one bit and suggested they move on.

As they drove away from Emily's Bridge Edward Rhodes asked his friend whether he had heard what the voices had said. In reply Jim told him it seemed to be mostly a female voice calling, 'Help! Help!' Edward looked at his friend and said he thought they ought to go back in case it was someone in need of assistance.

They turned the car round and went back to Emily's Bridge. Once inside Edward, now being roughly in the position Jim had been previously, saw a white light flashing on and off at the side of the bridge where it would be impossible for any living person to be. They didn't wait to see whether they heard any voices again but drove quickly away into the rain.

Edward Rhodes told Arthur Myers, one-time assistant city editor of *The Washington Post*, that he subsequently collected a wealth of evidence for odd happenings at Emily's Bridge, and he had unearthed some interesting stories about Emily herself.

Different people on different occasions have remarked on warm areas on the bridge in the cold months of January and February and, conversely, icy cold spots in the hot months of July and August. There have been other happenings, slight in themselves but taken collectively worthy of serious consideration: hats have been blown off when there is demonstrably no wind whatever; strong breezes have suddenly sprung up from nowhere; voices have been heard when the whole bridge has been deserted and there is no one anywhere near; objects have appeared on the bridge, sometimes dropping from space in front of witnesses, like a piece of newspaper from the late 1800s or a portion of red calico; people have had the impression of someone being on the bridge on foot, a woman described as having long brown hair and wearing a red dress; and cameras have repeatedly malfunctioned.

The real Emily is thought to have been one Emily Smith who lived during the second half of the nineteenth century, but records are patchy. People died in those days in places like Vermont and were buried on farms and smallholdings with no records being kept, and this was especially likely to happen in the case of suicides and questionable deaths that those involved hoped would be quickly forgotten.

Thwarted love and sudden death are the two ingredients that crop up in most of the stories surrounding the death of Emily Smith – if that was her name. Some say that the day before her marriage she was trampled to death at the bridge by runaway horses; others maintain that on her way to her wedding her horse bolted at the bridge and Emily was thrown out of the vehicle and killed; yet another story has it that the groom failed to show up and Emily, in her grief and disappointment, sped away from the church and congregation in a wagon which overturned at the bridge and the bride-to-be was killed. Yet another story handed down is that she had arranged to meet her fiancé at midnight at the bridge when they planned to elope but Emily's sweetheart did not show up and Emily committed suicide at the bridge. Finally one researcher thinks that Emily was 'fat, 36 and not very pretty', but she was much in love with a young man who didn't really like her but he got her pregnant. Rather than marry her Emily's lover jumped off the bridge to his death, while pregnant Emily followed him a month later, wearing the red dress she planned to wear at their wedding. Whatever the reason and the story behind it all, it does seem that Emily's Bridge may be haunted by a ghostly lady in red.

THE MOST HAUNTED PLACE IN AUSTRALIA?

As I was putting the finishing touches to this book, in April 1996, I received a letter from John Godl of Summer Hill, Sydney, Australia, telling me about the haunted Quarantine Station at Sydney Harbour. Built in the middle of the last century on ancient Aboriginal burial ground and still in use in 1972, there have been scores of reported paranormal happenings there for well over a century.

Meticulous records have been preserved for the whole time this massive place, occupying 69 acres on the North Shore of the famous harbour, served its purpose, some 150 years – and not a few reports concern ghosts and ghostly happenings.

The old Quarantine Station had three cemeteries, an enormous hospital complex, its own post office, power and water supplies, paved streets lined by private and industrial properties, and a morgue.

Today guides lead the living through the dark wards and streets recounting tales of ghostly happenings and pointing out haunted places. There are stories of a ghost Chinaman, ghost doctors and nurses and patients wandering about hospital wards long devoid of any human occupants; and strange voices have been heard by responsible park rangers and ghostly lights seen.

John Godl says, 'the Quarantine Station is undoubtedly the most haunted place in Australia' and perhaps it is. I hope to collaborate with

John Godl in an exhaustive examination of all the evidence before the full story is published.

This brief look at places in the public domain that are haunted does appear to indicate that such places as churches, theatres, inns, hospitals and prisons, where all kinds of people in all sorts of moods gather together for a while, often in a contemplative attitude, do sometimes retain some essential element of those people in circumstances that enable 'something' to reappear or recur at later dates, perhaps in an identical atmospheric condition, or in the presence of certain sensitive people.

It has been suggested that we may all leave our footprints on the sands of time that remain dormant but can be reawakened. As we move about, creating our personalities within the constraints imposed on us by our genetic inheritance, we inevitably establish patterns of behaviour which we turn into habit. Dr Percy Seymour of Plymouth University maintains that all matter in the universe leaves an indelible trace in the form of what might be called a 'worldline', rather like the wake of a ship, showing where it has been, and these permanent tracks of energy could be what we call ghosts.

A person of firm and strong habits who has lived at the same place for a long time or visited a particular building many times may leave an imprint by means of the wordline that can be picked up by later sensitive people. The possibility of leaving indelible worldlines may be enhanced by the building affected, the concentration in volume and the company present. Such a theory would suggest an acceptable explanation for the paranormal that need not involve life after death. Perhaps it is now time to develop this theme and look at some specific haunted houses.

INVESTIGATIONS IN HAUNTED HOUSES

It has been said that all houses wherein people live are haunted houses and if that is so some are patently more haunted than others. I could present in this chapter a hundred remarkable, well-attested and convincing examples of haunted houses, but I will confine myself to some of the specific haunted houses that I have visited, investigated, explored, and where I have spent many hours in daylight and in darkness.

ELM VICARAGE

The nocturnal visit I made to Elm Vicarage near Wisbech in Cambridgeshire (later called The Old Shires) was probably one of the most interesting nights I spent in a haunted house. The rector at the time, Arnold Bradshaw, showed me over the seventeenth-century building. A Keble College man who had been a curate at Dartford and Wrotham; a chaplain of hospitals and in the RAF and a rector in Suffolk before coming to Elm in Cambridgeshire; he never experienced anything anywhere like the wealth of weird happenings that plagued his life and that of his wife for 16 years at Elm Vicarage.

The Elm Vicarage case, as with many other well-attested cases of haunting, seems to have begun with mysterious footfalls, perhaps triggered by the presence of sympathetic personalities. Certainly I heard footsteps at Elm that were not of human origin.

Both Arnold and Irene Bradshaw were repeatedly awakened in the middle of the night, almost as soon as they moved into the house. The rhythmic and seemingly solid footfalls seemed to originate from the upper part of the house and quite near, perhaps the next room or the attic space under the roof, they could not be sure. Suzette, their teenage daughter, sometimes heard the footsteps too and the family dog, Kik, seemed to be aware of something invisible to the human occupants of the rambling vicarage.

Night after night the Bradshaws were disturbed, and night after night the vicar would get up and go in search of the perpetrator but he never found any normal explanation for the footsteps and he never succeeded in locating exactly where they came from. During the night I spent at Elm Vicarage I too heard footsteps. It was just after two o'clock in the morning and the sounds seemed to be faint and far away, but as I listened intently they became clearer, more distinct and louder. I had arranged with Arnold Bradshaw that he would not investigate on this occasion; instead if he heard anything he was to inform me by three short touches on the bell-push I had provided with a lead to the buzzer at my side.

The buzzer sounded as the footsteps became clearer and quietly I prepared to face the perpetrator for they seemed to be approaching me along the upstairs corridor. But suddenly the sounds seemed to become stationary. They were just as loud and distinct as before, but they no longer sounded as though they were approaching. Soundlessly I moved to a position where I could see the length of the passage. The footsteps still sounded loud and solid and I could hardly wait to flood the passage with light and see the cause of the sounds. Without warning I snapped on the powerful beam of my torch: the passage was almost at once as light as day, and as deserted as it had been when I had first seen it – but the footsteps still sounded as loud and uninterrupted as ever. Switching off my torch I edged forward a few steps. Now the sounds seemed to come from the room on my left near the end of the corridor. With the persistent sounds still pervading the otherwise silent house I slowly made my way towards the door. The sounds really did seem to be coming from inside this room and I quietly opened the door and flooded the room with light. The room was completely deserted and still the footsteps continued; they seemed all around me inside the very room I stood in and also and at the same time in the room below and above me in the attic space.

I retreated from the room and tried to locate the origin of the sounds but I was no more successful than had been the Revd Bradshaw on the dozens of occasions when he had risen from his bed and sought to find an answer to the mystery. After about three-quarters-of-an-hour the footsteps – which I recorded on tape – began to get a little fainter and then fainter still, and within a few moments all was silent.

In the morning Arnold and Irene Bradshaw told me they had heard the sounds exactly as I had heard them and there had been no interruption when I had entered the 'haunted' room and the sounds had continued for three-quarters-of-an-hour, as was usual, something I did not know until then.

I say 'haunted' room because I had asked not to be informed of specific incidents or locales the evening before and now I learned for the first time that Irene Bradshaw had encountered a ghost monk and Arnold had found an ancient bell in the attic.

Irene informed me, in the presence of witnesses, that one evening she had been in the corridor where I had spent the night when she suddenly found herself face to face with a monk wearing a brown habit and sandals. He almost brushed against her as they passed and Irene found herself saying, almost without thinking, 'Do be careful...' When she turned the passage was deserted.

A few evenings later, in the same passageway, Irene saw the monk again. He was almost upon her before she saw him and, as they passed, before she could collect her thoughts, he had disappeared again. On several more occasions Irene saw the monk and she never felt afraid, rather she felt sorry for him and sometimes, as they passed, she murmured, 'Bless you.'

Then one evening, again in the same corridor, she saw the monk some little way from her and she decided to pluck up the courage to address him. Standing still as he approached she said softly, in a voice she hardly recognised as her own: 'Bless you. Can I help you? Can you tell me your name? You are very welcome here.' That first time she really addressed the monk he said nothing but seemed to give her a little smile.

Each time she encountered the monk after that Irene said the same words and waited hopefully for some reply but he passed without a sound. Then one night he stopped and she heard the story of the ghost monk at Elm Vicarage.

I should say here that it is extremely rare for ghosts to be reported to speak; in fact there is very little good evidence for any spontaneous ghost speaking but to be fair to Mrs Bradshaw she did not say that the ghost spoke to her in the normal way; she said she spoke to the ghost and as he stood before her, his answer came into her mind. By this means she gleaned a remarkable story.

She learned that the ghost monk was named Ignatius – Ignatius the Bell Ringer – and gradually over a number of occasions Irene Bradshaw became acquainted with Ignatius and learned his poignant story – and she learned she was the first women he had ever spoken to.

Some 750 years before a monastery had occupied the site of Elm Vicarage. It had been the responsibility of Ignatius to keep a watch on the treacherous Fen flood waters and to warn his brethren if there appeared to be any danger. On one memorable occasion Ignatius fell asleep at his post, the waters rose quickly and silently, Ignatius did not ring the warning bell and many of his brethren lost their lives. Ignatius was in disgrace and when he died his shame was not forgotten; for 750 years the sad and time-worn monk made his nightly pilgrimage along a succeeding passageway to protect his brethren, walking back and forth to watch the Fen waters – no longer visible from the succeeding building – and sometimes ringing a bell, loud and clear, at dead of night, a phantom peal that seemed to be a death knell.

I found no records to establish this plausible story although there were many pointers to the present vicarage having been built on the site of an ancient monastery – so who knows. I pressed Irene Bradshaw to tell me all she could remember about Ignatius: how he became visible, whether she only saw him in that upstairs corridor, whether anyone else had seen him, what days and times she saw him, what sort of person he appeared to be, and what condition and disposition she had been in when she saw him. She told me she had seen him dozens of times; at first he had seemed faint and shadowy but gradually he became more definite and solid. Most often she met him in that upstairs corridor but she had seen him elsewhere about the house, both upstairs and down-stairs. Once, in the lounge downstairs, when she and Suzette were sitting quietly talking, Ignatius suddenly appeared and sat down on a chair and Kik the terrier jumped up and sat on his knee! Irene had looked at her daughter but she could not see Ignatius; instead she pointed in alarm at the dog, sitting apparently in mid-air above the chair seat! Irene described Ignatius as a man of perhaps 33 years of age, with 'dark curly hair and thin ascetic features'; he was always dressed in the same manner and his clothes looked old and worn. There did not appear to be any special time of day when he appeared but by far the commonest time she saw him was at night. He always seemed quiet, preoccupied and a little sad. She encountered him any time, when she was busy and happy or sad.

The story Ignatius related made curious sense with the phantom bell-ringing that Mrs Bradshaw had been hearing. On no less than 31 occasions in 2½ years Mrs Bradshaw had been awakened by the clear tolling of a bell, often around three o'clock in the morning, yet her husband slept on and heard nothing. Once or twice she had awakened him but the tolling bell died away as he awoke and Suzette never heard it either. Mrs Bradshaw agreed with me that it was probably his own phantom bell that Ignatius rang, although her husband thought it might well be the old bell he had discovered in the attic. Mrs Bradshaw never actually saw Ignatius ring the bell and he never carried a bell when they met but the plain fact is that when Mrs Bradshaw heard that bell tolling in the night – 31 times in 2½ years – her husband was needed to officiate next-day at a death in the parish!

On the night I spent at Elm Vicarage, I saw the bell in the attic and I 'controlled' it so that it could not ring other than by paranormal means, without leaving evidence that it had done so; sadly Mrs Bradshaw heard no bell-ringing during my visit. I made a point of silently patrolling the 'haunted' passage from time to time during the dark night hours but apart from those puzzling footsteps all was quiet. Just once as I turned to retrace my steps, in plimsolls and completely noiselessly, I caught a glimpse of something at the other end of the corridor, outside the 'haunted room', but even as I peered to satisfy myself that either something was there or there was nothing, I thought I heard the rustle of a long garment and the hint of a tinkling bell and then all was quiet again and the corridor was completely and utterly deserted.

I refer to the 'haunted room' because what had once been a comfortable visitors' bedroom was not occupied again for as long as the Bradshaws were at Elm Vicarage after Irene Bradshaw's frightening experience there.

One hot September night Irene prepared to sleep, as she occasionally did, in the pleasant and cool bedroom usually reserved for visitors; a room that was afterwards used only as a box room with the door securely locked at night.

Kik, as ever, was welcomed into the bedroom, for he usually slept at the bottom of Irene's bed but on this particular occasion he whimpered and cried and repeatedly tried to get out of the room. Three times he was brought back and only very reluctantly did he at length settle down on the bed.

Irene Bradshaw read for a while and then put out the light and settled down to sleep. She didn't know how long she had been asleep but it was pitch black when she found herself awake with the frightening feeling that something was being tied around her neck! She reached for her torch and discovered, to her immense relief, that a tendril of wisteria from the wall outside the bedroom window had found its way through the open window and lay across her throat. She tore it away and was preparing to return to sleep when she felt her bedclothes being pulled from her bed. As she turned she felt herself violently picked up and thrown sideways across the bed as she heard Kik snarling and whining and seemingly fighting something invisible to her.

Terrified as she had never been before she tried to scream but a vague black shape appeared above her and almost through a haze she saw a pair of gnarled hands materialise and clutch at her throat. Again she tried to scream and found to her horror that she could not make a sound. The hands on her throat increased their pressure and powerless to defend herself Irene Bradshaw felt her end had come when suddenly she saw Ignatius. He came purposefully towards her, reached for the twisted hands clutching her throat, and pulled them away.

As the awful pressure on her throat relaxed Mrs Bradshaw dropped back exhausted, but she hardly had time to breathe before she became aware of the horrible, vile creature again bending over her; this time she was aware of a huge head and a very red face. Again Ignatius seemed to come to her rescue and with a tremendous effort Irene Bradshaw tore herself free, rushed past the frightened, yapping Kik and burst into her husband's room. The marks on her throat remained for almost a week and I talked with her doctor who said he had never seen anything like it.

The first Arnold Bradshaw knew of the alarming episode was when he was awakened by his wife, and he and Suzette confirmed to me that Irene's throat was very badly bruised and that the marks remained for days.

A few nights later Mrs Bradshaw saw Ignatius in the usual corridor. Somehow he seemed less sad than usual and when she asked him who had attacked her, he told her it was a man who had himself been murdered in that room. On a later occasion Ignatius told Irene Bradshaw that she would not be seeing him so often in the future; his having saved her life had gone some way towards compensating for his lapse so many years before; he felt his penance had been partly lifted and he was hopeful of complete forgiveness.

At all events for the rest of her days Mrs Bradshaw was completely convinced that her life had been saved by the ghost Ignatius.

DOCKACRE HOUSE

Following a broadcast on the BBC dedicated to haunted houses, I received a letter from Mrs Dennise Buckeridge of Dockacre House, Launceston, Cornwall who told me all about the ghost or ghosts that have long haunted her house. Subsequently I visited the house several times and spent a lot of time there interviewing and investigating this interesting and in some ways unique case of haunting.

Dockacre House was originally built in the reign of Elizabeth I and extensively 'modernised' in Georgian times. The house is built 'on the slope of the hill, clinging to its side, a quaint property with a long narrow range of gables, roofs and walls encased in small slate-like mail armour; the foundations of the house in the street above being higher than the tops of the chimneys of Dockacre House'. A secret passage, now blocked by the foundations of the road at the back of the house, once ran towards the eleventh-century castle reportedly haunted by a *kergrin*, the Cornish word for ghoul.

The story of the ghost at Dockacre House goes back to the time when the Revd Sabine Baring-Gould lived there and concerns Nicholas Herle, a barrister, and his wife Elizabeth, daughter of the rector of Northcote. Herle, it should be noted, was a man of substance, being High Sheriff of the County of Cornwall and Mayor of Launceston. In the church there is a monument to Elizabeth Herle that tells it all: 'Depart ye life 25 Dec 1714 by starvation or other unlawful means'. There are two stories concerning the death of Elizabeth Herle: the first says she went mad and her husband locked her up in an upstairs room and starved her, then the recommended cure for madness. Unfortunately she was kept too long in confinement and she died. The second story has it that Nicholas either accidentally or intentionally shot Elizabeth on the stairs. In evidence of the latter story a large and immovable bloodstain was to be seen for many years, and only when the staircase treads were renewed was all evidence of the 'everlasting blood-stain' removed from mortal sight.

Strangely enough it is the ghost of the murderer and not the ghost of the murdered who haunts Dockacre House, notwithstanding the fact that Nicholas Herle died at Hampstead in 1728. His ghost has reportedly been seen in the main hall, beautifully panelled in the Queen Anne style. Nicholas Herle is also credited with playing a flute that is heard inside the house just before an occupant is about to die. The flute that is played is one no mortal can in fact play for one end has been blocked up and it has been made into a walking stick. Walking sticks play a big part in the traditions of Dockacre House for it has long been incumbent on the owner of the house to hand his successor a walking stick and when I was last there the number of sticks was 13. Also the collection of walking sticks kept in a sack in the attic was, apparently, subject to supernatural activity, for if they were not put away in a particular order, they have been known to sort themselves out into the correct order, with much rattling and tapping noises. Other reported activity here has included pictures falling from the walls without any good reason for doing so, strange bangs, raps and thuds, inexplicable footsteps and the unexplained opening and closing of doors.

I talked with a number of local people who had personal experience of the flute-playing 'Man in Red' (as he is called) and even more who had heard footsteps on the deserted stairway and had witnessed doors opening or closing, untouched by human hand. I examined the flute stick that plays by itself to herald the death of an occupant of the house. During my visits to Dockacre House I heard no flute-playing, no rattling of sticks and witnessed only one silent and unexplained opening and no closing of doors. I did hear footsteps that echoed strangely in an empty room and I had the distinct impression that something invisible brushed past me on the haunted stairway. Why are so many stairways haunted? Can it be they form a sort of vortex or whirlpool that sometimes gathers up psychic energy and becomes the centre of such activity in the house? Certainly it is a fact that the most haunted part of a house is likely to be the stairway area and there are far more haunted stairways than any other individual part of a house. One has only to recall places like The Queen's House, Greenwich; Raynham Hall; Newark Park; Longleat; Wolfeton House; Zeals House; Great Missenden Abbey; Old Battersea House; Farnham Castle; Salisbury Hall; Manderston House; Levens Hall and Ethie Castle, but it is an intriguing question. Perhaps when we climb or ascend stairs we unconsciously detach ourselves from the everyday world and become briefly autonomous, enabling some part of us to remain in the environment of the stairway, something that occasionally manifests itself. Perhaps stairways, existing as they do between two or more areas where people usually concentrate on one thing or another, provide a temporary region where we are relaxed, free from serious thought, inattentive, abstract in a way that is necessary, the requisite perhaps, and in this atmosphere forces or powers about which we know little and over which we have no control can record or register feelings and impressions and unconscious thoughts that may be picked up by other people at a later date.

During investigations carried out at Dockacre House I established that one area of the staircase registered a lower temperature than the rest and I wondered whether this was where the 'everlasting bloodstain' had once been in evidence. It was precisely in this part of the fine old staircase, I learned, that several visitors had suddenly and for no apparent reason felt ill or faint.

During the course of our investigations a door that had remained closed for hours abruptly swung open with a suddenness that startled everyone. There was no wind, no draught and we were unable to offer any explanation. Later we learned that previous and present occupants of the house had reported the inexplicable opening of that particular door. Naturally we controlled the door immediately, but there was no further movement during the course of five hours.

Twice automatic warning lights on our apparatus told us 'something' was interfering with our instruments but nothing showed up on immediate automatic photographs or registered on the running video-camera and nothing was visible to the naked eye. There was no unexplained movement of objects during our vigil.

TESTWOOD HOUSE

Most ghost guides include Testwood House (Rumasa), Totton, Southampton, ever since the publication of my *A–Z of British Ghosts* (1971), the first ever gazetteer of British ghosts and the first book to include the story of this and many other specific haunted houses.

Once a Tudor farmhouse and later a royal hunting lodge, and then the offices of sherry shippers, Testwood House is a medley of architecture; it stands gleaming white amid its green lawns and bright flower-beds, serene and peaceful, but it has been the scene of violent happenings and ghostly activity.

Over the years it is indisputable that heavy footsteps have been heard on many occasions walking along passages, footsteps that sound as though they are walking on echoing floorboards, although at the time the flooring of the passages was covered by thick carpeting. In particular such footsteps have been repeatedly reported from an upstairs corridor where dogs are very reluctant to go, a fact I can vouch for. I traced witnesses back to 1960, but then I heard from Mrs J.M. Ricketts of Southampton who told me in a letter of 7 September 1995 that she had been brought up with stories about Testwood House as their family home was situated nearby. She went to dancing lessons there during the Second World War and her grandfather had been a coachman there; he used to walk a big Alsatian dog as part of his duties and he always said there were parts of the house, upstairs, where the dog simply would not go.

In 1961 the caretaker's son and daughter returned home late one night from a dance and were surprised to see a tall man seemingly trying to get into the front door of Testwood House. They both plainly saw that he wore a frock coat and a tall hat, before the figure suddenly disappeared as they approached. About the same time, I discovered, the chef, working late in the kitchen, became aware of someone standing beside him – a figure that vanished almost immediately. Later, as he set out for home (nobody, I was told, at that time slept at Testwood House), the headlights of his car picked out the figure of a man on the drive. Aware that nobody had any business to be there at that time of the night, the chef stopped his car and got out to see who the intruder could be. As he approached the figure, clearly visible in the car headlights, he was surprised to see that the stranger wore a top hat and a long jacket or cape, but almost as soon as he was aware of these details, the figure was suddenly no longer there. Interestingly enough the unexplained figure of a man 'wearing a frock coat and a top hat' was seen later the same evening by another witness at the back of the house, a witness who was completely unaware of the previous sightings. A month later another staff member saw a similar figure standing by one of the drive gates in daylight.

I talked with the caretaker and his son who had been alerted one night by the barking of their dog into thinking that an intruder must be on the premises. They both ran across the yard to the main building where they found the back door rattling violently, although this particular door usually fits tightly; something I immediately tested and I have to say I could see no possibility of that door ever rattling. But no one was in sight and the pair circled the house, playing their torches on the windows and doors. When they reached the pantry window which, like the kitchen where the chef saw or sensed someone watching him, is in the oldest part of Testwood House, they saw that a face was looking down at them through the unglazed window that was protected by a mesh and bars. There could be no question of reflection (the answer to a number of reported 'ghostly' appearances on windows), and both father and son plainly saw the pale face of a young man, staring out of the window. They quickly established that no living person was inside the house and that the room in question was padlocked and deserted.

I had been told of a murder at Testwood House many years ago and without bringing the matter up myself I was informed by several of the people I interviewed on that and subsequent occasions that there had once been a manservant, a coachman some said, who had murdered the cook of the time in an upper room at the back of the house; he had then dragged the body along a corridor (subsequently shunned by dogs – notoriously psychic animals) and away from the house, across a road and finally dumping it in the byway known to this day as Cook's Lane.

On one occasion I took some friends to Testwood House, without telling them anything about the place and not mentioning a possible murder or ghostly activity of one sort or another. I wanted to see whether any of them had any reaction. Several found the upstairs room at the back of the house (where the murder may well have taken place and where the caretaker and his son saw someone's face at the window) most unpleasant, disconcerting and harbouring a strange 'waiting' feeling which none of them liked. Some of them said it was almost like the feeling of being strangled. Two members of the party refused to walk along the 'haunted' corridor. I had borrowed the caretaker's dog and he too refused to enter the corridor, even when I called his master and he tried to entice the dog to follow him along the corridor. My two reluctant friends were in front and they may have sensed the apprehension of the dog following on behind but, as we were about to descend the stairs to the ground floor, *all* of us heard the distinct sounds of someone walking down the stairs ahead of us, although we could plainly see that the stairway was deserted and that it was carpeted. The footsteps sounded as though they were walking on bare floorboards and discussing this afterwards most of us felt that they had sounded hurried and secretive; but the fact that footsteps which had no rational explanation were heard by eight alert and fit people on that occasion cannot be questioned.

Five years after that visit I was back at Testwood House talking to a company secretary working there who had heard nothing whatever about any haunting, being new to the organisation. He had been in the entrance hall at about 7.30 p.m. when he saw a man in a caped coat and tall hat sitting on a chair at the reception desk. At the same time he found himself inexplicably shivering with cold. He felt suddenly frightened and dashed blindly out of the front door where he quickly came to his senses and went back inside, but of the man he had seen there was no sign.

During this visit I talked with an elderly woman who had been a servant at Testwood House before the First World War. She told me she knew nothing about any ghost coachman or any murder, but she had always remembered hearing on just one occasion a noise that sounded like a team of horses galloping up the drive towards the house and she had hurriedly gone to the front door but she never saw or heard anything to account for the loud sounds. She had been in the upstairs room at the back of the house when she heard the sounds and afterwards she was told it was the room in which a murder had taken place. Could it be that the traumatic events that may have taken place in that room were preserved in some way and very occasionally anyone in the room heard the sounds and experienced the 'watching' and frightened feeling that one occupant must have felt?

BUCKINGHAM STREET, LONDON

Very occasionally ghostly figures are recognised and it is all the more interesting when it is established that the 'person' seen was in fact associated with the 'haunted' property; something not known at the time by the person seeing the ghost.

During the course of a series in a London national newspaper in April 1972 Tom Pocock wrote on the subject of Victorian enjoyments, saying, '... If the stairs in 14 Buckingham Street are haunted, I hope the gentle ghosts are of the buxom girls who climbed them to strip for Mr Etty. When nudity was permissible and popular so long as it was dressed up as something mythological, Etty shocked and delighted the Victorians by painting his models simply as beautiful bare bodies. Samuel Pepys who lived in a house on this site would have enjoyed calling on Mr Etty.' William Etty, RA (1787–1849) was a highly successful painter and life-long student of the nude; his oil studies are now highly valued. Samuel Pepys (1633–1703) lived in the house still standing at 12 Buckingham Street.

Gwyneth Bickford wrote to the newspaper from a West Kensington address as follows: 'I don't know about there being buxom girl ghosts at number 14 Buckingham Street but there is a ghost at number 12. I was running down the stairs there at about 7 o'clock one evening when a few steps from the bottom I gave a gasp and stopped. A man was standing beside the staircase. We just stood there looking at each other for what I suppose was a couple of seconds, and then he was gone.

'Soon after I moved my offices to number 22 so had no chance of seeing him again. The clothes were the right period, he lived at number 12 and the original staircase is still there ...'

Adele Butler, who is much interested in both psychic activity and seventeenth-century history, wrote to Gwyneth Bickford and asked her a few simple questions about her experience which was duly answered point by point. Adele Butler was particularly interested to note that Gwyneth Bickford jumped immediately to the conclusion that the person she saw was Samuel Pepys, and knowing that he was a tiny person in stature, she asked Miss Bickford about the height of the gentleman she saw. Miss Butler told me, 'I did not know that Pepys lived there until I saw the article ... the lady seems remarkably clear as to events though not to the actual appearance of the figure ... I have often wondered if (should I have the good fortune or otherwise to see a ghost) in similar circumstances I would painstakingly sum up every article of dress and figure, or whether I would speedily vanish myself!'

Gwyneth Bickford wrote: '... Number 12 is a very old building and I was told the staircase was original ... I have told various of my friends over the years about the experience. The date I saw the figure was somewhere around 1953–4 as I moved to number 22 about 1954. The stairs are wide and very shallow. I was about four steps from the bottom. The hall was reasonably lighted. I was alone although there were cleaners on the floors above.

'I was running down the stairs (probably anxious to get out of the building as the cleaners did not like us staying there after 6 p.m.) when I suddenly saw a figure standing against the wall between two doors. I stopped dead with fright but did not think of a ghost – just that someone was there when I didn't expect anyone to be there. It wasn't until I got out in the street that I began to realise what I had seen.

'He was not a bit transparent. In fact he did not look at all what I would have imagined a ghost to look like. He was very solid on his feet, very stocky build, his height, five feet, five inches maybe but I could be wrong about that as I am quite tall and I was standing on the stairs and looking over the banisters at him, although as the stairs are so shallow we were nearly at the same height. His outline was slightly blurred and his whole appearance grey but at the time I took this to be the colour of his clothes.

'But what struck me most and what I can remember so distinctly is the expression on his face. He was smiling with his lips *and* with his eyes as if he was tremendously pleased to see me. I can't think why I was so startled as no one could have looked kinder. It was just the unexpectedness of seeing someone there. I really don't know whether he disappeared or whether after stopping and looking I just ran on.

'I did know that Pepys had lived there but I never thought about seeing his ghost and I was certainly not thinking of him that evening. I had never thought of the house being haunted and we had never talked about it in the office.

'He was wearing knee breeches and stockings. His coat I would say was open although I can't be sure and I can't describe it. He did not have a hat on his head, neither did he have a full bottom wig. I have had a look at some books in the library and the clothes, as much I saw of them, do seem to be the right period.

'Whoever he was he must have been a very solid person when alive because his ghost was standing very firmly on his feet. I don't know why I got such a strong impression of his being so firmly on his feet – perhaps he had his feet slightly apart...'

In reply I said to Adele Butler: 'It is good to have all relevant details first-hand and I agree that there is probably little more that Miss Bickford can now add to the story. The account really is extremely interesting; I have never come across any reference to either the ghost of Pepys or any haunting at 12 Buckingham Street, a district I happen to know very well for over 20 years. I feel Miss Bickford's account has the ring of truth. There seems little point in her relating such an experience if it were untrue and little things such as the apparent solidarity of the figure suggest to me that she did see something, whether it could have been a real person is another question. If it was, he was dressed very oddly and had a "slightly blurred outline". On balance, I would think Miss Bickford probably did see a ghost.' More than 20 years after writing that letter I am still of the same opinion. Gwyneth Bickford was what might be described as a good witness and as far as human testimony can prove anything, we know there are many ghosts only seen on one occasion and many people who only see one ghost in their lifetime – as far as they know.

ALDERTON HALL

Actor Jack Watling and his family had considerable evidence that their home for many years was haunted. The whole family became convinced that there was a ghost at sixteenth-century timbered Alderton Hall, Loughton in Essex.

Daughter Deborah said she was in no doubt about the house being haunted, certainly ever since she had been a child: 'We learned that the probable cause was a servant girl who at one time was dishonoured by the master of the house. When she was turned out she drowned herself and her newly-born child in a pool in nearby Epping Forest. Soon afterwards the squire's small son was found drowned in the same pool. For centuries the legend has been handed down and many local people have always believed that the Hall was haunted and also the pool where a number of people have sworn that a pair of arms have emerged from the water and attempted to drag them in.'

Jack Watling talked to Ghost Club Society member Eric Maple and told him: 'When we first moved in I didn't take much notice of the story, but events changed my mind. Twice I heard running footsteps and twice I heard something invisible play the piano keys. And once I saw the figure of a fair-haired man in a red cloak. The figure was there for a moment, clear and solid; then it vanished.' The whole area was searched immediately but no one was found.

Deborah, who usually occupied the bedroom known as the 'Haunted Room', awakened one night to find an unknown face peering intently at her; another time she felt an invisible hand take hold of her hand and, thinking she was dreaming, she sat up and was amazed to see the figure of a young girl dissolve into the wall!

Once, when they were children, Deborah and her sister Nicola were sharing a bed when they were both awakened by an almighty crash. Nicola jumped out of bed and turned on the light and they found everything that had been on the bedside table had been swept across the room and the bed they were occupying had been pulled half-way across the room! Once too Deborah felt an invisible arm grab her and she was dragged bodily across the room; and she thought she saw the face of a girl one night on her bedroom wall, a girl with an old-fashioned hairstyle, and a pale and worried complexion. Sometimes too she heard her name called and times without number she heard footsteps on the stairway when no one was anywhere in sight.

The Watling son, Giles, has spoken of seeing the figure of a young girl in an attic room; a figure dressed in white that vanished almost as soon as he was aware of the seemingly solid figure.

Among the stories associated with Alderton Hall is one involving highwayman Dick Turpin – who seems to be one of the most active of ghosts and certainly frequented the area. Turpin is said to have roasted an old woman in the now bricked-up fireplace until she revealed where she had hidden her money. A former owner of the house claimed to have seen the ghost of this old woman.

The Watlings lived more or less happily with their ghost or ghosts for many years and all the occupants say none of them were ever really frightened, feeling that the house had a friendly atmosphere for most of the time and in many ways they were sorry to leave.

GAULDEN MANOR

Gaulden Manor at Tolland in Somerset, occupied by Mr and Mrs James Le Gendre Starkie, is a house that has the reputation of having had visits from the famous phantom coach of the Turbervilles, immortalised by Thomas Hardy; such visits supposedly presaged the death of a member of the family, however since there are no longer any Turbervilles at

Gaulden Manor it may no longer have visits from a phantom coach, but that there are other ghosts at the house seems to be well established.

James Turberville, a Bishop of Exeter who refused to take the Oath of Supremacy to Elizabeth I in 1559, found himself imprisoned in the Tower of London with five other like-minded bishops. Released in 1563 he was allowed to spend the last years of his life quietly at Gaulden. Today the splendid plaster frieze in the Great Hall reminds us of the life and times of the bishop and over the massive fireplace can be seen the arms of the Turbervilles, James, Sir Robert and Sir Richard: who can doubt that the heavy footsteps heard so many times on the 'deserted' main stairway are those of a past Turberville, for they all came to love this house? The garden is haunted too. Some monks are said to be buried in the haunted Bishops' Garden and to walk there on occasions. Witnesses have included people who had no idea that Gaulden was in the possession of Taunton Priory in the twelfth century and that the phantom monks are walking where they used to walk in gentler times; perhaps when the air here is scented from the Elizabethan herb garden the atmosphere is conducive, enabling some people to see figures that were here long, long ago.

The ghosts at Gaulden are numerous and mysterious with half-forgotten origins and half-remembered experiences. There is the uni-dentified small woman whose ghost haunts the front stairs; the ghostly grey lady who sometimes sits on the right-hand side of the fireplace and the phantom female who appeared so often in one of the bedrooms that for years that room was kept locked and shuttered.

Off the Great Hall there is a small room that has always been called The Chapel, divided from the Hall by beautifully carved panels. During the course of one visit to Gaulden, late one autumn afternoon, my wife sat alone in the Great Hall for a while and when Mrs Le Starkie asked her whether she liked the room, my wife replied that she felt something very unpleasant had happened in the area of the carved panels and only then did Mrs Le Starkie reveal that on more than one occasion visitors have said they could see three Cavaliers standing in front of the panels, covered in blood. During the Civil War there was a bloody battle nearby and it is more than probable that some Cavaliers sought shelter at Gaulden, perhaps wounded, perhaps dying – and that they have left behind something that some people can detect three hundred years later. It is known that Cromwell's men were at Gaulden Manor for over a week at one turbulent period of the conflict.

As with many haunted houses the stairs at Gaulden Manor seem to be the centre of apparent phenomena, and past and present owners have heard loud and distinct knocks sounding from the door at the head of the stairs. Each time there are just two sharp knocks, usually in the middle of the night, loud enough to awaken anyone sleeping nearby. In spite of immediate and extensive examination and exploration at the time and later nothing has ever been found that might account for the knocks. I examined the door and could suggest no logical reason for the occasional sudden, loud, limited and frightening knocks. It is interesting that several visitors have become uneasy in the immediate vicinity of this door, one suddenly stopping and saying the hair at the back of his neck prickled and he was sure something terrible had once happened there.

Footsteps, firm and heavy, loud and unmistakable, have been heard mounting the main staircase and it has been noticed that there is never any sound continuing beyond the top of the stairs, as though whatever is manifesting or whatever sounds are heard, it or they are confined to the ancient stairway itself, imprisoned as it were for all time within the staircase itself. I have no doubt that if the staircase was moved or structurally altered the sounds would cease – although the same alterations might release something else such as a phantom form!

The room at the top of the stairs, the Turberville Bedroom, seems to be a delightful room, yet even here in such surroundings, the ghostly form of a monk has been seen. On one visit we talked with Mrs Hunter, who helped in the house and shop when the house was open to the public, and we learned that both she and her daughter had seen ghosts at Gaulden.

On another visit, to take part in a day's filming, my wife and I arrived about 11 a.m. After a few moments my wife left to explore some of the antique shops in the area and she returned to collect me about 3.30 p.m. Almost as soon as she returned to the house Mrs Hunter asked her whether she had changed and returned to Gaulden Manor at lunchtime, which of course she had not done, but Mrs Hunter said she had been working in the dining-room and had looked up around noon and had seen a woman with dark hair and wearing a blue costume of some sort standing in the hall by the front door; after a moment the figure was no longer there. My wife's dark hair and height suggested to Mrs Hunter that she was the only real person it could have been, the only person at Gaulden Manor that day who looked anything like the figure she saw, but my wife was miles away at the time. Mrs Hunter did admit that it appeared to be the same figure she had seen on other occasions, but this time she really thought it was a human being – until it disappeared inexplicably and she discovered the whereabouts of the only person at the Manor that day who resembled the form she had seen.

During our visits to Gaulden Manor knocks and raps and unexplained footsteps were all heard and I am satisfied they were all inexplicable in rational terms: the place, the time, the people present and everything involved in these experiences leaves me in no doubt that in all probability they had a paranormal origin. And of course there is the figure seen in the hall, a figure recognised as having been seen before.

NEW PARK MANOR

In November 1986 a correspondent from Cheshire wrote to me out of the blue concerning a 'strange circumstance' that occurred during a visit by his parents to a hotel, New Park Manor at Brockenhurst in the New Forest. I quote verbatim from his letter: 'Both my parents were kept awake by the unmistakable buzz of voices, none of which they could hear individually. There was nobody outside and the murmur seemed loudest outside their window on the first floor. Indeed my mother said that when she opened the window to investigate the noise became concentrated and appeared to burst into the room. She felt that it was as if a crowd of people were engaged in some activity. My father also heard the noise and could not explain it, although he does not believe in the supernatural. They did not feel that it was the noise of animals as the sounds were definitely in the air. I should add that I believe they were in a new wing of the hotel.

'The next morning another lady in the hotel said that she had heard the same noise and that it had frightened her. My parents did not ask for an explanation from anyone at the hotel but my mother was told by someone in another hotel that the place has the reputation of being haunted but with no explanation. The holiday was in September and they returned without finding out anything more; however, the incident really shook them ... my parents do not feel that the noise of dogs and horses would result in such a concentration, almost pressure, of noise on first floor rooms ...'

After spending a few days at the hotel (without disclosing exactly who I was) I made some discreet enquiries and obtained some confirmation of what I had been told previously. In a letter sent to me on 25 March 1987 I was told: 'The Hotel is, indeed, reputed to be haunted – all friendly apparitions I have been told! We did in fact have three mediums stay with us shortly after the Hotel came under new management two years ago, who all saw and "spoke" to the sightings, though apparently there was no time to talk in great detail. I have spoken to those people who have seen and/or felt a presence and attach a brief resumé . . .' The appended note was headed 'Ghosts at New Park Manor' and read:

1. A stagecoach is heard rumbling along in the distance, the feeling of it rushing past (similar to the approach of an underground train); it stops by the stables which used to be the coaching stop *en route* to London.

2. 1700s: an old lady in the public rooms (which used to be her front room – the old entrance to the house) gazes out of the window (Cobbitt's time).

3. An old man (not related to the old lady, nor did they know each other), short with pure white hair in pageboy style receding, round shoulders, dressed in black suit with white collar, in his seventies. Seen both during day and night in restaurant and lounges. Also heard during night shuffling along the corridor.

4. In one of the bedrooms which used to be a nursery – a very pretty lady, in grey flannel dress, sitting at window (which no longer exists) writing letters – circa 1900s.

5. Cellar – eleventh century and the oldest part of the building; no actual sightings but definitely a presence – not friendly. The dogs refuse to go down there: their hackles rise, etc.

6. There is also supposed to be a crouching serving wench in one of the bedrooms, with horrible teeth, a vile smell and what appears to be a purple haze: only one person has seen this appearance but many guests refuse to sleep in this room reporting they feel a presence and/or general unease.

The upshot was that I took a party of 15 friends to New Park Manor for a couple of days in the following July. During that investigative visit presences were sensed, disembodied voices were heard, unexplained scents were experienced, footsteps were heard from unoccupied rooms and passages (in one instance when a passage was under surveillance from both ends) and a figure was seen by two watchers who were among those who stayed up overnight and encountered rather more than they had anticipated. The investigations included careful monitoring of the allegedly haunted areas, night vigils in different parts of the property and the use of various instruments and recording apparatus. We managed to record a snatch of conversation that had not originated from anyone present, the sound of footsteps from an empty stairway and the sound of a panting animal, although no animals were present at the time. As so often in these regions we are faced with relying on human testimony and while that may often be unsatisfactory it has to be accepted, as it is in a court of law, when it is corroborated, comes from a reliable witness and is established beyond reasonable doubt. On these criteria New Park Manor has been the scene of paranormal activity witnessed by serious and experienced investigators, by people who have little or no knowledge of the history of the property, or that such happenings had been reported previously, and by staff and local people who may have heard stories but are sceptical. It all adds up to a formidable array of evidence.

SUTTON PLACE

A ghostly Lady in White has long been said to haunt Sutton Place in Surrey. When I received reports of other apparently paranormal activity there I wrote to the then owner and resident Paul Getty about the possibility of bringing some friends interested in ghosts and ghostly activity to Sutton Place, and I was a little surprised to receive a reply asking whether I could go and see him. I found him very interested in ghosts and after a chat he readily agreed to a visit. I set about inviting selected friends, including F.R. Maude, Dr Letitia Fairfield, Glanville Squiers, Eric Wookey, Lt. Gen. Sir Kenneth Lock and Hope Alexander, former head of copyright at the BBC; all of them visited Sutton Place with me.

Paul Getty and I talked of ghosts at some length and, amid the priceless Brussels tapestries, the gold candelabra and the wonderful art treasures of that Elizabethan mansion, eventually I persuaded him to talk of the ghosts of Sutton Place: the unidentified ghost in the long gallery, mentioned by a visitor as long ago as 1777 and by another visitor as recently as 1980; the Lady in White (also unidentified) who, I was told, had been heard and not seen, and on other occasions seen and not heard, both inside the dark and gloomy mansion and outside in the garden.

Our visit to Sutton Place, 'that dark and gloomy and scary place' as one of Getty's grandsons has described it, was almost uneventful from a psychic viewpoint but I shall always remember the loud crashing sound that preceded some of us as we entered the haunted long gallery and *again* as we filed into the great hall. In each case the tremendous noise seemed to originate from just beyond the door we were about to pass through – yet on both occasions there was nothing to show for the startling sounds and the rooms were patently devoid of any human being. In the garden two of my party said they had 'almost' glimpsed a fleeting form that sped with remarkable agility behind a bush and then completely disappeared.

Paul Getty told me he was worried by what an American psychic had told him: that he would die on foreign soil. Later I heard that he sent confidential letters to a number of his friends in different parts of the world asking them to ensure that he was sent home to California if he ever looked like dying while in their part of the world. Sadly two of his sons predeceased him and Paul Getty himself lies buried in California beside them, after dying 6000 miles away, alone, wrapped in a blanket in his study at Sutton Place.

During the course of a stay at Sutton Place even the Duke of Windsor wrote of being alone in a 'huge room which felt spooky'.

OLD BATTERSEA HOUSE

One day I happened to remember a visit I made many years ago to Old Battersea House in London and on the spur of the moment I contacted the administrator at that time, Patricia McCaldin, who lived in the house and had done so for the past 13 years. She told me it was now a family house owned by Malcolm Forbes and his family and used on their frequent visits to the UK. She added: 'It is a large house and I am entirely on my own and I am rather concerned that any investigation you have in mind may upset our "resident" who accepts me totally and I have no wish to cause her distress...'. In reply I said that she need have no fear of our upsetting the 'resident', on the contrary in fact, I felt sure our sympathetic and understanding approach would be accepted and might well work wonders. So it was arranged and again I asked a few friends whether they would like to join me; they included scientist Dr Vernon Harrison, former President of The Royal Photographic Society; and shipping company director and Society for Psychical Research Council Member, Ken Lazenby; also musician Shirley Shaw; and researchers Philip Moore and Dennis Moyses.

I had previously visited Old Battersea House more than 30 years before in the company of Alasdair Alpin MacGregor who was working on one of his 'ghostie' books, as he liked to call them. He chanced to mention his friend Wilhelmena Stirling, saying she lived not far away at historic Old Battersea House. Mrs Stirling, who died not very long after our visit a few days before her hundredth birthday, was very curious when she learned that I was interested in ghosts.

I was spellbound at the beauty of Old Battersea House and its contents, altogether a veritable Pre-Raphaelite treasure house. Certainly the house had seen better days but housing, as it still does, the truly remarkable De Morgan Collection of pottery, paintings and porcelain within the superbly suitable setting of Old Battersea House itself, it really was and still is something quite exceptional. After the death of Mrs Stirling, her husband having predeceased her, the house was in poor condition and things looked bleak until Malcolm Forbes offered to restore the house at his own expense, if he could then use part as private accommodation; and so Old Battersea House was restored and refurbished to its former glory and to present-day standards of convenience.

Malcolm Forbes (1919–90) was a millionaire publisher, art collector, hot-air balloonist and one of America's richest eccentrics. His influence at Old Battersea House is obvious but laudable; quite literally he saved the house and its irreplaceable collection. Yet it has been suggested that Wilhelmena Stirling might have found the American ownership and some of the alterations, improvements and embellishments not to her liking, and if it was possible for her to do so, might she return to the house she loved and lived in for more than three decades?

One object that had attracted my attention on that first visit to the house had been a fine, carved, fifteenth-century Italian wooden armchair. After examining it for a few moments I went to sit down in it but Mrs Stirling stopped me. 'No. No,' she said. 'Not that chair dear, I keep it for the ghosts.'

Among many people who had felt the chair to be haunted, either seeing someone sitting in it who disappeared or having a strange experience while sitting in it themselves, was, I learned, Lady Churchill, mother of Winston. She was often at Old Battersea House and once called Mrs Stirling's attention to a man sitting in the chair, 'a man with a little pointed beard and a big Elizabethan ruff and with a rapier in his hand ...'. Mrs Stirling could see nothing but after that she avoided sitting in the chair herself and half-seriously dissuaded others from doing so. Once, a visitor sat in the chair before Mrs Stirling could stop him but he jumped up immediately saying the chair was icy cold and he had heard whispering close to his ear. For the rest of the time he was at Old Battersea House he could hardly take his eyes off the haunted chair.

Alasdair Alpin MacGregor always considered children good witnesses and on one occasion at Old Battersea House he and Wilhelmena Stirling were in the Garden Room talking to a mutual friend whose little daughter was playing in the hall. Suddenly the child ran up to her mother and said: 'Who is the man in the chair? He's wearing funny clothes and he won't talk to me ...' By the time they went into the hall the haunted chair was deserted, even to the eyes of the child. 'Man gone now,' she said.

Another time, also in the Garden Room, a visitor sitting facing the arched doorway leading into the hall and stairway suddenly rose from her chair, smiling, as if to welcome someone and then, an astonished look crossing her face, she resumed her seat. Looking very puzzled she said she had plainly seen an elderly lady about to enter the room but as she stood up the figure had completely vanished. She knew nothing about the ghostly form of an old lady that had long haunted the environs of the hall at Old Battersea House.

Wilhelmena Stirling related to me another incident concerning Lady Churchill. They were having tea in the Garden Room one Sunday afternoon when Mrs Stirling was called away. When she returned she encountered Lady Churchill in the adjoining hall, silent and preoccupied. After a moment she asked: 'Do you have a friend staying here who is going to a fancy-dress ball?' 'At 4 o'clock on a Sunday afternoon?' replied Mrs Stirling. 'I should hardly think so, why do you ask?'

Lady Churchill then explained that she had glimpsed a man half-way down the stairs looking over the banister. She saw to her surprise that he was wearing a plumed hat and a bright blue coat with oddly positioned diamond-shaped buttons. She also noticed that he was carrying a sword and wore long boots, which she saw gleaming through the balustrades of the landing. As she watched, he stood erect for a moment and then slowly walked down the stairs towards her, the end of his sword striking each step as he did so. Reaching the bottom of the stairs he took no notice of Lady Churchill but walked past, almost brushing against her as he did so, and turning to his right, disappeared into a closed door!

Lady Churchill was reminded of a portrait she had seen of the Duke of Marlborough, remembering in particular the positioning of the oddly shaped buttons on his coat. When she mentioned the Duke to Wilhelmena Stirling she learned for the first time that he had constantly visited the house, being a great friend of Bolingbroke, whose seat the house had once been: he called it Bolingbroke House. 'So it *was* the Duke!' Lady Churchill had exclaimed. 'And I suppose he ignored me because I'm a relative of his!'

Sadly the 'haunted chair' was no longer at Old Battersea House, Miss McCaldin informed me, but that the house was haunted there seemed little doubt. I don't think Wilhelmena Stirling ever saw any ghosts there (if she did she wasn't telling), but she certainly heard sounds and experienced happenings there that had no logical explanation. The distinct raps, taps and footsteps had nothing to do with the usual creaks and groans heard in any old house, and then there was the movement of heavy objects, furniture, paintings and articles of all kinds both inside and outside the house. Twice, she told me, she had been awakened in the middle of the night by a heavy bump in her bedroom exactly as though a person had thrown himself on to the bed beside her: a most alarming experience on each occasion and totally without any obvious explanation.

During our visit 30 years later Patricia McCaldin told me that just a few days before our visit, one Saturday, a complete stranger to the house was looking round when she came to a halt in the middle of the hall, saying she didn't like the atmosphere and could hardly bring herself to walk across to the stairs which she said were 'loaded with sad feelings'.

We learned that on several recent occasions some of the very heavy and very valuable paintings had been found safely leaning against the wall below where they were normally hung – no broken cord or wire or any obvious reason ever being found; once the picture over the bed in the 'haunted bedroom' and once the picture over the mantlepiece in the same room. Here too the electric lights had been turned on several times after the regular night visits to ensure that all lights were off, and in one instance the plug leading to an electric lamp was removed for safety when a four-year-old child was sleeping in the room but in the morning the plug was found to have been inserted, switched on and the lamp switched on. The same night one of the windows, kept closed for security reasons, was found to have been opened. After enquiries it was accepted that the child could not have been responsible for these incidents.

Among the furniture that had been found moved at night in deserted rooms, chairs seemed to be the most popular item. Sometimes different chairs in different rooms had been moved right across the floor the whole length of the room and once a large mirror was found broken, although no sound had been heard and it was established that it was undamaged and intact the evening before.

The haunted bedroom seemed to have been visited on several occasions by the ghostly figure of an old lady, occupants of the bedroom waking to see the phantom form standing beside the bed or sitting on the bed. In each case after a few seconds the figure disappeared. Once a young couple awoke and saw a shape in the room that disappeared before they could establish what it had been but they had the impression of a little old lady. They both had felt a shiver run through them as they had crossed the hall on their way upstairs earlier in the evening.

A mediumistic woman who visited the house said there was a 'presence in the hall' and, after remaining there alone for a time, she said she had made contact and the presence was an elderly lady who was not happy with Americans being in possession of the house and making a lot of alterations, like central heating and extra bedrooms, and she no longer felt settled and comfortable in her own home . . .

There does seem to be varied evidence that the ghostly form of an elderly lady has haunted the house for some 30 years and Miss McCaldin said she had become quite used to visitors asking about the old lady they saw seemingly looking at the pictures in the corridor outside the haunted bedroom.

During the night we spent at Old Battersea House two of my friends felt that an invisible woman came into the Garden Room; another kept having the impression of animals and repeatedly the name Margaret Pigg came into her mind; she too had the distinct impression of an old lady who hovered about the doorway and was always just about to come into the room from the hall, and several of us heard a swishing sound that we could not explain.

Just before midnight, two of us, stationed on different parts of the stairway, one on the top landing and one half-way down, both had the fleeting impression of a sweet scent that wafted down, but was there one moment and gone the next. Drops in temperature were noticed and duly recorded but they had no connection with any paranormal activity as far as we could establish.

Another member of our party, while resting in the Garden Room, had the overwhelming impression that an elderly lady was about to enter the room from the hall. So distinct was this feeling that my friend rose from the chair she had been sitting in, ready to welcome, as she thought, a visitor or someone associated with the house whom she had not met. A very similar impression was experienced by another of the party in the Cedar Room when he was there alone afterwards. Another, who knew what she was talking about, heard snatches of music emanating from an empty room, music described to me as 'probably Italian Renaissance'.

I have always found investigations in haunted houses quite fascinating and although such investigations usually comprise spending a great deal of time waiting for something to happen – and all too often nothing does – nevertheless there is always the possibility that 'something' might happen, an apparition might be seen under controlled conditions, a manifestation might be recorded scientifically and it is worth remembering that one has only to obtain irrefutable proof of some paranormal happening to have to face the fact that our present physical assessment of the world is incomplete. An example of that incompleteness which would be unanswerable in our present perception of the world would become apparent if it could be established that battlefields retain something of the agony that once existed there. So now we will go on to examine that possibility.

CHAPTER FIVE

HAUNTED BATTLEFIELDS

D oes the tension and agony of war create ghosts? Evidence suggests that there are battlefields restless with spectral soldiers, phantom armies and the sound of battle. While many psychical researchers feel that the phantom men and horses that are seen and the sounds of battle that are heard are not individual ghostly activity but reruns of traumatic events of the past, these collective hallucinations (to name an alternative theory) are varied in time and place and may be more dependent on the atmospheric conditions prevailing and the people present than has been acknowledged up to now. Some of these remnants of battle are invisible, but the sounds remain.

A case in point dates from 1951 when two English women on holiday in France near Dieppe were awoken by the sounds of gunfire that lasted for over three hours. They also heard the noise of dive-bombing and the cries of wounded men. A bloody battle had been fought on the Dieppe beaches exactly nine years earlier, during the same hours on 19 August 1942; a raid that had been seen as an essential rehearsal for the D-Day invasion two years later. The Dieppe raid was in fact a catastrophic failure with more than half the Canadian and British troops taking part being either killed or wounded. The Society for Psychical Research investigated the whole case over an extended period and came to the conclusion that 'a genuine psychic experience' had taken place.

CEDAR CREEK, VIRGINIA

The site of the Battle of Cedar Creek in Virginia, USA has been called 'one of the most haunted battlefields of the American Civil War'. In October 1864, Sheridan's 'Army of the Shenandoah' was camped beside the creek, completely unaware that a Confederate force under General Early had been marching day and night, determined to deal the Union army a stunning blow. The surprise attack came out of an autumn fog and after the initial fusillade the Union camp was overrun. The surviving soldiers fled and the ravenous Confederate troops fired at the fleeing men with their own artillery and then, ignoring their orders, fell upon the food supplies.

Sheridan awoke to the sound of musketry and cannon and within minutes he was racing towards the sound of battle, and there he met his disorganised and leaderless troops hurrying north in defeat. He rallied his men, turned them round, restored order and under his command they met the overconfident Southerners and broke their advancing line in a dozen places. The tired Confederate troops broke up, scattered and themselves fled. The Shenandoah campaign ended in a triumph won from the shadow of defeat.

This short, sharp and bitter operation saw pain, sudden death, violent action and strong emotions, all amid the clash of battle, and the screams and cries of the wounded and the dying. The effects of this violence and strong emotion still seem to linger at the site of the battle, and from time to time visitors and people with little or no knowledge of the event encounter some of the sounds of that battle: the clash of conflict, the call of bugles, the distant cries of wounded men, the whine of shots and the distant booming of cannon.

Vincent Gaddis, a much-respected Californian, has revealed that at a nearby church, used as a hospital outpost during the conflict, 'one can occasionally hear the cries and moans of the wounded'.

THE HAUNTED CALIFORNIAN RANCH

A ranch in California built on the site of a ranch that had been attacked by Native American Indians in 1820 was, according to the Revd Dr Kenneth McAll, very haunted at one time. All those years ago the Native Americans were rebelling against the Spanish soldiers who locked themselves in the church, knowing the Native Americans would not damage a religious building. The Native Americans meanwhile took refuge in the Spanish barracks, no doubt expecting similar restraint, but during the night the soldiers set fire to the barracks and allowed no one to escape. Today a heap of rubble still marks the site of the massacre. And the new ranch has been the subject of many curious happenings.

An open-air religious service took place at the site (the location of which I am obliged to keep secret) a few years ago when the new owners of the ranch apologised to the Native Americans from a neighbouring reserve. Nevertheless unexplained incidents continued to affect the family occupying the new ranch. Two of the family developed swollen, red and itchy skins, another was suddenly affected with breathlessness, palpitations and a feeling of great fear, and there were other health problems that might well have affected the imprisoned Native Americans more than a century and a half before. When the family left the ranch and returned to the city, all was well. Back at the ranch sights and sounds from the past continued, with whooping sounds of charging Native Americans, the clash of arms and sound of rifle fire and the occasional glimpse of a running Native American or a fleeing soldier being reported by local people and passing visitors. Things became so bad, Dr Kenneth McAll told me, that it was decided to see whether another religious reconciliation of some kind might be helpful.

Dr McAll's medical and religious experiences have led him to make sensational claims and he believes many ghosts, or 'haunted souls' as he calls them, are 'our tormented ancestors'. By holding a religious service he feels he can liberate such ghosts from their tormented states and stop them frightening people and haunting places. By drawing up a kind of family tree in respect of haunting entities he believes he can identify the ghosts responsible. So a religious service was arranged and this time included a retired Native American chief, a priest and a Spaniard, representing the chief protagonists, and at the end of the visit which included the sprinkling of holy water and the laying-out of flowers, the atmosphere seemed to be much improved and the family, who had suffered so much in one way and another, endured no more ill effects, I am told. Incidentally, Dr McAll, a consultant and psychiatrist for some 25 years, lived for some time in a house in the New Forest that was once the home of Sir Arthur Conan Doyle.

THE BATTLE OF SAN PASQUAL

Richard Senate, an American parapsychologist who goes out looking for ghosts, has reportedly said, 'Battlefields are known to hold ghosts'. Phantom armies, he believes, still march over some of history's best-known battlefields, such as the fatal confrontation between Mexicans and Yankees in 1847 at San Pasqual in San Diego County, California. Here, where the dead on both sides are buried in a mass grave, unnaturally cold draughts of wind have been recorded and strange cries have echoed through the canyon.

One of the last fierce battles of the Mexican-American War seems to have left what Richard Senate describes as 'deep psychic scars' on the land and 'many accounts exist of ghosts wandering the site'. Although not a tremendously important or a decisive battle it was the largest battle fought in California; who actually won is a question that is still hotly debated. But if the Battle of San Pasqual can be fairly described as a draw with no actual winner, there was undoubted bravery, grim determination and heroism on both sides, and all this is demonstrated by the battlefield site becoming a state park and a museum detailing the almost forgotten battle.

The tour and the museum are interesting enough, it seems, but the ghost lore is missing and no mention is made of the ghosts that are regularly reported on the night of each 6 December, the anniversary of the battle, of the screams and icy blasts of air that hover over areas of the battlefield. Even phantom Mexican lancers and American dragoons have been reported, locked in eternal combat. San Pasqual Battlefield Park is, by all accounts, a strange and mysterious place where visual memories linger of a half-forgotten war.

WAR IN THE CHANNEL ISLANDS

The Channel Islands, the only British territory occupied by Germany during the Second World War, may well be considered to be a battle-field, as indeed it was for five years, an uneasy tension existing between the islanders and the Germans, many of whom were terrified of being surreptitiously sniped at or killed as an enemy of the inhabitants or being discovered fraternising with the enemy or, worst of all, being transferred to the Russian Front, as many were. Because of the high rate of casualties experienced by the German armies in that battle area any such assignment was looked upon by the troops as a sentence of death.

Among the records of the Channel Islands Occupation Society there are a number of interesting reports of paranormal activity, particularly on Guernsey. Residents and newcomers to the island, not aware that German soldiers were billeted there during those five turbulent years, have reported seeing soldiers in German uniform in bedrooms and other rooms in houses that, it has subsequently been established, German soldiers had in fact visited for some purpose or other. Phantom German soldiers in their grey uniforms were occasionally reported by various people, including children, cycling between Bourg and the old airport. From time to time visitors to the Mirus gun site at Les Rouvets Farm on Guernsey have experienced an overwhelming feeling of panic and distress as we shall see in Chapter 11.

While making a film at La Vassalerie where the Germans had tunnelled into the hillside and built a two-part complex, half military hospital, half ammunition store, Peter Sellers himself told me he had never been so frightened in his life. He felt he could almost touch the total fear that surrounded him 'in that awful place which many people believe to be haunted'. Guernsey people don't go there and visitors giggle nervously when they get out. Whatever is required to produce a haunted battlefield applies equally to the Channel Islands where frightening paranormal activity has repeatedly been reported.

Dr Kenneth McAll has written of the hauntings associated with the German hospitals and defence on the Channel Islands, including voices, especially, he told me, a repeated guttural 'Ya'. Why there should be 'voices' may be explained by the enormous number of people murdered when these premises were being built and afterwards. Apparently anyone who offended the Germans in any way was summarily sent to their deaths, usually in view of other islanders, and their bodies thrown into the ever-presdnt concrete mixers.

Fellow prisoners and friends and relatives of the victims wrote their names with their fingers in the wet cement – and there were hundreds of them. When the building was completed the Germans, not wishing any of their secrets of defence emplacements to become known, killed all the remaining workers and threw their bodies into the concrete mixers. The Channel Islands Occupation Society rejects such stories, pointing out that no proof of such atrocities has ever been found and that placing bodies in the concrete would be practically impossible due to the steel reinforcing rods in the cement. Yet can it be the voices of anguished, murdered prisoners and their tormentors that are still occasionally reported?

THE BATTLE OF KILLIECRANKIE

The brief but bloody battle of Killiecrankie took place on 27 July 1689 when 2500 Highland Jacobites under Viscount John Graham of Claverhouse, better known as Bonnie Dundee, routed 3400 of William III's troops under General Mackay.

The battle was fought on the hillside above the main road a mile north of the Killiecrankie Pass through which King William's men advanced to engage the Highlanders, only to return in disarray soon afterwards as they fled from the torrent of bare-footed, tartan-clad, shouting Scots in the red glow of a summer evening.

Before the battle Bonnie Dundee had seen a phantom blood-stained head which he took to be a warning that death awaited him at Killiecrankie. So, on the day, he delayed things as long as he could and only ordered his men to descend from the high ground when sunset filled the pass. Within minutes King William's forces were defeated but as they fled a fatal shot struck Dundee.

Now, each 27 July, a supernatural glow is said to hang over the scene of the conflict; a phantom glow that many people, but not everyone, can see in that ominous valley; a ghostly glow that relates, perhaps, to the vivid sunset that lit the battle in that Perthshire pass.

Many years ago a party of horse riders approaching the Pass of Killiecrankie encountered a tall figure wearing a cowl or hood. As it moved towards them the horses panicked and their riders clung desperately to their steeds which they found refused to enter the Killiecrankie Pass. Enquiries ascertained that the mysterious phantom form was seen every few years, hovering about the same spot, but whether it has anything to do with the Battle of Killiecrankie, nobody seems to know. But perhaps it does suggest that there is something in the area that is sympathetic and conducive to psychic activity.

More recently a lone cyclist claimed to see the same figure, which appeared to bound after him and he had to pedal desperately to get away. Once actually in the Pass of Killiecrankie he was relieved to find the apparition or whatever it was had disappeared.

In August 1955 a correspondent from Dundee informed me that he and a friend explored the historic Pass of Killiecrankie on the evening and early morning of 27 and 28 July, the anniversary of the battle. Stuart Walker tells me that he and his friend had anticipated seeing or experiencing something of a supernatural nature but what followed, whether it was natural or supernatural, 'scared the life' out of the visitors. I quote verbatim: 'For a while we had argued about where the best place was to see possible phenomena. It was about 12.40 a.m. when we saw what looked like an old-fashioned lantern about a hundred yards ahead of us. We were not sure what it was but established that it was definitely coming towards us. We dived down the embankment as a result of being completely stunned. Moments later some five or six people walked past engaging in conversation, "Where do we go now?" was one phrase we heard. They wore clothes similar to those of yesteryear, cloaks and three-pointed hats. They passed without taking any notice of us. We asked at the Centre next day whether any re-enactment groups were in the area, anyone taking part in ghost walks, or any practical explanation for what we had seen. We learned nothing.'

The land of Scotland has seen much strife and bitter warfare and fierce battles over the years and many of the sites of these confrontations are haunted, as are some of the memorial cairns and hiding places of some of the contestants.

THE PSYCHIC AFTERMATH OF CULLODEN

The last pitched battle in Britain was fought on Culloden Moor in 1746 where Bonnie Prince Charlie's 5000 tired and hungry Highlanders met 9000 government troops and it was all over in 68 minutes. The Highlanders' losses were enormous with the victorious English massacring the wounded enemies. The English dead numbered about 50. Today a cairn and a green mound mark the scene of the tragedy in a setting that has changed little in 250 years.

However, on occasions, and especially at dusk, the dim form of a battle-worn Highlander has been observed in the vicinity of the cairn and one visitor, while looking closely at the Highlanders' graves, lifted a square of Stewart tartan which had blown down from the stone of the grave-mound and distinctly saw the body of a handsome, dark-haired Highlander, lying full length on top of the mound.

The visitor began to sense that the figure she was looking at was not of this world; his clothes were dirty, muddy and of old-fashioned cut and material; his face had an unnatural pallor – and as she fully realised that she was seeing something of a paranormal character, she turned and fled from that field of memories.

Mr J.W. Whyle of Glasgow is another person who is aware of the psychic aftermath of Culloden. He wrote to me: 'There are a number of small wooded islands on Loch Morar near Mallaig and it was on one of them that Simon Fraser, Lord Lovat, hid after the defeat of Prince Charles's forces at Culloden. He was eventually captured by Cumberland's Dragoons but he still "moves" around the little island where he once hid. I have seen him. A very heavy old chap, with a fat florid face and suffering badly from gout!'

ISANDLWANA MOUNTAIN, EASTERN ZULULAND

In September 1993 I received a most interesting letter from a reader of my books living in Marlborough and again I cannot do better than quote exactly: '... I am very interested in the theory that a place may become imprinted with occurrences of the past and I am writing to tell you about one such place I have visited.

'Earlier this year I was lucky enough to visit South Africa and some of the battlefields of the Anglo-Zulu War of 1879; the study of which is my particular hobby. One of these sites is the mountain of Isandlwana, an isolated, sphinx-shaped block of sandstone in Eastern Zululand. It was beneath this mountain, on 22 January 1879, that a Zulu army massacred over 1000 British troops and their Colonial allies. The bodies of these soldiers were left unburied for three months; and when the remains were interred, it was often impossible to identify the corpses. The white cairns that now litter the site each cover the bodies of between two and four soldiers, although the bones were naturally sometimes mixed up.

'The night before my visit to the battlefield, another tourist, who had been to Isandlwana that day, commented on the atmosphere at the site. Sure enough, once out of the car and walking around the various cairns and monuments, it is possible to experience an overwhelming sense of menace in the area. The mountain, rising over the plain in front of it, seems to sit brooding over its history, and exudes an almost indescribable atmosphere of despair. Although I am not aware of the battlefield being haunted, I feel that at least some of the violent history for which this mountain is best known remains in the strange mood experienced by most visitors. None of the other sites I visited, which included Rorke's Drift (of *Zulu* fame), Talana and Blood River, had the same feeling or held quite the same fascination after standing beneath Isandlwana.'

My correspondent, Matthew Adams, was kind enough to send me a photograph he took of some of the cairns in the area which extends for miles, following the path taken by the fugitives from the camp, together with a National Army Museum reproduction of a picture depicting the battle of Isandlwana on 22 January 1879 when six companies of the 24th (2nd Warwickshire) Regiment were annihilated by King Cetewayo's Zulus. Even just looking at these two pictures gives one an idea of the atmosphere of the area and the probably enduring sense of despair and misery and utter hopelessness that so many people have detected.

EDGEHILL

There have been sightings of phantom armies from Greece, Hawaii, Mexico, France, Germany and Ireland, but perhaps the best-known phantom army of all is the re-enactment and amply witnessed and well-documented Battle of Edgehill. Two months after the battle in October 1642 Charles I sent a group of investigators to report on the remarkable phenomenon, and I have reports as recent as 1994 of psychic activity there. Three and a half centuries have passed since Edgehill saw the first real fighting of the English Civil War, and still the battlefield, half-way between Warwick and Banbury, is widely regarded as being haunted by the sounds and scenes of the two-hour battle.

So regularly did the ghostly Cavaliers and Parliamentarians re-enact their combat soon after the event that, as the news spread, the credulous populace journeyed many miles to see the wondrous display, and see it many of them did by all accounts, and so the Royal Commission comprising six responsible gentlemen including Colonel Lewis Kirke,

Captain Dudley and Captain Wainsman visited the area and, according to their statements, they all heard and saw the arresting spectacle – even recognising some of the protagonists, Sir Edmund Verney, the king's Standard Bearer, among them.

Within weeks of the Battle of Edgehill a pamphlet was published certified by William Wood, Justice of the Peace for Warwickshire, Samuel Marshall, preacher of Kineton, and other 'persons of quality'. This certified that the events began with the sound of far off drums which seemed to come nearer and was accompanied by the noise of soldiers 'as it were, giving out their last groans' followed by a ghostly re-enactment in the sky of the recent hostilities of the battlefield below!

Since the evidence for something of the kind was repeatedly witnessed by reliable people one is forced to seek a possible logical explanation. Is it just possible that by some freak of nature the frightful noise and fearful sight of the brief but bloody battle became impressed on the atmosphere, to reappear at regular intervals that winter? Certainly reliable persons referred to 'full re-enactment' of the battle; each spectral event seems to have been identical and the whole occurrence vanished with the arrival of dawn. Of course there were those who believed that the re-enactments were caused by the unquiet spirits of the dead who had been left unburied on the battlefield, and indeed many bodies were so found and interred but still the visions continued for several weeks before getting fainter, less frequent and finally ceasing to appear with any regularity, but ever since the battle ghosts and spectral troops have been encountered there over the years.

There have been reports of other such visions. John Timbs, quoting from a pamphlet in the British Museum, described the event in March 1661 when hundreds of people congregated on London Bridge to watch an amazing spectacle in the sky. After seeing cloud-like substances assume such diverse shapes as cathedrals, whales, bears and mountains, 'there arose another cloud out of which issued forth an army, or great body of men, and to the left of this another army; each of these armies marching one towards the other, and the two armies seemed to approach very near to each other and meet in encounter, maintaining combat one against the other, and after a short combat, all vanished.'

Not that visions in the sky were confined to the seventeenth century. After 'The Leinster' was torpedoed by the Germans there were numerous reports of a cloud seen afterwards over the scene of the tragedy which took the form of an enormous cross with scores of human faces hovering in the background, according to many reports.

In 1860 several men reported seeing the Edgehill phantom army on the skyline from the vantage point of a ridge; and in the 1960s a young couple heard the frightening sounds of battle one winter night: it seemed to be coming from all sides and it grew louder and louder, and then suddenly faded and ceased. The date was 23 October, the anniversary of the battle.

The Revd John Dening (with whom I spent a night at Langenhoe Church, waiting for the ghosts that never appeared) has done much investigation into the ghosts of Edgehill and over the years he has located a number of local people who have heard the phantom sounds of battle and more than one has glimpsed something of the battle that took place three and a half centuries earlier. And John Dening has himself experienced something of the strange atmosphere there around the anniversary of the battle, as indeed I have myself.

In 1960 two soldiers posted to Melborough arrived at the camp late one afternoon that winter, knowing nothing of Edgehill and its ghosts. During one spell of duty they both heard screams and the sounds of battle. They were both so scared that they hurriedly retreated to the guard room where they remained for the rest of their spell of duty.

In the 1940s Bill Priest was a schoolmaster in the Edgehill area and he tells me that experiences of the disturbances were quite common among responsible adults and his pupils were full of stories of phantom horses in the area. He was also intrigued to discover a 'White Horse Road' running between the old battlefield and the burial ground where soldiers of both armies were buried. There are a number of reports of a phantom white horse seen galloping through the fields here and one theory is that the horse belonged to Prince Rupert, King Charles I's nephew and cavalry commander; another suggests the horse belonged to Captain Kingsmill, who died as a result of injuries received during the battle.

In 1965 the then chairman of Warwick Recording Society spent a year researching the ghosts of Edgehill. He said afterwards: 'Having spent a year investigating the battle and the ghosts I would still not like to say one way or another whether they exist, but we have uncovered a strange fact: during the few days surrounding the anniversary of the battle the guard dogs at the Control Ammunition Depot in Kineton will not patrol a certain area of the camp on the battle site.' He talked with some people who had heard the battle noise and others who had heard nothing.

In June 1960 Michael Romney-Woollard (Michaeli the concert pianist), whose Suffolk family trace their ancestry back to the eleventh century, fulfilled a lifetime's longing to see the site of the Battle of Edgehill. He did so with two friends, one a former army officer. Having obtained the necessary permission, he arrived and immediately felt that the scenery and the whole of the battle area was familiar to him; but at a burial plot where Cavaliers and Roundheads are both buried he became very disturbed and felt that hundreds of unseen men were watching him. His friends noticed his agitation and asked him why he looked so unwell and so frightened, but all Romney-Woollard could say was that he wanted to return home immediately.

Back home in London he believed overwhelmingly that he had brought back with him one of the dead soldiers from the battlefield. This unseen visitor, was, he felt, beside him everywhere he went and remained with him for a month or so. In his mind Michael Romney-Woollard saw a Roundhead, in armour, with a small moustache, deep piercing eyes and carrying a sword. After about a month the 'presence' or whatever it was left as suddenly as it had 'arrived'.

Looking back Michael Romney-Woollard wonders whether his experience was the result of a memory transmitted through his family generation by generation until he felt forced to revisit the scene of an ancestor's death; or was reincarnation the answer? He does not know, but that he recognised the countryside and the battle site, was conscious of being watched by hundreds of unseen eyes, and that he brought back to his home 'something' that seriously affected him he has no doubt, and what turned out to be the most terrifying experience of his life will be remembered always by him.

That there was intense emotion surrounding the Battle of Edgehill there can be no doubt. Both sides felt the war would be decided in this one great battle and so each soldier fought with all his might and with a single purpose. Furthermore religious feelings came into it: the Royalists believed they were defending God's 'substitute' on earth and the Puritans were equally convinced that they had divine approval. Such intense emotion on such a vast scale might have contributed to some kind of temporary psychometric impression in the local atmosphere.

The psychic echoes of the Battle of Edgehill present one of the more interesting and convincing examples of recurring psychic activity. The

Edgehill phantoms, incidentally are the only ghosts which the Public Records Office accept as authentic. With places like Bullet Hill and Battle Farm in the area the memory of the first pitched battle of the English Civil War will always be strong and perhaps 'experienced', for one correspondent reminds me that 'even today the area is rather mysterious . . .'.

PHANTOM SOLDIERS AT MARSTON MOOR

What has been described as the first really decisive battle of the English Civil War was fought at Marston Moor near York on 2 July 1644 when 18,000 Royalists fought 27,000 Roundheads, yet in spite of the numerical superiority it was actually the discipline of Cromwell's new Ironsides that won the day. For the first time infantry was able to withstand cavalry charges and the king lost the all-important battle.

Many times in the succeeding centuries phantom soldiers have been reportedly seen in the vicinity of the site of this conflict. In 1932 a motorist, Arthur Wright, was driving over the moor with a friend when they both saw ahead of them a group of long-haired men wearing cloaks and Cavalier-style hats. As a coach passed them Arthur Wright and his companion momentarily averted their gaze and when they looked back there was no sign of the people they had seen, soldiers who had appeared to be as solid and real as themselves. A very similar sighting, in roughly the same place, was reported in 1968 and yet another in 1992.

EXPERIENCES AT THE SITE OF THE BATTLE OF SEDGEMOOR

Something very similar has happened in the vicinity of the site of the Battle of Sedgemoor, fought on 6 July 1685, the last battle fought on English soil – with the crown of England hanging in the balance. Today there are few traces of the stirring battle on the Somerset plain, which

The Pass at Killiecrankie, Scotland, where echoes of a bloody battle seem to return each 27 July and a supernatural glow is said to hang over the former scene of conflict (see pages 99-100). © *Scottish Tourist Board*

Ronald Reagan at Old Battersea House, London, a few days after my visit to investigate the ghosts there (see pages 88-93). © *Kevin Harvey*

INSIDE OLD BATTERSEA HOUSE

LEFT
The haunted stairway and hall where Lady Churchill glimpsed a ghostly figure wearing a plumed hat and carrying a sword.
© *Peter Underwood*

RIGHT
The fifteenth-century Italian wooden armchair which was believed by many to be haunted. One person who sat in it jumped up immediately, announcing that the chair was icy cold and that he had heard whispering close to his ear.
© *Alasdair Alpin MacGregor*

The haunted tree in Green Park, London. Inexplicable sounds have been heard emanating from the tree and passers-by have detected a sense of sadness and despair underneath its branches (see pages 113-5).
© Chris Underwood

ended in the defeat and execution of James Scott, Duke of Monmouth.
The churches that were mute witnesses still stand, but the view from
their towers bears little resemblance to that of three centuries ago.
Some of the rhines, the large open ditches that played a part in the
battle, have long been filled in and their original courses can only be
detected by aerial photographs. But, over the years there have been
many stories of the ghostly remnants of Monmouth's brave army
struggling to leave the scene of frightful carnage that wet, sad summer
morning, being glimpsed and seen and heard. Usually ragged and
weary the figures of soldiers are seen, strangely attired, wandering about
the marshy fields and sometimes gruff voices are heard, and the distant
sound of desperate hand-to-hand fighting and the faint call of
something like, 'Come on over!'

Horace Robinson and his wife were motoring in the area when they
suddenly found themselves in the middle of oddly-attired fighting men,
a struggling motley collection of weary men who made not a sound.
Their son Philip recalled that his mother told her husband to stop the
car for fear of running into the people carrying staves and pikes but then,
as suddenly as they had appeared, the phantom men disappeared.

Charles Hugh Rose, James Wentworth Day's childhood tutor, was
driving in the Sedgemoor area when he encountered a ghost Cavalier
on horseback. He saw every detail of the figure; its face and uniform
were really clear and he was always convinced that he saw the ghost of
Monmouth himself. The date was early July and there has arisen a
tradition that the phantom form of Monmouth appears annually,
repeating his escape from the battlefield. He did indeed escape but fell
into the hands of the Sussex militia two days later and he was executed
on Tower Hill on 15 July.

Sax Rohmer, creator of *Fu Manchu*, told me he had collected a lot of
evidence for apparitions at Sedgemoor and said that 'without a shadow
of a doubt the unhappy Duke and some of his staff have been seen
crossing the path that skirts the moor...'. Apparitions at Sedgemoor
have been reported by bishops, rectors and people of integrity – not to
mention psychical researchers!

On the night of 6 July Trevor J. Kenward, a Council Member of the
Ghost Club Society, organised an all-night visit to the battle site on the
anniversary in 1994. The full story is told elsewhere, but suffice it to say
here that the investigating party involved four members and the apparatus employed on that occasion included three thermometers, a plumb

bob for vibration, an automatic camera, a tape-recorder and 'control' objects. The thermometers and the 'control' objects showed no evidence of any abnormality.

Among the odd happenings, however, all recorded in the log book at the time, were 'dull banging sounds' likened to musket shots; and other sounds, some likened to shots and others resembling drum beats; other sounds again were thought to resemble the beating of horses' hooves. At one point the ground vibrated for between two and three minutes, this being observed and checked by two observers. An hour and a half later a cry like a girl's voice was heard by all observers, from a westerly direction. All the dull bangs and other sounds were recorded on tape. In addition one member, perhaps more psychically sensitive than the others, had a strong feeling of unease, evil even, that lasted for the best part of 25 minutes. Photographs taken at the time resulted in some blank frames, then two frames with pinpricks of light and then further blank frames.

It does seem that ghostly soldiers from battles long ago are still seen from time to time in many parts of the world, usually silent reminders of days and conflicts and emotions and suffering long forgotten by mere mortals, but sometimes accompanied by the sounds of conflict. And such phenomena, it seems, are occasionally recordable with suitable instruments.

As we have seen the sounds of battle at Sedgemoor were recorded by Ghost Club Society Council Member and investigator Trevor Kenward and not only the dull boom of cannon fire but bangs, clangs, hoofbeats, human cries and other resonant sounds. And there have been other responsible witnesses to recorded paranormal activity from battlefields in Britain, Europe, the Americas and the Pacific Islands. Unless we resort to the possibility that imagined and hallucinatory sounds can become tangible enough to be recorded on an impartial and neutral machine – and perhaps that is a remote possibility – then we must accept that the sounds heard, and usually heard by more than one person, are objective and can have nothing to do with illusion. It would be interesting to have such sounds recorded at the same time from different areas of the battlefield.

Could it be that the trees that now grow on many of the old battlefields play a part in the retention and transmission of the sounds of battle? In Chapter 6 we will examine the phenomenon of haunted trees.

CHAPTER SIX

HAUNTED TREES

Trees, the oldest of all living things, have long been associated with the unknown and the unusual and have been regarded as possessing unearthly powers that it has been thought necessary to placate and pacify. The origin of trees, their growth, their foliage must have all seemed full of mystery to our ancestors. Compared with their lives trees must have seemed immortal and it is small wonder that trees were venerated. Soon there was tree-worship, sacred trees, trees that protected, trees that healed, trees of magic and of fertility, trees of evil, trees with oracular powers, and trees with magical properties; and we still carry out some of the routines and customs of our early, tree-fearing ancestors.

Stories persist concerning haunted trees. Are they simply stories, or do they represent folk memory, the experiences of reliable people, long dead and gone? One British psychical researcher and investigator, a man described on many occasions as 'one of the world's great ghost hunters', once compiled a book devoted entirely to haunted trees, wherein he detailed the best part of a hundred examples, including a Fatal Cherry Tree in Canada, the Haunted Nativity Wood near Cromarty, Scotland, the Screaming Phantom of Mannheim Forest in Germany and the Sinister Danmark Tree of the North of England.

Can it be, one wonders, that the absorbent quality of wood, and perhaps especially living wood, may possibly be particular and peculiar in that it can retain some traces of past events and can exude them in the form of psychic activity?

Trees, some authorities still believe, are the favourite dwelling place for ghosts of the dead. In India local shrines are built beneath trees to appease their resident ghosts, in fact the East is riddled with legends of ghosts and trees, while all over the world there are innumerable stories of tree spirits, tree worship, tree hauntings and even ghostly trees.

Trees look naked in the autumn and perhaps to restore their modesty there arose the ancient art of tree-dressing. Soon individual trees were regarded as having special properties: ash protected against evil; birch had magical properties and was a favourite with witches; elder protected against witchcraft; hazel was the tree of knowledge and used for dowsing; holly protected against the evil eye; oak has been the chief sacred tree since earliest times; the rowan protected against evil of all kinds; the yew restrained the spirits of the dead and so on. And there have always been trees regarded as being haunted.

HERNE'S OAK

One of the best-known haunted trees must be Herne's Oak in Windsor Great Park, Berkshire. There seems little doubt that the original tree, long known as Herne's Oak, was by 1796 in a very decayed state and that it was felled at that time, together with a number of other dead and dying trees. A replacement oak was blown down in a storm in 1863 and a further replacement was planted in or near the site of the original tree in the reign of Edward VII, after another, that became known as Herne's Oak, had been planted on the wrong side during the reign of Queen Victoria. But what was the story of Herne's Oak?

Herne the Hunter, that 'foul fiend of the forest' as Harrison Ainsworth calls him, is one of England's most famous ghosts. The story goes that the original Herne was a forest keeper in the reign of Richard II. Suspected of some long forgotten but presumably heinous offence he hanged himself, or at any rate his body was found hanging from a large oak tree. On the night of Herne's death a tremendous storm raged and a blast of lightning struck the tree, releasing the spirit of Herne to ride for ever about the forest. He is usually described as 'a wild, spectral object, possessing a slight resemblance to a human being, clad in the skin of a deer and wearing on his head a sort of helmet ... with a pair of large antlers' and mounted on a fast horse. The midnight rider is so depicted by George Cruickshank (1792–1878) in a famous engraving.

Herne was immortalised in Shakespeare's *Merry Wives of Windsor* and used to be regarded as a figure of ill omen that was seen whenever disaster threatened the nation. This may well be why Queen Victoria, who was certainly superstitious, had a new tree planted in 1863. She invariably began her letters to members of her family: 'Thank God and touch wood...'.

Herne's ghost was said to be most frequently seen in the vicinity of the old oak tree and especially before any threat to the royal family or the nation. The odd and surely unmistakable figure is said to have been seen in 1931 before the economic crisis; before the abdication of Edward VIII in 1936; and before the Second World War broke out in 1939.

There do seem to be a number of reliable reports of sightings. In 1926 Mrs Walter Legge JP, a responsible local resident, reported hearing at midnight animal sounds she was unable to account for and a fortnight later she heard the same sounds along with her daughter. Mrs Legge and her daughter lived at Windsor for many years afterwards but never heard anything like the midnight animal noises again. Lord Burton, who was born in 1894, is another witness and his experience took place shortly before the First World War so it may have been another premonition appearance.

In 1976 an army man, Robert H. Kent from Hertfordshire, stated that while in the area in 1941 (when the country was certainly in dire peril) he heard horses' hoofbeats in the distance and coming towards him, getting louder all the time, until they were close to him. He challenged whatever it was but the sounds of the invisible horse continued past him and faded into the distance. He saw nothing. Later he learned that other people had experienced similar sounds in the same place.

There is evidence to suggest that some spontaneous psychic activity fades, almost like a battery running down, over the years. At first the figure or form might be seen, clearly and distinctly, accompanied by sounds that would be clearly heard and be appropriate to the sighting, but over the years or perhaps depending on other circumstances and conditions, the picture might fade and become indistinct and eventually completely disappear while the sounds would still be heard as loud and clear as ever until, as the years pass, eventually the sounds too would become less distinct, fainter and fainter and finally cease to be heard altogether. An alternative theory for the whole Herne the Hunter legend would be that the answer to this riddle lies in an anthropological explanation and the story is a folk memory of some pre-Christian sanctuary where, as part of their apparel, the priests wore some kind of antlered head-dress.

GOFF'S OAK

Another well-known haunted tree is Goff's Oak at Theobalds in Hertfordshire. This tree, according to J.C. Louda in 1844, had a circumference of 32 ft and it gave its name to a nearby inn and indeed to the village situated 2 miles west of Cheshunt.

The tree, remains of which I remember seeing as a boy, was reputedly planted in 1066 by Sir Theodore Godfrey (or Goff'by) who came over with William the Conqueror. Nearby, another ancient oak, reputed to be a twin planting, stood in Beaumont Manor and the story goes that one of the early owners of the present manor, the previous one having been burned down in Elizabethan days, put his last penny on a horse which, failing to win, was shot by Major Grant and buried at the side of the oak tree. The groom, who was much attached to the horse, promptly committed suicide with the same gun and afterwards the area of Goff's Oak was said to be haunted by the ghosts of the groom and of the horse.

Why should a tree be affected by what happens nearby? Perhaps some trees have a property for absorbing the essence of traumatic happenings which took place in the immediate vicinity, as some trees and plants appear to be susceptible to humans talking to them, or perhaps some trees shade and protect the ground where something shocking once happened, enabling the ground about the tree to reproduce the event or parts of it on opportune occasions or to influence certain minds that such events are happening.

BLACK SALLY'S TREE

Dutch Elm disease resulted in the death and disappearance of a haunted elm tree in Hyde Park, in London, long known as Black Sally's Tree, a veritable magnet for ghosts, by all accounts.

Black Sally, it seems, was a Romany vagrant who frequented Hyde Park as a place to doss down for the night and she especially favoured the protective shade afforded by the gnarled trunk and twisted branches of an ancient elm tree, despite the warnings of other down-and-outs that the tree was haunted, several people having met their deaths in its shadows, either by their own hands or being found dead beside the 'tree of death' as it was also called. In addition there were recurring stories of phantom forms disturbing those who spent the night hours in its shelter, especially the ghost form of a man with protruding tongue and a cut throat who made horrible gurgling sounds...

Sally ignored the advice she was given and disregarded the stories she heard about the ghosts, indeed she always claimed to sleep soundly but her looks often belied what she said. One morning she was found dead beneath the tree that came to bear her name and thereafter an additional ghost was added to those associated with the tree, a dark-faced woman with matted black hair and ragged clothes who darted towards those who saw her in the dim moonlight – and then suddenly vanished to the sound of soulful moaning which seemed to come from the tree itself. Such reports have been noticeably fewer since the tree has disappeared.

Here it would appear that some great sadness, perhaps associated long ago with the tree itself, remained in the immediate vicinity and on moonlit nights was powerful enough to affect people who sheltered beneath its twisted branches.

GREEN PARK

Nearby Green Park was once part of St James's Park but anyone can notice the different atmosphere. Here, even on the brightest day there is a stillness, an air of quiet mystery and a sensation of sadness among the gnarled and ancient trees.

It is a place that has seen a lot of history and sad times and happy times. It was little more than a meadow with a few trees when the young Elizabeth I strolled there. In 1554 Royalist forces fought Wyatt's troops thereabouts; and there have been murders, robberies and rapes as well as beautiful moments in the shady arbours. It was once a favourite duelling place: one Earl of Bath was wounded in such a match; Count Vittoria Alfieri, the Italian poet, fought there in 1771; and Sir Henry Colt duelled with Beau Fielding over the favours of the Duchess of Cleveland who watched from Bridgewater House where she was staying; there have been attempts to assassinate royal personages there; Sir Robert Peel was thrown from his horse in Green Park and died as a result and I am sure there were many other less unpleasant happenings and affairs that lived long in the memories of those affected.

Can it be that something of the intensity and violence and passion of the rich tapestry that has been the history of Green Park has left something behind that can be sensed and perhaps seen by visitors centuries later?

When I was researching my book on *Haunted London* (published in 1973) I discovered that there was then, and still is in fact, one particular tree in Green Park that has always had a bad reputation. Vagrants invariably shun it, persistently refusing to sleep or even rest beneath its twisted branches; summer lovers never linger in its shade and even birds rarely alight on its old, gnarled and distorted branches, and they never seem to sing within its orbit. Since I carried out research there in the 1970s psychical researchers report that its malign influence appears to be reducing, but it was a very different story then. I talked with two park attendants who had no doubt that there was something very odd about that particular tree and they both told me, independently, that they had heard sounds, seemingly emanating from the tree itself that were quite inexplicable. On occasions the harsh and loud sound of a man's voice raised in anger would be heard, only to cease almost as soon as the hearer became aware of the voice. Then there was a low and cunning laugh that no matter how often it had been heard (and it was one of the more frequently heard sounds I was told), the sniggering peal of derision sent a chill through the hearer; and finally there was the groaning sound, sad, mournful and almost heartbreaking, as though someone was in mortal agony and utter despair.

I learned too that the tree was a favourite one for suicides in Green Park, and a sense of gloom, a sudden feeling of sadness and despair was experienced by many people who knew nothing about the tree or its reputation but who, for some reason they were totally unable to explain, were glad to move quickly on to less unwelcoming parts of the park.

Children rarely played in the vicinity of the tree; even animals gave it a wide berth. I asked whether anything at all could explain all this obvious and yet unconscious aversion and I was told, somewhat reluctantly, that occasionally, perhaps half-a-dozen times in the preceding couple of years, an unexplained figure, dark and ominous, had been reported, standing close to the tree, seeming to be almost a part of the tree. The silent, watchful figure disappears when the person who sees it looks a second time.

At other times visitors have reported the sensation of being followed when they pass near the tree although nothing is visible. Altogether it is not difficult to imagine a person contemplating suicide finding that when he reached the 'death tree' as it was widely known, he made his last decision and hanged himself.

THE WINDY OAKS

In Shropshire, not far from Newport, tall trees bordering the road are known locally as 'the windy oaks'. They are reputedly haunted by the phantom of one Madame Pigott (or Pigot), who was wed to a man who owned a large estate in the immediate neighbourhood.

One evening, so runs the story, she overheard her husband say something to the effect that if either his wife or their child had to die, he hoped it would not be the child. This so upset Madame Pigott that she rushed to a nearby pool and drowned herself, her shrieks and cries as she did so seeming to stir the leaves of the windy oaks that still night. Soon after the body was recovered the haunting began and continued intermittently for many years, perhaps preserved in some way by the timeless oak trees.

Richard Tauber, Austrian-born opera singer and composer who became a British subject, is one witness. Riding his motorcycle one stormy night through the windy oaks he saw the apparition of a distraught woman in front of him, an apparition that was suddenly and inexplicably no longer there. When he heard that other people had seen the ghost of Madame Pigott and heard her description, he became convinced that he too had seen the ghost of the unhappy Madame Pigott and his experience was published in the *New York Times*.

One night a colleague of mine, having heard the story and talked with some witnesses who claimed to have heard and seen something of the alleged haunting, arranged to spend some hours in the locality, accompanied by a young man who had seen the phantom form of Madame Pigott.

This young man had been cycling home from work one evening and was passing through the avenue of the windy oaks when he became aware of someone very near him. He glanced round and saw to his horror a tall female figure in white, striding along just behind him. He hurriedly increased his speed, fear lending him wings and giving him strength, but no matter how fast he cycled the tall figure kept pace with him. He kept trying to outpace the spectre but to his dismay he had no success and the road seemed otherwise to be completely deserted.

Just when he was beginning to give up hope and wondering what he could possibly do next, he noticed a pool almost bordering the road. As he passed the pool he heard a terrible, heart-rending cry and when he looked round the frightening form that had been accompanying him had completely disappeared. Hearing the story of Madame Pigott afterwards, he became convinced that it was her ghost that had followed him.

My colleague and the young man saw no spectral form during their sojourn in the vicinity of the ghost-ridden windy oaks but they did hear strange cries they were totally unable to account for and as they made their way towards the pool where Madame Pigott had drowned herself, they looked back and both saw ghostly lights glimmering through the foliage; lights that seemed to follow them for a time and then disappeared.

The pool had a distinctly eerie feeling about it and my colleague, very experienced in these matters but sensitive to psychic atmosphere, needed little encouragement from his young companion to leave the area and seek the lights of Newport.

Those windy oaks always had a strange, haunted atmosphere and the pool was no better. Perhaps it is not surprising that some sort of combination between trees, the subject of awe since the beginning of recorded history, and water, long regarded as a conductor of psychic activity, should result in a singularly haunted area.

MARY BLANDY'S TREE

Perhaps certain trees do attract ghosts. The Kenton Theatre at Henley-on-Thames in Oxfordshire has long been haunted by the ghostly form of Mary Blandy, a local girl who was hanged at Oxford for poisoning her father who would not give his consent to her marriage. For years her ghost and that of her intended husband were repeatedly seen in the garden of the house where she had lived, especially favouring the vicinity of a mulberry tree. Joan Morgan based her play *The Hanging Tree* on Mary Blandy's crime and when the play was staged at the Kenton Theatre a 'ghostly female form' was seen at the back of the stalls. The form was never identified and it appeared and disappeared in mysterious circumstances. Oddly enough a few years earlier when *The Hanging Tree* had been dramatised at Henley Town Hall there were reports of a similar ghost form being seen at the back of the audience.

So here then we have two of the most powerful attractions for ghosts, or at least two of the most haunted items in the realm of psychic activity: trees and theatres.

WALFORD'S GIBBET

There is a haunted tree near Walford's Gibbet in Somerset where the ghost of dark and popular John Walford walks, a young charcoal-burner who was in love with a local girl named Ann Rice. His occupation took him away from Ann for periods that they both found difficult but a country girl named Jenny pestered John day and night. In the end he succumbed to her advances and soon Jenny was pregnant. John dutifully married her in June 1789 – and murdered her 17 days later.

The judge is reputed to have wept as he sentenced John to death, but he had no option and faithful Ann Rice was by no means the only one openly in tears on the day that John was hanged and his body strung up in a cage for a year and a day as a warning to other would-be murderers. Walford's Gibbet marks that spot.

Before his death John was allowed a brief reunion with Ann and they both swore eternal love for each other. Ann desired above all things that somehow John would not suffer the agonising death that she had seen reflected in the faces of other hanged men and it is a fact that John remained dignified and as handsome as ever for a week after he had been hanged. History does not relate the fate of Ann Rice but when John's body was eventually taken down and buried in its iron cage at the foot of the gibbet where he had met his death, his restless ghost began to haunt the vicinity.

A nearby tree seemed to especially attract the phantom form of John Walford and the area of his burial at the foot of the gibbet (once a tree) became known for the putrid smell of rotting flesh that hangs in the air to this day. Late on summer evenings the ghost form of a handsome young man in the coarse clothes of a charcoal-burner has been encountered on the path between the site of the gibbet and the haunted tree: can he be still looking for his one true love, Ann Rice?

HEDDON OAK

Another haunted oak is the locally well-known Heddon Oak situated at a crossroads in the West Country. Some 50 miles west of the site of the battle of Sedgemoor, legend has it that some of Monmouth's men were caught by mounted Royalist soldiers and summarily hanged on the spot. For years the immediate neighbourhood has been haunted by the sounds of hoofbeats and running footsteps and the sound of frantic panting. Often, according to first-hand witnesses, and there are three on different occasions in 1989, 1992 and 1994, the ghostly sounds of panting turn to that of choking and then to the frightening sound of strangulation.

THE FOREST OF ILLUSION

Roger Courtney used to lead safaris in the wild country that was once known as Abyssinia. The strangest experience he had ever had in a lifetime of odd happenings was to the west of Gedi, he told me, in a certain dark forest area which he found oddly attractive, a place he learned was called the Forest of Illusion. An account of an experience in that strange place was given to him by a government official stationed in the area. This is what Roger Courtney was told: 'Ever since I arrived in the district I had been hearing tales about this forest, native stories, you know. They said the trees were not real, but came and went like shadows, were mere illusions, and that travellers were often confused by them and accordingly went hopelessly astray. I didn't pay much attention to the tales at first, thought it was just some silly yarn or other. Then one day Miss Randall, a white lady who had lived in East Africa since she was a small child, and was extraordinarily well informed in all matters concerning local customs and lore, put a different complexion on the matter. Finding herself near this mysterious forest one day, and having heard the story of the illusionary nature of the trees, she determined to test the matter there and then.

'With a hunting knife borrowed from one of her boys she sliced away a portion of the bark of one of the trees, leaving a large and clear mark. She then walked away a hundred yards or so and turned and walked back. There was no sign of the marked tree. There was not even a sign of the path along which she had originally gone up to the tree in order to make the mark.

'That was the story Miss Randall told me and my first reaction was that she must have made a mistake, had in some way become confused as to the position of the marked tree and had gone looking for it in another direction. I decided to try things out for myself and one day I did just that.

'I must say that at first glance it looked just like any other forest, and I almost convinced myself that Miss Randall really had made a mistake and it was in this sceptical frame of mind that I took a sheet of paper, torn from one of my official memobooks, and fastened it to a big and curiously twisted baobab tree that stood out from its fellows. Making sure that the paper was securely fixed and could not fall off or be blown off, I turned and walked away, a hundred yards or so, as Miss Randall had done. Then I turned and walked back.

'Now I want you to get it quite clearly in your mind that I hadn't made any mistake as to the position of the tree I had marked. I went right back to the spot where it should have been and I am as certain that I was in the right place as I have ever been certain of anything in my life; but there was no sign of the tree, nor of the piece of paper. They had disappeared as completely as though they had never been there at all.

'Not only that but the whole character of that part of the forest seemed to have altered, the individual trees all seemed to have changed their positions. I did notice a strange shimmering effect about the forest, not unlike that of a mirage. In fact there was a threatening effect about it all and I left the place as soon as I could.'

That is the story of the Forest of Illusion as told to Roger Courtney by the government official. Later Roger told me he met Miss Randall and she confirmed the story of her experiment of marking the tree. During his sojourn at Gedi, Roger had no opportunity to visit that mysterious forest for himself, but he hoped some day to do so and to walk into the forest and perhaps camp there for a while. A year or so later I learned that he had gone back to Africa, but I never heard any more from him, indeed he seemed completely to disappear and I have often wondered whether he found that strange forest and disappeared into it.

FISHER'S GHOST CREEK, CAMPBELLTOWN

There is or was a famous haunted tree in Australia. When Alasdair Alpin MacGregor was seeking ghost stories worldwide he came across a well-known Australian ghost associated with a tree near Campbelltown, south-west of Sydney. There in the shade of a tree beside a bridge the ghost of an early settler, Fred Fisher, was repeatedly seen, seemingly pointing to the nearby creek. Fisher had disappeared in mysterious circumstances and investigations by the police eventually uncovered a corpse buried in the creek with its skull fractured. The body was that of Fred Fisher and at the subsequent trial his one-time partner George Worrall confessed to the murder and was hanged for the crime – a murderer brought to justice by the intervention of a ghost! The place is now known as Fisher's Ghost Creek.

Is it surprising that so many trees seem to be haunted? Of course much depends on the credibility of testimony and one must not lose sight of the frailty of human memory, inaccurate observation and an unconscious tendency to 'improve' a story. A dozen witnesses to an event will all give different accounts of that event, each convinced that their story is the correct one; although there can be no doubt that the event itself did occur. After all, whether or not human testimony is a type of evidence acceptable to science, it is what we build our lives on. If human testimony can prove anything, it has proved beyond reasonable doubt that some trees are haunted.

There is overwhelming evidence for haunted chairs, haunted grandfather clocks, haunted pictures, haunted coffins, haunted stairways, haunted chests – all items made from wood. Perhaps there is something special about wood that attracts and retains something of traumatic events that occur in the vicinity that can be glimpsed at a later date. It is an idea that deserves to be explored. The curious fact that ghosts seem to be attracted to famous people and vice versa may be more difficult to explain, but we will go on to look at the phenomenon in Chapter 7.

CHAPTER SEVEN

GHOSTS AND FAMOUS PEOPLE

I have never really understood why ghosts of well-known people and ghostly experiences of well-known people cause others to think twice about the paranormal, but then we are all influenced by those we admire or feel we know personally.

One in ten of us has had the good fortune – some would say the bad fortune – to be around when a ghost has walked. This is a remarkably high figure and something in itself, if true, that causes us to stop and wonder. It is almost what has been called 'evidentiality': strong evidence that what is purported to be true is in fact true.

ROBERT GRAVES AT BERRY POMEROY

'The commonsense view is, I think, that one should accept ghosts...' So said Robert Graves, poet and literary legend. Graves lived for five years in Devon, and he was fascinated by Berry Pomeroy Castle and its ghosts. Once, he told me, he had arrived at the castle to find it closed to visitors, and he sought and discovered a gap near the main entrance that he wriggled through. He never forgot the feeling of being 'overwhelmed by a nameless horror' as soon as he found himself within the castle precincts. However he pressed on, and with his heart in his mouth he explored the haunted dungeons and other parts of the atmospheric ruins until he could stand it no longer, and he fled back through the gap and home to safety. 'I have never forgotten that awful feeling of absolute terror,' he told me. 'And I never shall. There is something not of this world at Berry Pomeroy.' I know just what he means and I have written elsewhere (*Nights in Haunted Houses*, Headline 1994) of this remarkable place with its ghosts reliably reported for more than two hundred years.

IDA LUPINO'S STORY

Many people have only one ghostly experience in their whole lives but it is something they never forget and they usually try to find a logical explanation to account for what has happened. A case in point is British-born actress Ida Lupino who died in Hollywood in 1995. Ida herself related to me her one 'ghostly' encounter.

At the time they were living on the outskirts of London with Ida's grandparents and one of the great friends of the family, a man whom Ida always called Uncle Andy. Her parents Stanley and Connie Lupino were appearing on the London variety stage and Ida was nine years old at the time.

One night, about half-past-ten, she found herself awake and unable to get back to sleep so she went downstairs to tell her grandmother, who was in the kitchen preparing a meal for her son and daughter-in-law.

While she and her grandmother were talking the telephone rang and Ida picked it up. She heard a man's voice on the line, so faint that she could hardly understand the words. Then the voice became stronger and said over and over again: 'I must talk to Stanley ... it is terribly important. I must talk to Stanley ... it is terribly important...'

Ida suddenly recognised the voice and said, 'Oh, it's you, Uncle Andy! Daddy isn't home yet...' But the voice kept repeating the same enquiry for Stanley and Ida passed the telephone to her grandmother. Ida heard her say: 'Why, Andrew – are you ill? I'll ask Stanley to call you the moment he comes in.' As she finished speaking the line went dead and Ida's grandmother was quite cross. She flashed the telephone switchboard operator and told her a call had been cut off, but the operator insisted there had been no call during the past hour. They had no idea where 'Uncle Andy' had been telephoning from so could do nothing but they presumed Stanley would know where Andrew was.

About half-an-hour later Stanley and Connie arrived home and Ida, still up, gave her father Uncle Andy's message. Her mother overheard and dropped suddenly into a chair and looked as though she was going to faint.

Ida's father told her she must be mistaken but her grandmother confirmed the call and said, 'You'd better call Andrew; he sounded as though he could be ill.' 'Mum,' Stanley answered, and Ida always remembered how tense and puzzled he sounded, 'Andrew is dead. He hanged himself three days ago.'

Ida never found an acceptable explanation for this. The obvious answer to the puzzle is that it was not Uncle Andy's voice on the telephone, and that both Ida and her grandmother had been mistaken. I remember putting that point to Ida Lupino who said, 'No way'. Both she and her grandmother knew Andy well, they had often talked with him on the telephone and there was no possibility whatever that they could have mistaken his distinctive voice. Anyway, had it been someone else, surely they would have rung again – no one ever did. Ida Lupino and I both agreed to accept it as a mystery unsolved and insoluble.

THE WILD GOOSE AND JOHN WAYNE

Anchored at Newport Harbour, Rhode Island, USA is *The Wild Goose*, a sleek, purposeful-looking converted naval minesweeper, a sister ship to Jacques Cousteau's world famous exploring vessel, *Calypso*. *The Wild Goose* is nearly 140 ft long, boasts a luxury stateroom and several bedrooms, and requires a staff of six to operate it. For 15 years *The Wild Goose* was the pride and joy of movie actor John Wayne (the 'Duke') and he only sold it a month before his death in 1979. Wayne sold his yacht to lawyer Lynn Hutchins who, within a month of the actor's death, came to believe that he saw and heard the phantom form of John Wayne on *The Wild Goose*.

The first incident, as with so many genuine haunted houses, was paranormal footsteps. The first time he slept aboard the yacht Hutchins slept in the stateroom and the lawyer found himself awakened by measured footsteps that appeared to come from overhead. Immediate investigation failed to reveal their origin. In the morning Lynn Hutchins spoke to the yacht's engineer who had been on the yacht in John Wayne's days. Hutchins was told that the actor was in the habit of walking 20 laps round the deck every night as a constitutional exercise.

'It happens every time I sleep in the stateroom,' Hutchins said in 1982. 'It also happens when guests use the stateroom.'

Lynn Hutchins, by this time, had twice seen the unmistakable ghostly form of John Wayne and he had felt the actor to be near him on the yacht on numerous occasions. One night, sleeping aboard, he found himself suddenly awake in the middle of the night. It was very dark and very quiet. As his eyes became accustomed to the inky blackness of his surroundings he became aware of a form standing by the doorway to the port gangway.

Knowing he was supposed to be alone on the boat Hutchins leaned out of bed – and the big, tall and seemingly quite solid figure immediately vanished. The figure had seemed to almost fill the doorway, there was a half-smile on his face and he wore a cowboy hat. The experience lasted no more than three or four seconds, but in those few seconds the figure was quite distinct and he could somehow see the features clearly. Talking afterwards about the experience to Bert Minshall, a former captain of the boat, and describing the height and stance and appearance and position of the figure he had seen, Minshall said, simply, 'That was John Wayne'.

A year later in the main salon, reading a book with his back to the doorway, Lynn Hutchins gradually became aware that someone was standing behind him. He turned suddenly and as he did so a sudden gust of wind came from nowhere and Wayne's personal beer glasses, hanging above the bar, began to shake and tinkle wildly so that Hutchins thought they must shatter. Looking at his reflection in the mirror behind the bar he saw a second reflection: a man with a craggy, weather-beaten face and a twinkle in his eye, a man much taller than himself, a man wearing cowboy apparel and a stetson hat. He was looking at the unmistakable phantom form of John Wayne. Within a second he swung round but there was nobody behind him. He looked again in the mirror but the reflection of the ghost had disappeared. It was indisputably the same 'man' he had seen previously.

The Wild Goose is not just a boat, it was, as everyone knew, 'John's boat'. Even when it had changed hands it still housed the actor's books and many of the plaques and awards he had received in a long and respected career. In a way it was a floating museum; a memorial to the life of John Wayne whose ghost, according to reports, has also been seen at the historic Alamo in San Antonio, Texas, a place he certainly knew during his lifetime; and at The White House, Washington, which seems less likely, but as American author Arthur Myers puts it, 'If Ronnie Reagan could make it to The White House, I wouldn't be surprised to find the Duke floating around there too!'

Hutchins became convinced that the 'spirit' of John Wayne was on the boat. Not that he was at all scared; in fact he experienced a feeling of 'protective warmth' in parts of the yacht, as did a caterer who knew the yacht well.

William G. Roll, a prominent American parapsychologist, visited *The Wild Goose* with four psychics from the Patricia Hayes School of Inner Sense Development and while they scored with several impressions in various parts of the boat and in subsequent 'communications' with Wayne, Roll questioned whether John Wayne had really returned from the other world to continue his perambulations around the yacht he loved or was there another possibility.

He concluded that it was necessary to look beyond the phenomena witnessed: the apparitions, the footsteps and the other incidents that might well be related to Wayne, it was also necessary to consider the person at the centre of the occurrences, Lynn Hutchins.

William Roll (who has formulated the interesting idea that there may be a connection between psychic phenomena and forms of epilepsy) says you could not be with Hutchins for long without becoming aware of his emotional attachment to John Wayne. He talked about the actor as he would one of his family and he talked about *The Wild Goose* as his and Wayne's family home. In a way he needed Wayne's protective presence on the boat and when he saw a form he immediately identified it with Wayne and when he heard footsteps where Wayne had walked he solidly identified them as coming from Wayne.

But why the cowboy hat? Roll argues that psychic impressions are rarely photographic reflections of reality. The intention behind the impression is what counts and the cowboy hat is universally associated with John Wayne. The invisible traces of Wayne that Hutchins picked up could have included place memories. Events not only leave their traces in a person's brain but also in the things and places where the events took place. Should such trace images remain and be picked up by a sympathetic or psychic person, that place memory may be mistaken for a person's spirit form – so reasoned William Roll.

Late at night and early in the morning a hormone, nocturnal melan-tonin, reduces the usual inhibition of the brain, and we may see and hear things of which we are usually unaware. These impressionable times were when Hutchins had his apparitional experiences and when he heard the footsteps. In addition the sense of purpose and protection exhibited by Hutchins could have played a part in the experiences.

It is comparatively common for people to project their mental images into their surroundings. We call such images hallucinations and when other people experience the image that is projected, this may be telepathy; when the image appears to be solid some people term it a thought form.

It may be that in some cases of haunting it is really thought forms that we are dealing with and the ghostly form of John Wayne on *The Wild Goose* could be an example. Hutchins said he never felt alone on the boat and there was always a warm feeling of protection. Therein may lie the secret.

THE GHOST OF MARILYN MONROE

12305 Fifth Helena Drive, Brentwood, was the first home Marilyn Monroe ever owned and it was the home where she died on 4 August 1962. Her ghost has been reported walking in the secluded garden there, very early in the morning, as she was in the habit of doing. Little has been written about the unmistakable apparitional form of the most famous of all Hollywood stars who might well be expected to return as a ghost if anyone does. She had a strange, haunted, secretive and yet over-publicised life, and after more than 30 years the manner and precise details of her death are still debated. When I was collecting information for the part about Marilyn Monroe in my book *Death in Hollywood* (Piatkus, 1992) I received a number of reports pertaining to Marilyn Monroe and psychical activity. Her well-known preference for little or no clothing in the privacy of her home makes likely the possibility of Marilyn being the naked female phantom that has been glimpsed within the sheltered confines of her garden.

Marilyn Monroe lived for a brief time in the Hollywood Apartments that were once a dormitory for the nearby Paramount Studios' young starlets. Here the *ingenues* were safe from scandal and from the adoring fans who flooded to the building where a strict 'No men on the premises' policy was always adhered to. On the ground floor a trap door led to a small and rather damp tunnel through which the actresses were ushered on to the lots.

Strange and unpleasant happenings, mostly of a minor kind, have been reported from this seemingly cheerful building for years with objects moving of their own volition, electrical appliances switching themselves on and off, and cold pockets of air being encountered. Tenants have also found themselves tipped out of bed in the middle of the night and have walked into the heady aroma of carnations in deserted rooms and corridors. The trap door, permanently secured by the authorities in 1978, has been known to produce strange scrabbling noises, and raps and taps that have nothing to do with variation in temperature or rodents.

John Myers, who has been described by Hans Holzer, a well-known American psychic investigator, as 'America's leading psychic photographer', was also a practising medium, a clairvoyant and a healer. He met Marilyn Monroe on several occasions and gave her 'spirit healing'. Soon after her death odd happenings occurred in Myers's healing rooms; the lights being switched on and off when no one was around and objects appearing and disappearing from the locked room.

Soon, says Myers, Marilyn manifested several times clairvoyantly, conveying her distress at the accident which caused her death. She insisted she did not commit suicide (the coroner's verdict was 'probable suicide') but said she took pills when unable to sleep and in a semi-conscious state she could not remember how many pills she had swallowed and she kept taking more. 'I did not understand what I was doing,' she explained, reported John Myers, 'And then it was too late...' Recent research into her death tends to confirm this scenario.

Marilyn Monroe had a photographic session at the pool of the Roosevelt Hotel on Hollywood Boulevard in 1951 and she stayed in Room 1200 in the mid-1950s. Here, there is a famous 'cold spot' in the grand ballroom and the reflections of deceased guests have been reportedly seen in mirrors in the lobby. The ghost of actor Montgomery Clift haunts the ninth floor, sometimes practising at playing the trumpet – as he used to do. On some occasions the ghostly reflection of Marilyn Monroe has been reportedly seen in a mirror here that used to belong to the star.

During her all too short life Marilyn Monroe was a restless soul and between 1926 (when she was born at 5454 Wilshire Boulevard – now the Caravan Rug Corporation) and her death in 1962, she lived at 35 addresses in Hollywood, and 7 addresses in New York and the surrounding area. After her death, alone and uncomforted as she had been so often, reports imply that her ghost was restless too.

GHOSTS AND
BORIS KARLOFF

COLDWATER CANYON

In the mid-1930s Boris Karloff, Hollywood horror film actor, was living with his then wife Dorothy, in a Mexican-style former farmhouse in Coldwater Canyon in Beverly Hills. Here he created, as he used to say, 'a little piece of England' but he had also bought a ghost.

When I talked with Boris Karloff he learned of my abiding interest in the subject of ghosts and hauntings, and then he told me he had once lived in a haunted house and that he and his wife had seen the ghost on many occasions; 'a harmless shade from the past' was how he put it, 'revisiting the place he had loved'.

Soon after they had moved into the house in Coldwater Canyon, the Karloffs, busy with their two Scotties, Violet the pig, a pair of ducks, some chickens, an aged turtle and a parrot, realised that often the animals seemed preoccupied, to be aware of something invisible and to be repeatedly looking at what appeared to be empty space. Before long they both began to glimpse, usually out of the corners of their eyes, the shadowy form of a short, tubby man who always seemed to be just disappearing round a corner or behind some bushes.

Boris told me he made enquiries, both of the people who had sold the house to them and to his somewhat scattered neighbours and friends, and he learned that he and his wife were not the first people to report such a figure. Previous occupants, it seemed, had often talked of 'their lodger' as they called him, a harmless and rather shy 'ghost' who just seemed to be there when he was least expected. Boris also discovered that long ago, when the place was built, the original owner had been a sort of smallholder or farmer in a small way; a short, bulky sort of man who lived on his own and always said he would never leave the place.

Their ghost never really worried the Karloffs, for he never seemed to put in an appearance when they had guests and they became quite used to him and more or less accepted him 'as part of the furniture'. Other occupants of the house had not been so fortunate.

In Charles Higham's biography of Katharine Hepburn the author relates that after appearing in the film *Morning Glory* (released in 1933) Kate lived for a time in 'an odd, triangular house set against a hillside' in Coldwater Canyon. Kate and her friend Laura Harding both noticed something strange about the house from the beginning. In the early summer Joanna, the maid, kept insisting that a small guest apartment under the house was haunted.

Although the apartment was unoccupied and kept locked, whenever Joanna went in there she said the furniture had been moved. One night Kate telephoned Laura, who was away staying with her family in New Orleans, from her bedroom saying that 'someone was in the house'. Kate's close friend and stand-in, Eve March, had actually seen the latch on Kate's bedroom door move by itself and when the two women opened the door there was nobody there.

Laura could tell that Kate and Eve were terrified, and she suggested they call the police, but Kate was horrified at the thought of the inevitable publicity and she refused. Next day, Kate and Eve were at the pool turning off the hydraulic pump when they noticed the figure of a man turn and walk into the lower apartment of the house. When they went to check, the door was locked and no one could be seen inside or outside. Kate rang Laura again, asking her to come out as soon as she could.

Laura soon arrived with her dogs but the animals failed to flush out the mysterious intruder and the haunting worsened and the sense of a foreign presence became increasingly overpowering. Kate's brother Richard arrived and he was housed in the guest apartment, having been told nothing about the apparent haunting.

After he had been there a week, he said to Kate, 'There's something wrong with this house. I haven't slept a single night since I've been here. I'm always having the feeling that someone is standing at the foot of the bed, looking at me . . .' Later, when Boris Karloff took over the house, Laura said: 'We felt rather sorry for the ghost!'

BORIS IN BRAMSHOTT

Boris and Evie Karloff moved into flats in Knightsbridge and Kensington after they returned to their native England in 1959 and a few years later they found a cottage in Hampshire where they were to happily spend his last years. This cottage, Roundabout, Bramshott, was only haunted after Boris died - by the ghost of the great actor himself!

Bramshott has the reputation of being one of the most haunted villages in England and I know from personal experience that there are indeed many ghosts there. The old manor has its White Lady, a priest from Elizabethan days and a Quaker; a cottage in the village harbours the ghost of what appears to be an Elizabethan gamekeeper; in the same lane a fair-haired shepherd boy plays ghostly pipe music; the slow-moving stream is haunted by the sad ghost of Elizabeth Butler who drowned herself there and a little girl in a poke bonnet haunts the church. Here too there is reputed to be a Grey Lady, a phantom pot boy, a cavalier, a coach-and-horses and what about the 'tall, dark figure with an unusual bow-legged gait' seen and heard in and around the cottage that the Karloffs settled in?

I once asked Boris Karloff whether he had ever seen or heard any of the ghosts of Bramshott and he replied, 'No, but from my experience of human beings, when they see me in the flesh, the ghosts would probably be so scared that they would disappear before I did!' Be that as it may not long after his death and intermittently in the succeeding years I have received reports of the unmistakable figure of a tall man with a mechanical and familiar gait, and more rarely the snatch of conversation in a soft, slightly lisping, well-trained voice that disappears almost as soon as one is aware of it.

BARBARA CARTLAND'S GHOSTLY STORIES

When I met Barbara Cartland, prolific romantic fiction writer, she told me she believed completely in an afterlife and not only for human beings, although her dead husband had returned to her with some flowers and to tell her that there was indeed life after death and that it *was* possible to return. She also told me about the ghost dog she often sees at her Hertfordshire home, a favourite pet whom she could not bear to lose and who couldn't bear to leave her, a cocker spaniel called Jimmy, and his ghost still walks at Camfield Place, in the hall, on the terrace, upstairs – sometimes her two other dogs see him too.

In Somerset Dame Barbara once lived in a house that had a haunted staircase; she never felt alone there and whenever she went upstairs there was someone ahead of her or following close behind. She learned that years ago a Cavalier, wounded by Roundheads, had returned to his home to die. She also told me the story of when she was a young girl on holiday with her brother Ronald, in northern Italy. They went for a walk one day through lovely countryside and found themselves walking beside a large lake. On the opposite bank they both clearly saw a magnificent castle with spires and turrets.

When they got back to the village where they were staying they described the castle they had seen and its whereabouts and asked to whom it belonged. They were astonished to hear that the castle by the lake had been destroyed many, many years before and was now only a ruin, and what remained of it did not stand higher than 6 ft in any part.

When Dame Barbara and her brother returned to the place they had visited the day before they could find no trace of the castle that they had both seen so clearly 24 hours earlier.

CONRAD VEIDT'S HAUNTED HOUSE

Conrad Veidt, the legendary film actor, lived in London in a haunted house. He was always interested in occult matters and he never tired of talking about the exorcism carried out in his house and its aftermath.

Conrad Veidt and his wife Lily discovered that the house was haunted very soon after they moved in. They heard the sound of raised voices, sudden bangs and crashing noises from empty rooms at all hours of the days and night, and disembodied footsteps. They would suddenly become aware of the voice or the noises and then, perhaps half-an-hour later, the sounds would completely cease. Occasionally they glimpsed phantom forms, sometimes a man, sometimes a woman, and sometimes the pair of them together, usually at the top of the stairway but occasionally in one of the back bedrooms.

Conrad Veidt, interested and sympathetic as he was, found the disturbances interfering with his work and concentration, and when he mentioned the matter to a friend, the idea of an exorcism was discussed. Meanwhile a friend of Lily's, on hearing that the house was haunted, had a word with a clergyman friend who agreed to do what he could. So it came about that two clergymen, with bell, book and candle, attempted to cleanse the Veidts' home. Conrad Veidt said afterwards that he was much impressed by the pomp, solemnity and sincerity of the event which began with the two clerics blessing the house with prayers and words of benediction. They visited every room in the house and performed a ritual in each, sprinkling holy water, leaving open Bibles and ringing bells.

All was quiet during the ceremony and the atmosphere seemed to improve until they arrived at the 'haunted' back bedroom. As the party entered the cold and empty room they all saw, momentarily, the ghostly forms of a man and a woman standing together in one corner of the bedroom. They seemed to be adopting a defiant and almost threatening attitude but, after a moment's hesitation, the two clergymen walked towards the figures with words of blessing and as they drew near the forms seemed to dissolve and disappeared. Suddenly there was a loud and piercing shriek that reverberated through the whole house and then there was silence.

Afterwards the house was much better to live in, and as the days and weeks passed, and the occasional sound of distant voices, or footsteps, became fewer and fewer, Lily and Conrad Veidt felt, for the first time since they moved in, that the house had a peaceful atmosphere. A clairvoyant told them that a woman had been murdered on the stairs and a man had committed suicide in the back bedroom, and the Veidts did come across a number of stories about the house, about an unhappy couple and either a murder or a suicide pact, but they were pleased that the house seemed so much improved so they did not pursue the matter.

Several months after the exorcisms Lily and Conrad Veidt really felt that the house was peaceful but then Conrad had occasion to visit the 'haunted' back bedroom. As soon as he entered the room he knew the ghostly couple were there. The old atmosphere of tension, hatred, unhappiness and frustration filled the ice-cold room. He hurriedly collected the item he had come for and made to leave the room when he saw the couple standing in his way in the open doorway. The man seemed to be glaring at him with ill-concealed hatred, while the woman cowered beside him. Conrad stopped in his tracks facing them; then he closed his eyes and concentrated, using all his willpower in an attempt to remove the forms from his path and from his house. He soon found he was becoming drained and exhausted by the efforts he was making, and when he felt he could no longer continue and he opened his eyes, the ghostly forms had disappeared, and neither Lily nor Conrad Veidt ever saw them again.

DENNIS WHEATLEY'S OCCULT EXPERIENCE

I met Dennis Wheatley, the best-selling novelist, at his home in Lynd-hurst. Inevitably our talk turned to ghosts which had intrigued Dennis for almost as long as he could remember, but he would never agree to accompany me on visits to haunted houses for he could never forget an experience he had as a child.

While at boarding school in Broadstairs he was going up to bed one night when he came face to face with a ghost. Thinking it was a burglar he screamed and the staff instituted an immediate search, but no trace of anyone was ever found. Dennis told me 'I found myself staring into another face within inches of my own and beyond was the dark outline of a man's figure; the face was round, white and horrible. I was petrified ... and I have never forgotten it; I can see it now. As I plunged downstairs it swiftly and silently glided up the stairs and out of sight...'

Years later he met one of the teachers again in France and she told him that what he had seen was a ghost. She said it was some sort of elemental that had been conjured up and had begun to haunt the place. Later he used the true incident in his book *The Haunting of Toby Jugg*.

Whatever the facts of the matter this personal and unsought experi-ence convinced him beyond all shadow of a doubt 'that there are planes outside our physical world, and disembodied intelligences, which in certain circumstances impinge upon it'. To Dennis Wheatley the existence of occult manifestations was proved and he would never, but never, visit a haunted house or become engaged in any sort of psychical investigation – 'in case something might be conjured up...'.

CHAPTER EIGHT

HAUNTED INANIMATE OBJECTS

There are many people who can just about accept the possibility of ghosts being people who are dead; be it their 'spirit forms', a type of atmospheric photograph, a projection from a living person or whatever – but haunted inanimate objects? Can inanimate objects, such as furniture, really become imbued with something of the emotional charge generated by people who have come in contact with that object? And is this something, whatever it is, picked up by certain, perhaps sensitive, people by some process comparable with telepathy? Impossible you say, yet there is considerable evidence that some inanimate objects are indeed haunted.

TUTANKHAMUN'S BATTLE TRUMPETS

The Egyptian boy king Tutankhamun's two ceremonial battle trumpets may be haunted in a singular fashion, not associated with any apparitional appearance or affecting the person handling them, but the sounding of them meaning nothing less than inaugurating a harbinger of war.

Fashioned 1300 years before the birth of Christ they were reputed to have been sounded to herald wars in ancient Egypt; folk memory asserting that these powerful battle trumpets had triggered awful battles long centuries ago and their reputation had ensured that neither had been sounded for over 3000 years. One was eventually sounded in the

spring of 1939, for the first time in three millennia, and the world was
devastated by the Second World War. A fantastic suggestion surely . . .?

Rex Keating, who had charge of the European Division of Egyptian
State Broadcasting in 1939, was responsible for the first broadcast, after
many difficulties, of the sounding of one of those battle trumpets.

They had been discovered in the tomb of Tutankhamun in the Valley
of the Kings and after the opening of the tomb and the disclosure of its
many treasures several attempts were made to broadcast the sound of
the battle trumpets. Rex Keating and I talked about those days and the
remarkable trumpets.

Rex described to me the eeriness of the scene when the broadcast was
eventually made; a broadcast I remember all too well. The electricity
supply in the Cairo Museum inexplicably failed, and by the light of
flickering candles in one of the long galleries, the figures of gods
and Pharaohs loomed out of the shadows, shadows that flickered and
curled away into utter darkness. The announcement before the trumpet
sounded is still impressive: 'The trumpets of the Pharaoh
Tutankhamun, Lord of the Crowns, King of the South and North, Son
of Ra!'

After a moment of expectant silence the harsh and haunting sound of
the trumpet was broadcast to the world. For Rex Keating it was a
tremendous occasion, the sort of thing that happened once in a lifetime;
but there are those who say the ancient curse of the Pharaohs reached
out that spring day in 1939 and within a few short months the world was
plunged into an awful world war.

Today the trumpets, one of copper, the other of silver, chased with
delicate designs and seemingly in perfect condition, reside in the Cairo
Museum among the multitude of priceless objects from the tomb of
Tutankhamun – I say 'seemingly' because in fact only one of them is in
the condition in which it was recovered, as revealed to me by Rex
Keating.

Having obtained permission for one of the 18-inch trumpets to be
sounded and broadcast, a search began for someone who could blow
them – a very difficult task. At length a bandsman from one of the
British Hussar Regiments was selected. Early attempts to blow the
trumpet resulted in ear-splitting screeches, but the broadcast was arranged and rehearsals were held in one of the workshops at the back of
the Cairo Museum, where the noise would be less likely to disturb
visitors.

On the morning of the second rehearsal the bandsman made a valiant but unsuccessful attempt to extract three notes from the copper trumpet, as Engelback, the keeper of the Cairo Museum, and Rex Keating stood by, watching and telling themselves that all would be well on the day. Suddenly the door opened and in walked King Farouk. Apparently during the course of an unofficial visit to the museum he had heard the extraordinary noises and had insisted on knowing what was happening. Engleback at once moved to greet the king and momentarily the careful watch on the trumpets was relaxed. Out of the corner of his eye Keating saw the bandsman pick up the silver trumpet. There was the sound of a short, sharp crack, followed by a tinkling noise. Everyone looked towards the bandsman who stood, a picture of stupefaction, with the neck of the trumpet in his hand and at his feet the shattered pieces of that priceless relic!

There was a stunned silence and then everyone, including the king, was on his knees searching for fragments of the silver trumpet in the dust of the workshop floor. No one knew at the time but the silver had become crystallised with the passage of 3000 years and was as brittle as glass. The bandsman had thought it might help if he fitted a modern bugle mouthpiece into the end of the trumpet. Unfortunately the mouthpiece was slightly too large so he had placed the mouthpiece in the trumpet against the palm of his hand and sought to ram it home – with disastrous results.

Reverently the shattered pieces of silver trumpet were placed on the table and then the king spoke. Not a word of what had happened, he commanded, must leak out. To reveal that the precious trumpet had been smashed by a British soldier, in the presence of the king, might easily result in civil disturbances. Meanwhile every effort must be made to repair the trumpet.

After this regrettable incident the Egyptian Department of Antiquities, understandably perhaps, decided to withdraw their permission for the broadcast and it took days of patient argument from Rex Keating to persuade them to allow the broadcast to go ahead. The damaged trumpet would never again sound a clear note.

More difficulties were encountered but eventually the broadcast went forward as arranged. For a moment time and space were bridged. The gulf dividing the twentieth century from Ancient Egypt was crossed and for a few seconds life was breathed into dead bones. In common with many people who heard that historic broadcast I am sure

I shall never forget the strange, haunting and almost unearthly sound of that trumpet from the tomb of Tutankhamun.

THE CAMPBELLS

Sir Malcolm Campbell and Donald Campbell were the most remarkable father and son speed kings the world has seen. Malcolm Campbell was the son of a jeweller from Chislehurst and even as a boy he loved speed and motor cars. Starting work in an insurance office he spent all his spare money on cars and motor cycles, and in 1908 he made his first appearance on Brooklands Racing Track. Later he bought a big Darracq car which he painted blue and called it *Bluebird*. It was the first car with which he won a race; after that all his important cars and yachts were called *Bluebird*.

In motor racing he won over 400 trophies, from 1925 to 1938 he frequently held the world's motor speed record and in 1937 he established a motor-boat speed record which he subsequently broke himself. He bought from Sax Rohmer the haunted house 'Little Gatton' near Reigate with its panelling from the *Mauritania*, panelling that creaked and groaned inexplicably in times of bad weather, as it must have done when the old ship met heavy seas. Elizabeth, Sax Rohmer's wife, told me she always felt the beautiful gardens to have the feeling of 'a valley of death' with a deep and strong sense of tragedy and sadness. Meeting Sax after he had been in the house for a while Sir Malcolm Campbell told him: 'I would never buy that bloody house of yours now you know – talk about bloody haunted . . .'

Sir Malcolm Campbell believed in an afterlife from which it was possible to communicate with people still in the land of the living and his son reflected his father's convictions in these areas. I talked with Donald Campbell and his wife Tonia about ghosts and the afterlife. Donald was completely convinced that he had seen his dead father many times, and he *knew* that Sir Malcolm watched over his son during his attempts on land and water speed records.

Always on those occasions Donald told me he was afraid of what might happen, and he was right to be apprehensive for very little had to go wrong at the speeds Donald used to travel for it to be curtains for him. Always on those occasions, he told me, just as he was prepared to

Within a month of his death, the ghost of John Wayne was reportedly seen aboard his beloved yacht, *The Wild Goose*, anchored at Newport Harbour, Rhode Island, USA (see pages 123-6). *Author's Collection*

The author sitting next to Dulcie Gray at a dinner he organised at London's Oriental Club where she recounted personal ghostly experiences.
© *The Ghost Club*

The haunted battle trumpets of Tutankhamun - trumpets that allegedly carry the curse of the ancient Egyptians (see pages 135-8). © *Rex Keating*

Skull House, Appley Bridge, Greater Manchester, one of a number of houses harbouring a 'screaming skull' - see left. Removal of the skull (known as 'Charlie') from the house led to frightening disturbances and a run of bad luck. Once when it was thrown into the nearby river, the skull reportedly made its own way back to the house!
© Lancashire Life

go for the record, he would see his father who would comfort him and say, 'It's all right, Donald, it's going to be all right' and of course it always was. Donald Campbell was the first man to hold both the land and water world speed records in the same year.

We will never know whether Donald saw his dead father before he made that last attempt to beat his own water speed record in 1967 on Coniston Water, and if he did, what he 'said'. Ten years after Donald's death Tonia told me, 'Donald is still guiding me from the other world. He has helped me in all sorts of ways. I have awakened in the middle of the night to find him standing there but he is always helpful and never scary. I often see him in front of me yet I'm not psychic in any way. I really have seen Donald,' she said. 'But I fight against it; I don't want to encourage this sense . . . I used to feel that Donald was very strongly guiding me and looking after me. I never felt that I was seeing a ghost or that he was trying to come back. He was simply giving me help and encouragement.'

Donald Campbell had some curious experiences in his last racing car, *Bluebird*, and perhaps that remarkable and history-making car qualifies as a haunted inanimate object. Donald always said it was a haunted machine with a life of its own and if it felt like doing its best nothing could beat it. He felt that he was an insignificant part of the record making; it was the machine that was the real winner. Often he felt he was guided by the machine to drive it to victory and many times he had seen his father's face in the windshield of the car. At times it seemed that his father was actually there, and controlling both Donald and the car.

HAUNTED CLOCKS

Clocks seem to have a curious affinity with their owners and there are stories without number about clocks stopping when their owners die or long-silent clocks ticking for a while when their owners depart this life – but surely these must be coincidences?

Dennis Bardens, first editor of the BBC's *Panorama* series, has related such a story from Denver, Colorado, USA concerning a haunted clock owned by Helen Verba, a clock that had been in her family for five generations and on several occasions had stopped at the minute that a member of the family had died. This happened in the case of Helen Verba's great-great-grandfather, Charles Spelman; the next owner of the clock, her great uncle Emerson Spelman; and the next owner, Helen Verba's grandfather R.J. Spelman.

When her father inherited the clock he put it away out of sight and some time after both her parents had died she found the clock in the basement wrapped in a blanket, and as she moved from apartment to apartment, she kept it wrapped and stored away. After her last move she decided to get rid of the clock and took it to a local antique dealer but at the last check made by Helen Verba it was unsold.

General Sir Ian Hamilton, the man who led the Gallipoli campaign in 1915, died in 1947 in his Victorian home – and every clock in the house, according to Miss Mary Shields, his secretary for over 30 years, stopped one after the other.

When Fred Cartman died at his home in West Sussex in 1985 his favourite cuckoo clock stopped at the exact moment of his death. Fred Cartman always had a horror of being cremated and his ashes scattered; he wished to be buried but his widow and other members of the family decided on cremation. At the announcement a picture in the room fell off the wall and the cuckoo clock started working again, but erratically. The family decided on a compromise: Fred Cartman would be cremated but his ashes would be buried. When this was done there were no further disturbances.

GHOSTLY INFLUENCES ON DOMESTIC OBJECTS

Will Goldston was a world-famous magician who invented many illusions for other magicians. Founder and vice-president of the Magicians' Club, he took psychical research very seriously. A complete sceptic when he began to investigate the subject he found himself confronted with conditions which he 'could not attempt to explain'. 'There are many magicians,' he once said, 'Who like myself are not entirely sceptical about mediumistic manifestations. I have attended more than 300 seances and I have seen things which could not possibly be reproduced by an illusionist.'

On one occasion Goldston took a music-hall performer with him to a seance. The man carried a knife which he handed to the medium to see her reactions. As soon as she touched the knife she screamed: 'This knife has killed a man – your partner...'. The performer confirmed that this was indeed so. 'She is right,' he said. 'My partner took his own life with this knife.' So perhaps some objects can be haunted in the sense that their qualities can be perceived by sensitive people and perhaps in certain circumstances they can 'perform' independently.

Pictures seem to be susceptible to these influences, if influences they are, and there are innumerable instances of pictures apparently moving by themselves. My wife and I once visited the home of a well-known dowser who said his house was haunted. He, his wife and their two sons had all experienced incidents for which they could find no explanation: footsteps, raps and taps, touchings, movement of objects, 'shadows', odd odours and the day after our visit he rang to say he had got up in the morning to find all the pictures that hung on the stairway wall had been taken off their hooks and neatly leaned against the wall on the stairs. Nothing was broken, all the wires and hooks were intact, but 'someone' had been very busy during the night. I told him to replace the pictures and to say, repeatedly and firmly but not unkindly as he did so, 'Leave us alone. This is our house. Leave us alone.' They never had any more trouble!

A Miss Hislett wrote to me from Scotland. She had bought a painting of Queen Victoria at an auction sale for £50. She didn't go to the sale to buy the picture and had no intention of buying it but when it came up for sale something seemed to impel her to bid for it; she suddenly felt that she had to have it and she bought it.

She took several photographs of the picture to send to relatives and while doing so noticed for the first time that there seemed to be bubbles on the right-hand side of the face which did not always seem to be visible. A friend looked at the picture and died very shortly afterwards; an antique dealer looked at it and he had a bad accident the next day; and a neighbour looked at it and her garage collapsed on her that night.

Miss Hislett then had a vivid dream in which she saw the picture, and the subject had been cut and stabbed on the right-hand side of her face.

Miss Hislett went to see her doctor thinking she must be going mad but her doctor said she was perfectly sane. She decided to get rid of the picture and the antique dealer who agreed to sell it had it in his shop only a short while when he telephoned to say he was afraid there had been an accident and the picture had been badly damaged. Miss Hislett told him there was no need for him to tell her where the portrait was damaged – on the right-hand side of the face of Queen Victoria. And so it was, a deep cut marked the face, rendering the portrait useless and it was destroyed.

In North Korea in 1989 an elderly farmer died and all his family said they repeatedly saw his reflection in his bedroom mirror! The farmer's daughter, Kim Min-sook, said that the reflection of her father spoke to them. The body of the farmer was mummified and burial was being prepared when the family members carried the corpse in front of the 'talking' mirror and heard their father's voice coming from the mirror again and, when they turned, they found his image looking at them!

Their dead father asked them to leave his body there in the bedroom for a while as he wanted to talk to them. The family were really frightened but he spoke calmly and requested that the body be placed in front of the mirror each day so that he could chat with the family.

The authorities in Pungsan heard about the matter and asked Kim's family to co-operate with the burial laws but the family refused saying, 'We'll never bury him as long as his reflection comes alive and speaks to us from the mirror'. When the 'reflection' faded and no longer spoke to the family, the body of the old man was buried and the mirror reverted to being just an ordinary bedroom mirror.

What might be classed as haunted inanimate objects are the famous Min Min Lights near Boulia, Queensland, Australia. This well-attested phenomenon is named after a hotel that once stood in this remote area; luminous balls of light that have reportedly been seen on a number of occasions and first recorded in 1912. In 1981 the Queensland Commissioner for Police received an official report from one of his detectives, Sergeant Lyah Bowth, who had himself seen the balls of light. He saw them at 1 a.m. and Detective Sergeant Bowth watched them for fully five minutes before they dived groundwards and disappeared from view. He said the lights started out as bright white in colour and then seemed to become yellow before disappearing. This description corresponds with many other sightings over the past 80 years.

SKULLS

There are probably more haunted skulls than any other haunted inanimate object. At Wardley Hall in Lancashire I examined the skull of Ambrose Barlow, a Benedictine monk who was hanged, drawn and quartered in 1641 for professing his Catholic faith under a Protestant state, a skull that is said to have provoked screaming sounds and thunderstorms and is today carefully preserved.

At Calgarth Hall in Cumbria the skulls of two hanged people are still thought to be buried somewhere in the walls resulting, it is said, in a weird atmosphere, odd noises and movement of windows, doors and electrical switches; similar incidents having been reported by many people over many years.

At Warbleton Priory in Sussex two skulls, one that of a murderer, were preserved for many years and their removal is widely believed to have resulted in fearful screams, doors and windows rattling and farm horses showing every sign of terror for no apparent reason. When I was there some years ago there were plenty of local people with weird tales to tell and ghost hunter Thurston Hopkins had examined both skulls and told me he had originally heard their story from his friend Rudyard Kipling.

The skull of Theophilus Broome has been preserved at his house in Chilton Cantelo in Somerset for over 300 years, where I have examined it. Attempts at burial have resulted in 'horrid noises' being heard throughout the farmhouse.

Burton Agnes Hall in Yorkshire possesses a famous 'screaming skull' (which I have also examined), that of Anne Griffith who met an untimely end, but before she died she made her sister promise that her head would always be kept at the Hall, which she loved passionately. When groans, moans and other unaccountable noises were persistently heard throughout the house following burial in the usual way, the remains were dug up and the head brought into the Hall where it has resided ever since, apart from a brief period when the skull was thrown out of the house by a servant and again terrible sounds were reported until the skull was replaced inside the house. It is now bricked up in a wall of the house so that it can never be parted from beautiful Burton Agnes Hall.

I have handled the 'screaming skull' at Bettiscombe Manor in Dorset. Removal of the skull (possibly that of a black servant) from the house has resulted in appalling and continuous screaming immediately filling the house and making life for the occupants unbearable. I hoped to test the properties and efficacy of this particular skull, but the then occupants Mrs and Mrs Michael Pinney (there had been Pinneys there for more than 300 years) would not permit me to take the skull out of the house under any circumstances. This may have had something to do with the tradition that if the skull is ever taken out of doors the householder will die within a year.

My friend Eric Maple once spent a night at Bettiscombe Manor. He told me, 'Never again!' He spent most of the night listening to strange slithering noises outside his room; at 2 a.m. his door creaked open and again half-an-hour later when he saw what appeared to be a grinning skull. Next morning he left the house as soon as he could.

'Dickie', the skull at Tunstead Farm in Derbyshire, thought to be that of a murdered ancestor of a former owner, although no one really knows, is believed to cause disaster and difficulties of all kinds if removed from the house, so it is studiously preserved therein.

Appropriately named Skull House in Lancashire contains a skull that may belong to someone murdered in the interesting old house which I have visited. Obscure and mysterious happenings may or may not accompany the removal of the skull from the house, but again the owner/occupier was taking no chances. There are other 'screaming skulls' preserved and jealously guarded against possible calamities but surely it is all nonsense, this fear of the skull, the symbol of mortality and the vanity of earthly life, but also the centre of psychic energy and the alleged dwelling place of the soul?

THE GHOST AEROPLANE

There is a well-known aeroplane that is known as 'Old Willie'. It was a Canadian SE5 First World War biplane. British RAF nightfighters racing to intercept German bombers during the Battle of Britain would find themselves joined by Old Willie and he would keep up with their much faster machines. When the German bombers were sighted Old Willie would fly straight at them until they were forced to swerve to avoid hitting him, often hitting each other in the process.

No one has ever explained this recurring avenger seen by dozens of pilots, British and Nazi, but strangely enough a phantom red Fokker triplane from the First World War apparently flew for the Germans in the Second World War. RAF Lieutenant Grayson was chased by such a machine and he had a clear view of it in bright moonlight. He escaped and when he reported the incident he learned that many of his squadron had also seen the ghostly Red Baron aeroplane. Martin Caiden, recounting the story in his book *Ghosts of the Air*, says the triplane was also seen in daylight by a group of German pilots.

QUEEN MARY'S GHOSTS

Although there were few, if any, reports of ghostly happenings when the majestic liner *Queen Mary* ploughed her way back and forth across the Atlantic in peace and war, there have been innumerable stories about odd happenings since she has been berthed as a floating hotel in Long Beach harbour, Los Angeles, USA.

There have been persistent reports of women in old-fashioned costume, a bearded engine-room worker and even the recognised form of Sir Winston Churchill being seen on the luxury passenger liner, usually at night.

A female security officer was alone on deck one night when she came face to face with a woman wearing a bright 1930s or 1940s swimsuit. 'She was poised as though about to dive into the swimming pool,' said Nancy Wazny. 'But the pool is empty these days and I was about to stop her when she suddenly vanished. One second she was there, as large as life, and the next second - nothing!' Strangely enough there is a record of a woman drowning in the ship's pool in the 1930s.

Another phantom form, seen on the upper deck this time, is a man in overalls; he appears to have dark hair and a black beard. One witness met him and stepped to one side to let him pass and suddenly he was no longer there. No sound, no feeling of a presence, no sudden coldness, nothing. Oddly enough a 'greaser', one of the ship's workmen who died in an accident, fitted the description given by several witnesses. There were in fact 35 deaths aboard the *Queen Mary* during the 33 years she was afloat.

Another reported ghost did not die aboard her. No less than three times guests occupying the Winston Churchill Suite have reported seeing the unmistakable form of the famous British wartime leader. The same figure has probably been seen by others who have not reported the fact for a variety of reasons, not least the fact that those who have spoken of seeing the apparition say he 'just stood there looking at them' and then faded away.

There is also a ghostly girl in a 1950s dress who is encountered walking along the main deck. She wears a swirling skirt and seems to be the personification of youth and happiness until she completely vanishes behind a pillar. Other, possibly psychical, disturbances aboard ship include hammering noises in the bowels of the ship late at night, although immediate investigation has found nothing that could have been responsible; doors locking by themselves; the sound of running footsteps, of voices, of a man clearing his throat; movement of a chain guarding the entrance to the engine room and random movement of objects in several areas but especially the kitchens. That the *Queen Mary* still holds a few secrets is indisputable.

HAUNTED TRAINS

Laurie McQuary of Lake Oswego, Oregon, USA has sent me information about a haunted train. In August 1935 a railroad bridge support collapsed just west of Cochran in Washington County, resulting in seven deaths when the engine, tender and two passenger cars crashed down into Little Baldwin Creek. The train was Southern Pacific's *Spirit of Oregon*.

Today the historic dinner train travels between Roy and Cochran, and is owned by Vickie and Bob Steele. A year or two ago, during a benefit party on the train, Vickie noticed a strange blue haze, an eerie shape that was captured on a photograph. Soon the form of a blonde woman wearing an old-fashioned hairstyle was seen coming out of the train galley and the train crew began reporting mysterious clanging sounds on the track, glasses breaking for no reason and unexplained pockets of cold air in the train's dining room. In 1994 Vickie Steele, walking outside the train, and suddenly feeling icy cold, saw a shadow in the doorway of the bar car.

Some people who have seen the photograph think it represents a bleeding man carrying a railway lantern; others glimpse a second face on the photograph. A radio programme and a filmed documentary suggest, beyond reasonable doubt, that it is possible for a train carriage that has been involved in a death crash to be haunted. It may even be possible for long-vanished trains themselves to return in phantom form!

A case in point is President Abraham Lincoln's special funeral train. After the assassination his body was taken back to Illinois for burial on a special train and all along the route people lined the track to see the train pass. For several consecutive years, always and only on 27 April, a phantom replica of the funeral train was seen retracing its slow and melancholy journey from Washington to Illinois.

According to local and national reports, including the *Albany Evening Times*, hundreds of railway workers and members of the public made a point of waiting alongside the track in the early evening of that day and many reportedly saw the ghost train that passed noiselessly by. Year after year the phantom train was seen, it is said, and then it missed a year, then two years, then three years and gradually it came about that the train was seen no more. Lincoln's funeral train has been likened to the phantom armies of Europe: scores of people know someone who knows someone who saw the phantom exhibition, but of actual first-hand witnesses, as Scott would have said, came there none.

CHAPTER NINE

AERIAL PHENOMENA

There is much evidence that stress, in one form or another, plays an important contribution in the appearance of spontaneous psychic phenomena. The human mind has an incredible capacity and capability, and in times of extreme stress it is by no means impossible that very powerful influences on the brain may result in the projection of images which can be received at later dates by receptive individuals.

Our conquest of the air has resulted in some amazing mysteries. Men and women have taken off and never returned and no trace has ever been found of them or their machines: Captain Albert Ball VC disappeared in curious circumstances during the First World War, and there are mysterious aspects of German air ace Baron von Richthofen's death – that honour being claimed by the British, the Australians and the Canadians. There was also American Amelia Earhart, Australian Kingsford-Smith, British Amy Johnson and the 'flying' Duchess of Bedford among dozens of strange disappearances. Perhaps among the *less* curious happenings are disappearances. After all people do vanish in war-time, but even the briefest look at just a few examples is sufficient to puzzle anyone.

Glenn Miller disappeared on a flight from England to France in 1944 – not long after I saw him in London. The plane involved is not known to have landed anywhere and no body has ever officially been identified as that of the popular band leader. Two US naval officers named Cody and Adams disappeared from the airship L.8 in 1942 while patrolling off San Francisco, looking for Japanese submarines. Having spotted an oil slick they radioed that they were going in for a closer look. Fishing and patrol boats in the vicinity watched the airship descend, hover for a second and then lift and disappear among the clouds. Two hours later the airship came down but there was no sign of Cody or Adams and only their bright yellow lifejackets were missing from the craft. No one saw anything drop from the dirigible and subsequent searches found no trace of the two men or their lifejackets.

Among the *more* curious happenings are those concerning aerial phenomena, from phantom airmen to haunted airfields. Somewhere in between are the many unsolved mysteries concerning unidentified flying objects (UFOs). Some of the best pilots and most advanced aeroplanes have set out to challenge reported UFOs and not a few have inexplicably crashed.

UFOs

In 1948 there were numerous reports of a giant machine seen hovering over Kentucky in the USA and after it was also seen by the control tower at Goodman Field airbase USAF Captain Thomas Mantell set off to investigate. He soon radioed back that he had found the 'disc . . . it looks metallic and is tremendous . . .' He said he was going to climb to 20,000 ft. The radio suddenly went dead. Two hours later the wreckage of his plane was found scattered over a wide area.

In 1953 a jet fighter-interceptor took off from Otis Air Base at Cape Cod, USA, following reports that a UFO had been sighted. At 15,000 ft the engine cut out and the electrical system failed. As the jet hurtled towards earth the pilot and his radar officer baled out. The pilot landed in the garden of a house but of his radar officer there was no sign – or of the crashed jet. They had seemingly disappeared and the mystery has never been solved.

Also in 1953 another jet set out to intercept a UFO spotted over Lake Superior, USA. The plane was guided to the UFO from the ground and this plane was seen to close in on the UFO, then it seemed to merge with it and disappeared. Nothing was ever seen again of the jet or its occupants. I could go on, almost indefinitely, indeed several books on UFO mysteries have been published.

HAUNTED AIRFIELDS

Haunted airfields may have ghost airmen or ghost aeroplanes or both, or they may simply harbour the sounds of men and machines. In the golden days of late summer many people have heard the unmistakable whine of a well-tuned Merlin engine in the clear sky over Biggin Hill airfield in Kent. The pilots and staff at Biggin Hill Flying Club look at each other and remember that individual whine: it can only be a Spitfire fighter.

In 1940, at the height of the Battle of Britain, RAF Biggin Hill was a famous frontline base with Spitfires and Hurricanes setting off to intercept the invading German fighters and bombers; and from time to time a distinctive whine would herald the return to base of a Spitfire and maybe there would be a 'victory roll' over the field. More than 50 years after those frantic days people looking skywards at the familiar whine have caught a glimpse of the recognised shape of the manoeuvrable and beloved Spitfire. This ghost Spitfire has most frequently been seen in the late afternoon of a still, shimmering, summer day; an incident caught in a psychic whirlpool that has no option but to reappear when the atmospheric conditions and everything else are just right.

Since the infancy of aeronautics phantom aeroplanes and their phantom pilots have featured in reported paranormal activity. At Hendon RAF museum in North London vast hangars house Spitfires and Messerschmitts, Tempests, Typhoons, Mosquitos, a famous Avro Lancaster and the last surviving Wellington. Aware that buildings of the size and age of those at Hendon can be affected by temperature differences, especially at night, causing all sorts of odd bumps and cracks and bangings, nevertheless good witnesses, including directors of the museum, are at a loss to explain the distinct footsteps, the unmistakable sound of engine cowlings being lifted and the throbbing sound of running motors. More than a few of the staff, service personnel and visitors look back to the sudden death in 1917 of Lieutenant Shepherd who was killed when he crashed here in his trainer aircraft.

At RAF Cosford, Shropshire, an Avro Lincoln aircraft has been at the centre of a number of unexplained incidents including crew members being seen inside the empty aircraft, ghost voices, unexplained Morse blips, droning engines, switches and levers being operated, clanging hangar doors, temperature variations and even a spectral airman dressed in Second World War battle kit. What made the matter especially interesting was the fact that this particular Lincoln bomber never saw active service in the Second World War, although it had seen service in Africa during tribal disturbances.

Together with some members of the Ghost Club Society I spent several hours of darkness in the otherwise deserted enormous hangar that houses the haunted aircraft. During our vigil we caught sight of the figure of a man in the empty hangar; objects we carefully placed and frequently checked within the aircraft were moved under controlled conditions and a man wearing flying gear was photographed, twice, in the front observation dome. Philip Moore, during one observational period, climbed aboard at the rear of the plane and was immediately confronted with what he described as 'a sudden wall of static electricity'. 'It felt as though a wall had been erected', he said afterwards. 'The air was alive and although I saw nothing the feeling of expectancy remained and lasted for two minutes before everything returned to normal. It was something I had never experienced before and something that I am at a total loss to explain.'

As for myself I thought I saw a shadowy yet distinct figure, a man in flying uniform, from my vantage point near the tail of the Lincoln. My wife was underneath the cockpit at the time and I quietly drew her attention to the figure silently approaching the bomber. She saw it too. Also another member of our team, unbeknown to us at the time, glimpsed the same figure in the same place at the same time from an entirely different position. When one of the occasional loud clanging noises sounded from the other end of the hanger it seems that we all looked in that direction; when we looked back there was no sign of the phantom airman.

A former curator of the museum Flight Lieutenant Derek Eastwood admitted that 'extra' crew members had been seen in and near the Lincoln by various people on different occasions, adding, 'I don't pretend to understand these things and I prefer to leave them alone ... when people have pried into them in the past, unpleasant things have happened here. On one occasion we allowed a television crew to film the aeroplane. They were being on the humorous side about the whole thing when suddenly their camera was picked up and hurled across the hanger – no one was near it at the time. They packed up and left!'

GHOSTLY ACTIVITY AT MONTROSE AERODROME

During the Second World War Montrose Aerodrome in Scotland housed a flying training school and there too there have been a number of interesting ghost sightings and reports of ghostly activity, from that period and much earlier, during or before the First World War.

The sound of flying aircraft, seemingly returning to the airfield, has been heard on many occasions and when nothing that might account for the sound had been seen. In 1943 a NAFFI (services canteen) employee heard the sound she had come to know well and poured tea ready for the returning pilot and his crew but no one turned up and no aeroplane had in fact landed. On another occasion a uniformed airman entered the canteen, a stranger to the NAFFI assistant, but when she spoke to 'him', the figure suddenly disappeared.

In 1987 a woman driving near the aerodrome saw a khaki-painted aircraft flying low, close enough for her to see every detail of the machine that she thought was a Hurricane, yet she heard not a sound. She reported the sighting to the Montrose Aerodrome Museum Society which, she discovered, had information about a number of aircraft that had crashed when the place had been an RAF station; one of them was a Hurricane.

In 1913 Lieutenant Desmond Arthur of the old Royal Flying Corps crashed his biplane, an accident that the subsequent enquiry established was due to negligent repair work. Whatever the cause the result was the death of Desmond Arthur and his subsequent reappearance as a ghost, more especially after publication of the court's findings. This 'strange officer' appeared to other officers in and about the officers' quarters at Montrose and invariably vanished completely when approached too closely. The number of officers who claimed to see the apparition grew and there were stories of the form appearing in the night in rooms shared by two officers – and the phantom form was seen by both. It was also seen by Major Cyril Foggin, by the Commanding Officer of the day and by some flying instructors. Sir Peter Mansfield, a former Director-General of the Ministry of Civil Aviation, told me he saw the 1913 accident re-enacted in May 1963, 50 years to the day after it happened.

Those seeing the ghost of Desmond Arthur began to believe that he was unhappy with the finding of the court of enquiry and, according to

Major P.L. Holmes 'it was largely due to the ghost that the original findings were altered by a second court'. At all events the appearances of the ghost of Lieutenant Arthur grew less frequent, although there were still stories of encounters with the ghost both indoors and over towards the south end of the aerodrome in the 1940s.

Another ghost at Montrose seems to date from the summer of 1942 when a Flight Lieutenant stationed at Montrose, the RAF's first operational air station, crashed within seconds of taking off and was killed instantly. Before long responsible airmen reported seeing a ghost, a figure in flying suit and goggles, and sightings became so commonplace that new arrivals at the station were warned to watch out for the ghost airman. One experienced serviceman laughed at the stories but during a night ground duty he saw an airman with a dead-white face and wearing goggles, helmet and flying suit suddenly appear close to the control tower – and as suddenly disappear.

Witnesses for ghostly activity at Montrose include a RAF policeman, Norrie Webster, who heard disembodied footsteps and followed them; the footsteps stopped, turned and began to approach him – Webster desperately shone his torch everywhere but nothing showed up. He reported the incident officially. Airman Alex Kettles heard first-hand accounts of a figure in a flying suit suddenly disappearing. Alexander Hendry, a civilian, met a figure in flying clothing one night on the airfield and as they passed he made some comment about the weather. Receiving no reply he looked over his shoulder at the 'man' he had just passed: the figure had completely vanished and there was no sign of anyone in the immediate area and not a sound broke the stillness of the night . . .

Ian G. McIntosh of the Montrose Aerodrome Museum Society informed me that the aerodrome is still active, with light aircraft using it very regularly, especially at weekends, and the hauntings continue. In 1990 a woman walking her dog on the airfield heard a voice that 'came out of the air' say four times, 'I'm here'. There was no one in sight and nowhere for anyone to hide. Twice, once at the end of 1990 and once early in 1991, an unidentified figure has frightened people off the airfield at dusk. Three girls saw 'something' beside one of the old hangars and left, fast; and in 1994 footsteps, door opening and door handle rattling were experienced and a shadowy figure was seen by the Museum Society principal's son. If special areas attract ghosts and ghostly activity Montrose Aerodrome seems to be a special place with a powerful attraction.

OTHER HAUNTED AERODROMES

Other haunted aerodromes include Whitchurch where the ghost of a German airforce officer was seen by a cleaner and other personnel at what used to be part of the aerodrome; RAF Binbrook, Lincolnshire, with its haunted bomb dump and ghost airmen; Bircham Newton, Norfolk (closed in 1962) with its ghostly laughing airman, its Women's Auxiliary Air Force suicide, its ghostly footsteps and ghost in RAF uniform in the old squash court; Kimbolton with its ghostly American airmen and crashed B17 bomber; RAF Kelstern, Lincolnshire with its ghostly drone of Merlin engines; Coleby Grange near Lincoln with its haunted control tower; RAF Laurbruch in Germany, once a Luftwaffe base, with its phantom German soldier; Wellesbourne Mountford in Warwickshire with its ghost of a wartime air navigator; RAF Strubby in Lincolnshire with its hangar haunted by the ghost of a headless airman and Holmsley South Airfield with its ghost voices, music and roar of planes taking off: quite literally the list is endless.

There is also the story long associated with the Second World War RAF Station at Honington in East Anglia, concerning a Canadian pilot who was nursing his badly damaged aircraft back across the Channel after a raid on Germany when, as he was in sight of the airfield, he realised his plane was on fire. There was no chance of landing, even crash landing, and he sought an open space where he could bale out. As he did so his parachute caught fire and he fell like a rocket, landing on the roof of one of the aircraft hangars. He slid to the ground, picked himself up and, according to eye witnesses, calmly walked about 100 yd before dropping down dead. His ghost has been seen on many occasions.

THE HAUNTED AIRMAN'S HOUSE

In March 1995 Basil Wright of Dartmouth wrote to me about his personal experience of a haunted house bordering an airfield. He writes: 'As a First Mate in the Royal Maritime Auxilliary Service, I was posted to their HQ in Bath and was allocated a semi-detached house in "officer country" at what had been RAF Colerne. At that time the RAF was withdrawing from the station and the MOD (Ministry of Defence) was using the quarters to house staff posted to the area from away. My house was in the middle of a row overlooking the airfield, but apart from me, only the house at each end of the row was occupied.

'One evening, having had a very hard day, I went to bed early, but awoke just after midnight to the sounds of a lot of chattering and laughter. In my sleep-befuddled state I decided that a party must be going on next door. I settled down and eventually went back to sleep.

'In the morning I remembered that the houses on either side of me were empty so I mentioned it to the Military Police who told me that if I heard anything during the night it was probably their patrol checking the empty houses as in the past they had had trouble with squatters.

'I thought no more about it until one night when I had been working late and got home at about midnight. There was quite a storm blowing and, having garaged the car, I was glad to get indoors. Having checked that the doors and windows were secured, I went to bed. I had no sooner turned out the light than I again heard a lot of chattering and laughter. I tried to locate where the sounds were coming from until I realised, to my horror, that they were emanating from my own front room downstairs!

'As I lay wondering what to do the bedclothes were suddenly and sharply pulled across me, tightly, and the mattress at the side of the bed sank as though someone had sat on the edge of the bed to remove his shoes and socks: but there was no one else in the house! I am not usually a praying man, but that night I prayed. By gosh I prayed. I have never prayed so hard.

'Then, as I prayed, the pressure on the bed eased, the voices and laughter faded and even the raging storm outside was stilled and I was overcome by a feeling of all-pervading peace.

'A few months later, I was giving a colleague a lift to the office. At the start of our journey, we had to drive along a lane with the airstation on our right and thick woodland on our left. Towards the end of the lane we passed on our right the eastern end of the East/West runway and on our left a large gap in the woodland. The trees surrounding the gap were badly scorched, having obviously been subject to a very fierce fire.

'My colleague informed me that he was living on the station when that crash happened. It was the last Hastings aircraft on the station and it was taking off for a series of practice "circuits and bumps". Unfortunately, someone had omitted to replace a bolt in one of the tail aelerons and the pilot could not get sufficient lift to clear the trees. The plane ploughed into the woods and, with a full load of fuel on board, it blew up in a fireball killing all the crew.

'He added that the pilot was very popular with his crew and on the evening before any flight he always invited them all to his house where they would discuss and work out the flight plan for the following day. When that was over the drinks would come out and they would get down to yarning and joking. "He lived along your road," he added.

' "Oh?" I said. "Which number?"

' "Number ten," he replied.

'All at once everything seemed to be answered. I lived at number ten!'

PHANTOM PLANES

A ghost Wellington bomber has been seen by many people flying along the Towy valley between Llandeilo and Llandovery in Dyfed, Wales. Martin Green, a former London publisher, was walking along the valley road one morning when he saw an unmistakable Wellington bomber flying towards him at tree-top level. He saw it quite clearly, its propellers were spinning and the tops of the trees bent in the slipstream as it passed but he heard no sound. Thinking it rather odd he mentioned the sighting to friends and acquaintances here and there, and then discovered that other people had seen it too.

A few weeks later Martin Green was driving up the same valley with a friend when they both saw the mystery aircraft flying towards them. As it passed they stopped the car and got out at the same time as another car drew up on the other side of the road and the occupants, a middle-aged couple, got out to watch. All four watchers saw the silent aircraft, then the other driver looked puzzled and said it looked like a Wellington bomber but it couldn't have been because there were no flying Wellingtons left. He was more than a little shocked to think that he might have seen a ghost!

He was quite right, of course, in saying there are no flying Wellingtons, in fact the only Wellington left in Britain is an exhibit in the RAF museum at Hendon. But the bombers did train over the Brecon Beacons and around the Towy valley during the Second World War. Why this particular one should revisit that Welsh valley is a puzzle, but if we are to accept human testimony, an extinct and silent Wellington bomber has been seen flying there as it did half a century ago.

AVIATORS' EXPERIENCES

CHARLES LINDBERGH

A number of well-known aviators have heard voices and had other experiences that they are convinced could not have had a natural or rational explanation. Charles Lindbergh, once a pilot in the American air mail service, made the first non-stop flight between New York and Europe. During the 33 hours of flying Lindbergh's outstanding memory was during the 22nd hour of the journey when he had the most extraordinary experience of his life.

Enveloped in dense fog and battling against sleep Lindbergh felt he became weightless and even formless – almost like a ghost. He said afterwards, 'I existed independently of time and matter... I felt myself departing from my body as I imagine a spirit would depart – emanating into the cockpit, extending through the fuselage as though no frame or fabric walls were there, angling upward, outward, until I reformed in an awareness far distant from the human form I left in a fast-flying trans-atlantic plane. But I remained connected to my body through a long-extended strand, a strand so tenuous that it could have been severed by a breath.'

Aware that his experiences would be attributed to extreme fatigue the aviator said in his autobiography 50 years later: 'My visions were easily explained away through reason, but the longer I live, the more limited I believe rationality to be.'

Lindbergh was almost 25 years of age when he made the historic flight and he had more than 4 years of aviation experience. Writing later he maintained that at one time the fuselage of his plane became crowded with ghostly presences, ghastly figures that came and went, dissolving through the walls of the plane.

While staring at the instruments the fuselage behind him became 'filled with ghostly presences – vaguely outlined forms, transparent, moving, riding weightless' with him in the plane. 'I felt no surprise at their coming,' he said. 'There was no suddenness to their appearance. Without turning my head, I saw them clearly...' First one and then another pressed forward to speak above the noise of the engine and then drew back to the group behind him.

At any other time Lindbergh knew he would be startled by the visions he was witnessing but on that fantastic flight he felt so far separated from the earthly life he knew that he felt he could accept whatever circumstances might come along. In fact he felt 'these emissaries from a spirit world' were quite in keeping with the mysterious blending of day and night that he was experiencing.

Looking back the name of Lindbergh's plane, *Spirit of St Louis*, and its appearance, steel-grey, all give it a somewhat ghostly quality. As the journey progressed Lindbergh felt more and more fatigued and helpless in the blackness of the Atlantic at night, but he was not alone or helpless. 'One and then another of the forms,' he said, 'pressed forward to my shoulder to speak above the noise of the engine ... conversing and advising me on my flight, discussing problems of navigation, reassuring me and giving me messages of importance unattainable in ordinary life.'

Lindbergh was not a man accustomed to flights of fancy or inclined to the mystical. He had to be analytical in his airmail piloting and in his military training. Later, he was to take part in combat missions over the Pacific Ocean during the Second World War. One could say that Lindbergh's perceptions and apparent experiences were caused by sleep deprivation, that his unconscious mind took over during hours of fatigue and isolation accompanied by the hypnotic drone of the engines. Aware of these possibilities Lindbergh, 25 years after his historic flight, still looked back on the experiences as objective and the 'messages' he received stayed with him for the rest of his life. 'Death,' he said. 'No longer seems the final end it used to be, but rather the entrance to a new and free existence which includes all space and all time.' Yet the awful fatigue must have played a part.

SHEILA SCOTT

Aviatrix Sheila Scott also encountered something she had not expected during one of her epoch-making flights. She flew three times round the world solo and held over 100 World Class Light Aircraft records. She was the first person in the world to pilot a light aircraft solo from the Equator to Equator via a pole and the first woman in the world to fly the Arctic Ocean and the true North Pole solo. During that flight the North American Space Agency used her and her aircraft for experiments in the biomedical, environmental and positioning fields via the Satellite

Nimbus. Her major awards included the USA's Harmon Trophy 1967 and UK's Britannia Trophy 1968. She died almost in poverty.

During one of her record-making flights Sheila Scott became aware that she was totally lost. It was the middle of the night, a cloudy night with no stars visible; she had somehow lost track of her route and her instruments seemed to be telling her different things. As she began to panic she heard a voice, although she knew that it was not possible and decided that it must be something inside her head. She went back to trying to make sense of her irregular instruments and the deep, deep darkness all around her. Out of that darkness, it seemed, the voice came again. Almost before she realised what was said, another voice told her to alter course; she did so without question. She was told to alter the route on her instructions, which she did, and then she was told to follow a certain course for the next hour. She did so and at the end of the hour she was astonished to see all her instruments lined up, as they should, and everything seemed to be in order. She kept to the route she had been given and in due course found she had diverted for a while but had then regained her set route and all was well.

'I was finished,' she told me. 'I was flying over hostile forests and rapidly losing height, without knowing I was doing so. A few more moments and I would have been down and probably not found for years. Where those voices came from I have no idea. I didn't recognise them but they saved my life. Of that there is no shadow of a doubt.'

THE 'GHOST CHILD' ON THE FLIGHT TO AUSTRALIA

A somewhat similar experience has been recalled by Dr and Mrs J.N. Haldeman of Pretoria, South Africa. The doctor and his wife flew in their private plane to Australia and back, a 30,000 mile trip.

Before taking off from Pretoria, a photographer took a picture of their aeroplane. There was no one in it or near it, but in the resulting picture, in the cabin, as plain as can be, was a little girl of about six years old.

'We felt her presence throughout the trip,' Dr Haldeman said. 'The "ghost child" guided us repeatedly in times of danger. Flying from Masirah to Salah, we hit a monsoon and gave ourselves up for lost. It seemed, however, that the child took over from us and guided the plane to safety. We took the photo with her in it along with us.' No one has ever been able to identify the child in the photograph and the

Haldemans never had any subsequent impression of the presence of the ghost child who, they certainly felt, saved their lives on that unforgettable trip.

THE 'GHOST VOICE' ON THE PLANE FROM SPAIN

A haunted aircraft flew between Spain and England in 1984 and among the passengers who wrote to tell me about a ghost voice crying for help in the middle of the night in the middle of nowhere was Andrew Murphy of Glasgow. He said: 'I would like to tell you of a strange experience that happened to my wife and I aboard a plane that was taking us home on 27 December 1984 from an airport in Spain.

'My wife and I and some of my family were spending a month in Lanzarote over Christmas. I was taken ill, was in terrible pain, and had to be put on the first available flight out which was on the Thursday night at 10.30 on 27 December to Gatwick. We were delayed by paperwork and airport officials but somehow they got me aboard the plane which had been held up by all this. The stewardesses came to meet me and Dorothy, my wife, and they could not have been nicer and more helpful. They asked me how I felt and if there was anything they could do to help me. I told them I was all right, just a little pain, and if they could show us to our seats, everything would be fine. They said they were sorry it was not a direct flight to Glasgow. The plane was half empty and we decided to sit on the port side half-way up the aisle, just next to the wing.

'It was pitch-black outside as the plane took off at 10.35 p.m. I told my wife to stretch herself out on the seats and rest her head on the window. I took my jacket off and covered her and told her to try and get a bit of sleep. I was still in pain but I did not want my wife or anybody else aboard the plane to know that. I had no pain-killing drugs or anything else to ease the pain and I don't drink any form of alcohol. Within the hour most of the lights on the plane were dimmed, except one or two reading lights, including my own. I was trying to read a novel but found it hard to concentrate. After some time I looked at my watch and found that it had stopped at 1 a.m.

'I went up aft to where the stewardesses were sitting and asked for a glass of iced water to drink and for the correct time; they told me it was 1.30 and they were quite upset because I had not rung for them . . . I told them it was all right and wanted to stretch my legs. I then went back to my seat where my wife was dozing.

'I sat down and continued to try to read my book; then at 1.40 I heard the eerie voice of an Englishman calling for help! This was repeated several times, then the voice said he was on the wing, and he kept saying, 'Help! Help! I'm on the wing, let me in, let me in ...' This lasted a couple of minutes maybe and by this time the hairs on the back of my neck were standing up and cold shivers were running all over my body.

'I looked down at my wife who was wide awake and looking at me. I asked her if she had heard a voice and she said, yes. After a few moments the voice seemed to fade away in the distance and my wife asked me if it could have been the pilot playing a joke on the stewardesses; if so it was in poor taste. I told her it was more than the pilot's job was worth, as it could have caused a panic. Within minutes all the passengers were putting their lights on and everyone was obviously concerned but I don't think anyone said much about the voices; they were too relieved that the flight was nearly over. When we arrived at Gatwick I never saw a plane empty so quickly in all my life!'

THE *FLYING DUTCHMAN*

The *Flying Dutchman*, probably the most celebrated of aerial phenomena, a ghost ship in the sky, is supposed to date from the seventeenth century when a Captain Hendrik van der Decken (although the name varies in different versions of the story which seems first to have been written up in about 1821), rounding the Cape of Good Hope, encountered such unfavourable weather that he had the greatest difficulty in making any progress. Stubborn and determined, as sea captains had to be in those days, a man who boasted that he feared nothing in this world or out of it, he tried again and again to round the Cape but refused the pleas of his passengers and crew to seek a port until the storm blew itself out.

Cursing and shaking his fist at the dark heavens he swore he would round the damned Cape if it took till Doomsday. The *Flying Dutchman* sank with only one or two survivors but the ghostly replica of the ship has been reportedly seen by many experienced and reliable sailors in the area, and this is a phantom that has some sort of official recognition for records of sightings are preserved in the files of the British Admiralty.

Among the alleged sightings are those in 1823, 1835, 1890, 1893, 1905, 1911, 1916, 1939 and 1942.

Among the witnesses are King George V when he was a naval cadet together with 12 other witnesses including his brother Prince Clarence, then heir to the throne. Prince George noted the appearance in a matter-of-fact way in his diary: 'At 4 a.m. *The Flying Dutchman* crossed our bows. A strange red light as of a phantom ship all aglow, in the midst of which the masts, spars and sails of a brig 200 yards distant stood out in strong relief ... the officer of the watch from the bridge saw her, as did the quarter-deck midshipman who was sent forward at once to the forecastle.' The formal entry in the ship's log reads: 'July 11, 1881 During the middle watch the so-called *Flying Dutchman* crossed our bows ... 13 persons altogether saw her ... *Tourmaline* and *Cleopatra*, which were sailing on our starboard quarter, flashed signals asking whether we had seen the strange glow and if we could account for it.'

During the Second World War Admiral Karl Doenitz, Hitler's Commander-in-Chief of U-boats, reported a sighting of the *Flying Dutchman*: 'Certain of my U-boat crews claimed they saw the *Flying Dutchman* or some other so-called phantom ship on their tours of duty east of Suez. When they returned to their base the men said they preferred facing the combined strength of Allied warships in the North Atlantic than know the terror a second time of being confronted by a phantom vessel.'

Among the evidence is that of Commander A.B. Campbell, one of the original members of the BBC Brains Trust, who told me that once, when he rounded the Cape of Good Hope, he saw the ghost ship. A storm was blowing but he and three companions saw clearly in the sky an enormous ancient craft in full sail and he just had time to notice the foreign and out-of-date line of the vessel and the strange billowing sails before the apparition disappeared. Afterwards he met a shrewd and sceptical old sea captain who assured him that he too had once seen the phantom ship when he had been rounding the Cape and Campbell also talked with an old seaman who had spent sixty years at sea and he too had seen the same ghost ship in similar circumstances.

Whatever the explanation there can be no doubt that for many years varied and reliable eye-witnesses have reported seeing a ship moving in the sky over the sea around the Cape of Good Hope, a ship with a strange square, squat hull, a high poop and an ancient rig. On the other hand the waters off the Cape of Good Hope have long been known for mirages and one must ask oneself whether this may account for all the sightings of *The Flying Dutchman*. The legend of the cursed ship achieved another kind of immortality from Richard Wagner's opera, *Der Fliegende Halländer*.

It is interesting that this famous apparition is seen in the air, almost as though it is preserved in the clouds and atmosphere, and affected by the prevailing climate and possibly by the ozone, a condensed form of oxygen. Another famous apparitional appearance in the air is of course the violent ghost battle responsibly reported at Edgehill which we have already explored in Chapter 5.

FLIGHT 401

Yet another remarkable example of paranormal activity in the air is the well-known case of the ghost of Flight 401. An Eastern Airlines jet crashed in the Everglades, the swampy subtropical region of Southern Florida, USA, 100 miles long and 50 and more miles wide, in 1972 with the deaths of 101 people.

Two crew members were seen on numerous occasions after their deaths, usually on sister aeroplanes which contained salvaged parts of the crashed plane. The ghost figures were seen and recognised by stewardesses, pilots, engineers and members of the public. In particular the apparition of dead flight engineer Don Repo appeared most frequently, sometimes apparently warning pilots of impending danger.

Seeking to learn how modern-day legends are born John Fuller soon realised that in this case the rumours and stories were remarkably consistent and that competent and intelligent people, trained engineers and level-headed pilots among them, were claiming sightings of the ghost figures. His attempt to investigate the whole case scientifically and present it objectively was made difficult by the airline companies whose employees, or some of them, refused to allow their names to be revealed for fear of disapproval and retaliation by their employers.

None the less his book on the case, *The Ghost of Flight 401*, sold over one million copies in the USA alone and the considerable anecdotal material and evidence is impressive with first-hand statements and a personal encounter with the dead flight engineer. It all sounds a little too good to be true, but I met and talked with John Fuller and I was impressed.

'Numerous reliable eye witnesses I spoke to have seen the ghosts on jets of Eastern Airlines,' he told me. The ghost of Captain Bob Loft was seen and recognised by a stewardess; on a different occasion and on a different jet the ghost of the dead pilot was seen and recognised by the captain and two crew members; on another flight cabin staff were checking the passengers and called their pilot when a man in captain's uniform ignored their questions and then suddenly disappeared, but not before the pilot recognised the man as Captain Loft.

The ghost of engineer Don Repo has also been seen according to extensive evidence. A flight engineer saw the dead man seated at his instruments, before he disappeared; and he was seen and identified by another flight captain on another TriStar jet.

'When I first heard of these and other ghostly appearances I decided to research the stories and explain the development of a modern legend but my talks with airline staff and my own experiences in contacting the dead flight engineer have convinced me that the legend is fact,' John Fuller told me.

Eastern Airlines' president rejects the story but liaison executive Doris Ahnstrom said that published reports of the appearances of the ghost of the flight engineer appeared in a safety bulletin in 1974, long before Fuller's book. These followed reports received by an experienced and trustworthy pilot; the bulletin also contained the report of a stewardess who had seen the dead flight engineer.

John Fuller interviewed scores of airline flight personnel and seems to have explored every facet of each report. As I say, I was impressed, although it is a pity that the anecdotal quality of the evidence and the fact that so much of it is anonymous make it impossible for other researchers to check.

CHAPTER TEN

GHOSTS AND ANIMALS

Many records of psychic activity have to do with animals, their 'sixth' sense, their influence, their telepathic powers and their ghostly attributes.

Much is still unknown about animal behaviour. How do homing pigeons and migrating flocks of birds unerringly wing hundreds of miles to their lofts or nesting sites? How does a family pet, lost or left behind when its owners move, find its way to them although it has never travelled the area or seen the new property? How do insects like bees, ants and termites co-ordinate their efforts for the good of the whole? How can chimps, gorillas, dolphins and other animals learn to understand our speech and be taught to communicate with us?

DOGS

Animals, especially perhaps dogs, do seem to have a perception of the wishes and wants of their human owners and companions far beyond that of human beings, and conversely the perception of animals can sometimes be picked up by humans. The best-selling novelist Dame Catherine Cookson, in her ninetieth year and having lost most of her sight, told me in August 1995 that 'the ghost in her house' recounted in her biography by Cliff Goodwin (Arrow, 1995) was really the fact that her dog felt the presence of someone in the house. Dame Cookson, knowing that Miss Harrison, the previous owner of the house, greatly loved the place, was convinced that she was present for a time, mostly as a feeling within Catherine Cookson herself who, although she does not think she has ever actually seen a ghost, has always been very sensitive to atmosphere and it would seem, the feelings and perceptions of her dog.

THE 'PSYCHIC DOG'

Dogs, perhaps because of their close connection with humanity, are most frequently mentioned in occult experiences. When the deputy features editor of the monthly magazine *Homes and Gardens* sent me an account of an Australian reader's experiences and her 'psychic dog' I must confess my heart sank a little for I get an awful lot of unsolicited correspondence, but having carefully read this particular piece several times I feel it has the ring of truth and deserves serious consideration.

I preface the account by stating that the writer, Mrs I.E. Will, avers that every word is strictly true and there is not one bit of exaggeration. She says, 'the whole episode is still absolutely clear in my mind... At that frightening period of my life I was perfectly well, happily married, my children had never given me a moment's worry and I had no financial worries. I had money of my own and a generous husband. I was delighted with the house when I had finished with it. Moreover I have always been a level-headed, sensible person although I confess to never discounting the unexplainable but nor have I ever tried to delve into it. I love beauty in all its forms but I can be very hard-headed over money. In short, a fairly "all round" person. So please take this letter seriously...'
I wrote to Mrs Wills several times but received no response. It does seem that some, perhaps all, dogs see and sense ghosts. This is the gist of Mrs Will's story:

'Something over thirty years ago we moved from a large, much loved, home to a smaller house which required a fair amount of renovation but which we felt at the time would fill our needs. We both had reservations about the purchase but for no specific reason. Eventually workmen moved in but not one single thing went right from start to finish although we were employing a reputable builder whom we had employed on various previous occasions and found his work good. Not this time! Everything went wrong and one day when I had looked in to check progress I went home to my husband and in sheer desperation blurted out: "That house is evil! It simply won't co-operate" – and I thought no more about the remark.

'We eventually moved in with the builders still coming and going but finally they pronounced "Finished" and I made what I thought an attractive and comfortable home. My late husband was a general medical practitioner and in those days GPs were at the beck and call of the general public and went when called regardless of time or payment. Our family at this stage were grown-up and both in England (my birth-place

and home for the first 27 years of my life). Consequently I was frequently alone for long periods but I had grown accustomed to this over
the years and it did not affect me one way or the other until we moved
into the house of which I have spoken. I soon realised that when I was
alone I became terribly restless and felt I must be on my feet doing
something, day or night, unless I was asleep.

'One evening when I was alone for what I knew would be a fairly long
call I was so restless that I pulled out the cleaner and began to vacuum
the carpet. Shortly after I began I looked towards a door, I have no idea
why, but I saw what appeared to be a nebulous, distorted shape vaguely
resembling a bulky figure. I looked down at the floor and closed my eyes
and then looked again, whatever it was was still there but this time I
thought it was slightly more distinct. For the third time I closed my eyes
and when I looked again the apparition, call it what you will, had
disappeared. I spent the rest of the time until my husband returned
busying myself about the house and trying to assure myself that nothing
had happened and nearly succeeded – except that I knew it had. I said
nothing to my husband nor to anyone else, just tried to forget, but that I
wasn't allowed to do.

'At the time we possessed a small mongrel dog, a wire-haired terrier.
His mother was a pure-bred spaniel, the pup we named Peter; he was
about the size of a small spaniel. He was a most affectionate little fellow
with plenty of intelligence. He was about nine at the time of which I
write, not given to wandering, definitely a house dog.

'I never saw the "whatever" again but at intervals after its appearance
I began to get an icy sensation which I can only say felt like something
quite literally passing through my body from back to front. I would risk
being disbelieved except that Peter, if he was with me, saw or felt it too. I
felt paralysed for the time it took the sensation to pass, Peter evidently
felt it too. He didn't utter a sound, crouched on the floor with terror-
stricken eyes fixed on me and every hair on his body standing erect. We
recovered together at exactly the same time. There was never any
premonition of the happening, never a change in Peter's behaviour,
only this dreadful sensation through my body and the utter sense of
terror while it lasted and an inability to move.

'Peter lived with us in three different houses before this thing
happened. After we sold he lived in three more but neither before or
after had he ever been anything but a very happy little dog nor had I ever
experienced anything of the kind before nor have I since. Now, seven

years after being widowed and in my eighty-fifth year I live very happily alone in a small flat which I bought at the time of my husband's death. I did hear, about two years after we left, that a very keen gardener had committed suicide there and had been found half-way down his terraced garden which he had evidently loved very much. I hesitate to make any conjecture as to whether that had any bearing on what went on during our residency. My husband was only once with us during a "visitation". He saw all that happened but when I tried to talk to him afterwards he rubbished the whole thing and suggested that Peter had probably heard a rat somewhere. Peter, with his part strain of terrier fatherhood would have raised Cain if a rat had been within half a mile of him! I tried once more to talk to my husband but when he suggested I saw a mental specialist, I clammed up. Nevertheless, he made no objection when I suggested putting the house on the market.'

CLASSIC GHOSTLY DOG STORIES

A classic story of a ghost dog dates back to the American Civil War when a Confederate spy was captured with his dog and sentenced to be shot. He asked for his dog for company during his last night on earth but this request was refused and the dog was slaughtered. Next morning, as he faced the firing squad, he saw his dog approach and greeted it. The firing squad saw nothing and thought he was mad and he was hastily blindfolded, but Colonel Panton, in charge of the execution, went deathly pale and apparently did see the ghost dog. Three times he tried to give the order to fire but no words came and at length, visibly shaken, he muttered, 'Execution deferred' and dismissed the firing squad. That night the Confederates attacked, Colonel Panton was killed, the condemned soldier was released and he then learned that his dog had been killed. To the end of his life he maintained that his dead pet had returned to save his life.

One of the most celebrated of dog apparitions is, or was, that at Peel Castle on the Isle of Man. Among the surviving ruins, close to the old Gatehouse, is the Guard Room, the haunt of the castle's Black Dog apparition; detailed in the official guide. Known as 'the Manthe or Moddey Dhoo or Doog', the form was that of a large black spaniel with a shaggy coat that haunted several chambers in the castle, once one of the most remarkable fortresses in the British Isles; its story certainly going back to the tenth century and probably far beyond.

It seems that the phantom dog would sometimes appear after sunset and lie in front of the glowing turf fire. It invariably disappeared before sunrise and some of the soldiers using the Guard Room, while being careful not to get too close or to interfere with it, became quite accustomed to its presence.

There was one part of their duties which they all disliked. Every night it was necessary for the keys of the castle to be carried from the Guard Room to the Captain's House, beyond the cathedral crypt and along a passage which was the regular route of the ghost dog. There being safety in numbers, the soldiers invariably performed this duty in twos.

One night, a soldier whom drink had made reckless, declared he had never seen the dog himself and had no fear of it and he would take the keys on his own. His comrades tried to dissuade him but off he went with the keys.

Before long there was a considerable commotion and the soldier staggered back into the Guard Room, sobered but speechless, and in a state of great distress and agony. He died three days later, his face contorted and still not having said a word about what he had encountered or what had transpired.

The haunted passage was bricked up but the legend of the ghost dog persisted and there have been periodical reports of the phantom dog being seen several times towards the end of the nineteenth century and in the middle and latter years of the twentieth century. A visitor who succeeded in spending a night in the Guard Room in 1988 assured me that he had seen the shadowy form of a large black spaniel lying on the floor, a form that completely vanished when he and his companion approached. The trouble here, as with many cases where the ghost watcher knows what to expect, is that he is half-way to seeing the haunting entity before he reaches the haunted room and the slightest shadow or anything of the kind can prompt such a person into accepting as paranormal the most natural object which merges with the reputed phantom and becomes a figment of the imagination.

BLACK SHUCK

Perhaps the best-known ghost dog is Black Shuck, Black Hound or Devil Dog. James Wentworth Day, ghost hunter extraordinary, regarded the enormous apparitional animal as the last relic of the Wild Hunt, that Teutonic myth that the storm-racked sky was the hunting ground of Wotan, the Wild Huntsman, and his spectral hounds ever in pursuit of human souls, the phantom black dog being the solitary survivor of the pack of demon dogs set loose to fend for themselves. He told me he had talked with literally dozens of people who swore they had seen such a creature

These ghost dogs are reportedly found in many parts of the country but seem to be especially prevalent in East Anglia and the West Country. It was while on a golfing holiday in Cromer that Sir Arthur Conan Doyle first heard about Black Shuck and the seed was planted for one of his finest books, *The Hound of the Baskervilles*. Later he went to Dartmoor and decided to set the story there and so came about the memorable story of the demon hound of Dartmoor.

Ghostly black dogs have also long been accepted in Devon, Dorset, Somerset, the Midlands, the Lake District – there was a public house in Lyme Regis, Dorset, named after the spectral dog that once haunted the area and the Black Dog of Bungay, Essex, seen as long ago as 1577 has a weathervane to commemorate it. Some ancient families have a tradition that an ominous black dog is seen before the death of a member, such as the Vaughan family. Spectral hounds are common throughout Europe, where packs of such phantom animals have been reported from the twelfth century onwards.

BLACK DOG AT SPINNEY ABBEY

Robert Fuller who farmed Spinney Abbey, a mile from historic Wicken Fen in Cambridgeshire, once saw the phantom black dog. Years ago now, in the company of Ghost Club Society Member Tom Brown and friend Bill Whitney, I spent a night at haunted Spinney Abbey where we had first-hand evidence of animals' apparent awareness of ghosts.

During the night we spent in the grounds of Spinney Abbey, we employed among other apparatus a number of delicate thermometers. We placed these in hopefully strategic spots, such as a part of the piggery where pigs were known to fight, seemingly aware of some invisible adversary; the spot where Harold Fuller had seen a human figure suddenly disappear in front of his eyes; the place where Joseph Fuller had seen a vague, white, ghostly form and had struck at it with his whip which he found went clean through the strange form, met no resistance and had no effect; and on the path where Tom Fuller had several times seen the figure of a monk glide silently along the path (possibly connected with the original abbey here in the fifteenth century, and the sound of music and Latin chanting heard on several occasions, once by all the six people in one room at the time), we placed a further thermometer.

Throughout the night readings were carefully checked and recorded every ten minutes and all the thermometers except one showed no abnormality, each of them steadily declining from around 32°F at midnight to 24°F at 6 a.m. as might be expected; but the thermometer placed where the ghostly monk had walked recorded a sudden and inexplicable drop in temperature of 7 degrees! This occurred at 2.10 a.m. and the reading was verified by all three of us; yet the other nearby thermometer showed no similar drop in temperature. One was no more exposed than the other and ten minutes later all the thermometers showed the same normal temperature.

Some horses stabled nearby were quiet throughout the whole of the night except at the exact time at which this sudden drop in temperature occurred. At exactly 2.10 a.m. the horses suddenly set up a terrific noise in their stable, kicking their stalls, whinnying and neighing loudly. After a few moments the animals quietened down, and by the time the thermometers showed normal readings at 2.20 a.m. all was quiet again. And at precisely the same time the pigs made a great deal of noise as though they were fighting to get out but again they were quiet by 2.20 a.m. We wondered then and I still wonder whether some shade of a ghost passed near to us that night, perceived by the heightened sensibilities of animals in the immediate vicinity. At all events that sudden and not inconsiderable drop of 7 degrees remains on my chart to puzzle me, and to remind me that we may encounter some inexplicable occurrence at any time and perhaps especially when we least expect it.

Jimmy Wentworth Day told me Jake Barton from Wicken Fen had seen Black Shuck too, and a Norfolk peeress and Lady Rendlesham who saw it together, and Mrs A.M. Osborne of Tollesbury and William Fell, a shrewd and alert gamekeeper – the list seemed to go on and on.

OTHER GHOST DOGS

Dr Kenneth McAll told me about a ghost dog seen in a new house. The occupants, a professional man and his wife and family, moved into the brand new house only to find that they were disturbed night after night by the sound of a dog running up and down the two flights of stairs and bounding about the landings. Heavy thuds, panting and the general sounds of a large dog kept the whole family awake. Subsequent discoveries suggested that a dog had been sacrificed before the house had been built, or possibly its predecessor on the same site. And novelist Jilly Cooper has revealed that her move from London to Gloucestershire was in part due to the death and subsequent ghostly appearance of her beloved Yorkshire terrier. 'I missed him so much. His ghost used to run round Putney Common, and I just couldn't stand it.'

William Oliver Stevens of New York told me about an unusual and thought-provoking instance of a ghost dog recounted first-hand by Bayard Veiller and his wife. They possessed a much-loved dog named Penn who in time became old and when he began to suffer the Veillers decided that the time had come to help him out of his pain. He was taken to a veterinary doctor who put him to sleep and Mr Veiller took him home and buried him in the garden.

One night Bayard Veiller was awakened by the sound of barking – and it sounded like Penn! The tone of the barking sounded excited and happy, and Veiller got up and went outdoors. The garden was bathed in bright moonlight and there he plainly saw Penn dash across the lawn as boisterous and carefree as he had done as a puppy. He said afterwards it was unmistakably Penn and he watched for a moment, full of happy memories, and then the 'dog' disappeared among the flowerbeds.

Next morning, before he said anything to his wife, she told him she thought she had heard Penn during the night and going to the window she had clearly seen Penn romping and playing in the garden, as he had done as a puppy; then he had suddenly disappeared.

They interpreted the apparition of Penn as a return on the part of the dog so that his master and mistress would know that everything was fine with him and that they must not grieve. The interesting fact of the experience is that the ghost dog was heard and seen by both Mr and Mrs Veiller independently of each other and from different vantage points, ruling out hallucination. The similarity in so many cases of human 'apparitional' appearances is unmistakable: the dead loved one seemingly returning to say that everything is all right, that they have survived death and are now alive and well in a marvellous new existence. Wishful thinking? The ample and varied evidence warrants serious consideration of the facts.

CATS

Phantom cats are legion. The Old Talbot Hotel at Worcester has a phantom feline that has been seen by the manager, his wife and various members of the staff and also by visitors. It is nearly always seen in the mornings between 10 a.m. and 10.30 a.m. and usually on the stairway in the bar. William Miller said it looked like 'a large bundle of steel wool' and it faded after a second or two. His dog was terrified. A housekeeper said she had never believed in ghosts but she never experienced anything like she had at The Old Talbot. As she went into Room 14 she saw a black cat sitting on an armless chair; it was sleek and healthy looking. It raised its head and she called out to her girls, 'There's a cat in this room' – but when she looked back there was no sign of the cat. The window was not open and it certainly did not go out through the door.

Downstairs she said, 'I've just seen the ghost of a cat' and then, for the first time, she learned that the hotel was supposed to be haunted by a ghost cat and that lots of different people had seen it in different parts of the premises.

On occasions the receptionist needed to visit the cellar, the oldest part of the property, and she would switch on the light at the top of the stairs before going down the steps. On this particular occasion she switched on the light as usual but as she reached the bottom step in the cellar she caught a fleeting glimpse of 'something' that could well have been a cat. 'There was definitely something there for a moment,' she said.

Julie Hurton of Cecil, Wisconsin, USA, was equally more than certain that she saw a cat when visiting a new neighbour. It was a beautiful creature. 'But we don't have a cat,' protested the neighbour. As Julie looked back at the cat – it disappeared in front of her eyes. When she described the animal the neighbour immediately recognised a cat that had been a nuisance and had been shot by her husband.

Also from the USA comes the story of Nancy Boswell of Burley, Idaho, who had an older sister who was dying. The whole family was gathered around the bed when the sister suddenly looked up and said brightly, 'Look, my kitten has come back!' Her kitten had died two weeks earlier. A deathbed hallucination? Certainly the sister died soon afterwards but she died happy in the 'knowledge' that her kitten had come back.

MUMMIFIED CATS

It has become traditional to deposit 'time capsules' containing coins, newspapers and other items beneath the foundation stone of a new official building. This ceremony may have its origins in the magical ceremony of sacrificing a live animal, representing the life force, when building a structure. Some call it an old heathen custom to drive away evil and witchcraft. Cats were often used in this respect and mummified cats are still found during renovation or demolition of old houses.

At The Mill Hotel, Sudbury in Suffolk, there is buried in the floor under a glass cover, a well-known mummified cat – a cat with a curious story. The 'Sudbury Cat' was discovered in 1971 when the 300-year-old millhouse was rebuilt as a hotel standing on the banks of the River Stour and retaining much of its original character including the century-old mill wheel which still works.

The cat was found immured in the roof, most likely the mill cat, buried in the structure after it had died. The builder discovering the Sudbury Cat obtained permission to remove it, but within weeks of the cat being taken away, there was a financial crisis and all building and refurbishment work was halted. The cat had been taken to a studio which suffered a mysterious and serious fire, although the cat escaped any injury. Next it was taken to a farmhouse at Wickham St Paul which also suffered a fire. The cat was then taken back to the old millhouse at Sudbury where a beam in the mill roof, where the cat had been found, collapsed, causing considerable damage.

When the hotel proprietors learned about the cat and its recent history they decided to reinter the cat in the building and after the reburial, it seems, all has been well.

The subject of mummified cats and other creatures being found in properties is interesting and all part of the cult of the dead. In the hope of averting the anger of the dead primitive peoples used to place food and drink within graves while more sophisticated societies provided women and slaves. Gradually the grave was no longer regarded as a kind of prison where the dead could be secured and confined, but instead it became a place of pilgrimage where the living paid respect to their ancestors. Yet underlying all these ceremonies was the ancient fear of the ghost's return.

Old graves have been discovered with bodies tied up tightly; other tombs have contained skeletons covered with red ochre representing human blood and we are reminded of barbaric times throughout the world where slaves were either killed and interred with their dead master or sacrificed over the grave itself in order that their blood would seep into the soil and placate the bloodless corpse, so that it stayed at rest within the grave. Societies ceased to draw hard and fast distinctions between human beings and animals, and the slaying of an animal formed part of the funeral rites in many parts of the world and in many religions. Soon animals were sacrificed when a building was erected to protect the property from evil and from wandering ghosts; a practice that became very widespread with ancient people and animal remains are still frequently found in old properties.

OTHER GHOSTLY ANIMALS

Other denizens of the animal world reportedly manifest as ghosts. Ghost fallow and roe deer have been repeatedly reported near Kingston Seymour and on Clevedon golfcourse in Avon, while a ghost bull long haunted a field in the same county. The farmer concerned always saw it very early in the morning on summer days and he was never frightened of the animal. 'I knew it wasn't a real bull because it was dark brown and had very long horns. I knew there was no bull like that on any of the farms round here', he said. Could he have seen a vision of a member of an ancient and now extinct British breed?

Anthony Dent, a member of the publishing family, was always deeply interested in horses and donkeys. He told me of an interesting ghostly horse experience of his. At the time Anthony Dent lived near Whitby in Yorkshire and owned a number of horses, all of them black or brown. He used to call them in each evening, feed them and settle them in their stables for the night. As he did so he began to notice a beautiful white stallion among his horses but as his animals pricked up their ears at his voice and galloped towards him, the white horse would disappear. Anthony thought this must be some kind of optical illusion but he began to see the white horse every night and one evening he took his wife and she too saw the white stallion and commented on its beauty. Yet again as his horses came running towards him the white horse vanished.

One evening, having called the horses and as he was feeding them, Anthony looked up and there was the white horse walking into the yard. It was a really beautiful animal and he gazed admiringly at the light step and proudly tossed mane. It walked unhesitatingly towards him and got within 15 ft or so and he held out his hand, offering it some grain. The horse took two more steps towards him – and completely vanished. And he never saw the white horse again.

POLLY'S STORY

When my wife and I travelled to Wales to buy a new Springer Spaniel puppy it was one of the happiest days of our lives. We brought Polly home and she was the most delightful little dog.

When she was about 18 months old we decided on a leisurely tour of the West Country. One afternoon, while chasing a butterfly, she fell hundreds of feet from the overhanging cliffs of Sidmouth Hill to the beach below. She was obviously badly hurt. We rushed her to a vet who said that due to internal bleeding they would have to operate immediately. There was nothing we could do. We returned to our hotel and waited to hear from the vet. When he rang he said he had operated on Polly and had stopped the bleeding but it had been a big shock for such a little dog. But she was fit and strong and he was hoping for the best – although the next few hours would be crucial. He promised to ring again the next morning.

My wife and I spent a terrible evening and a worried night. Eventually we dropped off to sleep and the next thing I remember was suddenly finding myself wide awake at twenty minutes past five in the morning. I woke my wife: 'She's gone . . . Polly's dead . . . she's gone . . .'. My wife tried to comfort and reassure me: 'No . . . she's a strong little dog. She'll be alright . . .'. But nothing she said had any effect. Somehow I knew Polly was dead.

The vet rang in the morning and said, 'Bad news, I'm afraid. Polly died early this morning.' Stunned, I asked, 'What time?' 'Just before 5.30' he replied.

Many times over the years people have told me about what seemed to them to be psychic experiences and they have often said, 'I just *knew* . . .'. After my experience of Polly's death I understood for the first time exactly what they meant. I *knew* Polly had died and nothing anyone said could or would have made any difference. At the moment of her death I felt it.

There is a theory that when a much-loved pet reaches the end of its life some kind of signal is emitted aimed at those closest to the animal. Perhaps there is a close relationship between telepathy as we understand it and the instinct of the animal world. I really don't have any other explanation, but what I do know is that the moment Polly died I knew she had gone. That knowledge awakened me and I have never been more certain of anything in my life. I like to think that in her last moments I was of some comfort to little Polly.

CHAPTER ELEVEN

TIME SLIPS AND CYCLIC GHOSTS

The derangement in respect of time and place, sometimes on a regular basis, forms the background to some of the most remarkable and convincing of psychic experiences. Most researchers in these difficult fields now accept that some accounts of ghosts and so-called hauntings do seem to involve what have been termed 'time slips'. These 'ghosts' or whatever you may like to call them appear to totally ignore the surroundings in which they are seen, walking through walls and closed doors, sitting or lying down where there is no chair or bed or *chaise longue*, walking up stairs and steps not visible to us and poring over invisible books or manuscripts or private papers that have long disappeared from the face of the earth. It could well be that a combination of circumstances and perhaps the presence of a certain type of person can sometimes result in a sort of atmospheric recording that occasionally or regularly replays itself.

THEORIES ABOUT TIME SLIPS

Evidence is mounting that in some circumstances traumatic happenings do leave significant traces on the atmosphere, almost like a cinematograph film, that again in certain circumstances, that we are not yet able to fully define, such happenings are replayed and the witness is in effect watching a recording of a previous happening. It may be that a person more 'sympathetic' and attuned to psychic happenings and aware of the unseen world is more likely to find themselves in a time slip or witnessing some other kind of psychic activity. We are all different, with varying attributes, skills and perceptions: some of us appreciate music and find it plays a major part in our lives, others, like me, are tone deaf and so music means nothing to us. It may well be that in some people a developed sense of some kind may make them more likely to be involved in psychic happenings. Although I am sure that in general anyone can see a ghost: it is just a matter of being in the right place at the right time, some people may stand a better chance of doing so.

The idea that such appearances are the result of a natural if unusual combination of circumstances resulting in what we call 'psychic phenomena' cannot help but suggest that perhaps all ghostly appearances are natural, the result of some cause and effect over which we have no control. Such an explanation would be a curiously satisfactory answer to a remarkable number of apparitional appearances witnessed by responsible individuals in circumstances which rule out deception, hallucination and malobservation. Scientists, like Dr V.G.W. Harrison, Dr Percy A.H. Seymour, Professor John Beloff, Professor A.J. Ellison and Professor A.E. Roy, and the more objective psychical researchers, such as Professor D.J. West, Dr Alan Gauld, A.D. Cornell and Dr Michael H. Coleman, are beginning to accept the distinct possibility that ghosts are a natural phenomenon, observed in all parts of the world by all kinds of people since the beginning of recorded time.

The idea that on rare occasions time, which we simply do not understand, becomes warped and out of alignment, resulting in previous happenings reoccurring, in vanished houses being seen again, in people in bygone costumes walking again, may seem far-fetched, but that such things have happened is indisputable, and that curious phenomenon time could well be responsible.

We conceive time as a true dimension, running straight and uninterrupted like a railtrack with the present time being represented by a moving train, yet no less an authority than Sir James Jeans, former Astronomer Royal, questions this assumption. 'The fundamental laws of nature, in so far as we are at present acquainted with then, give no reason why time should flow steadily on: they are equally prepared to consider the possibility of time standing still or flowing backwards ... the steady onward flow of time ... is something we assume ... out of our own experience; whether or not it is inherent in the nature of time, we simply do not know.'

TIME SLIPS ON GUERNSEY

As we have seen, the Channel Islands Occupation Society has a number of reports and records of paranormal activity in their extensive archives that suggest some sort of partial time slip back to the days when the islands were occupied by German forces.

In 1978 the Perry family decided to visit the Batterie Mirus gun site at Les Rouvets Farm on Guernsey, a property owned by Lt. Col. Patrick A. Wootton. As they were entering the tunnel the youngest girl of the family suddenly began screaming and saying she could see a man 'dressed in old clothes covered in blood'. The family dog also displayed extreme unease and reluctance to go into the bunker complex. On my behalf John Kiely interviewed the mother of the girl and told me he was 'left in no doubt whatsoever that her daughter witnessed what she had reported'.

Subsequently Lt. Col. Patrick Wootton enlarged on the incident in a letter from Canada, during the course of which he mentioned that the child's mother was the wife of a Guernsey policeman and the child was four years old at the time. She suddenly stopped in the entrance to the former battery and screamed, 'I'm not going in there – I'm not going in there – there's a horrid man standing there with blood all over his face.'

Her mother said, 'Don't be silly, dear. There's no one there.' 'Yes, there is,' the child replied. 'And there's another man behind him with a bucket in one hand and a knife in the other.' The mother did not persist but they sought out Lt. Col. Wootton, told him what had happened and asked him whether he would like to question the child. He declined to do so, feeling it might distress the little girl but said he would be happy to have a word with her in a few days' time if she didn't mind talking about it.

Accordingly a couple of days later the little girl returned with her mother and chatting casually in the tea rooms Lt. Col. Wootton asked the girl what colour was the suit the man was wearing and she replied, without hesitation, 'Green, and he had boots on like yours.' Col. Wootton was wearing Wellington boots at the time.

Afterwards Lt. Col. Wootton called on a neighbour who had been in Guernsey during the war and without telling him about the incident asked whether the Germans had any problems with the guns at that battery. 'They certainly did!' he was told. 'The first time they fired it (it had a range of 35 miles or so), they killed the whole gun crew from the recoil!'

Lt. Col. Wootton comments: 'It would seem that the girl saw something of this event, for on considering the matter it is obvious that the effect of recoil would have been pressure on lungs, causing vomiting of blood, etc. The "bucket" could well have been a helmet and the knife might have been used to cut away strapping...'

On the subject of the occupation of the Channel Islands there are a number of well-authenticated instances of German soldiers being seen in various places where they were in actual fact during those dramatic and stressful days. One concerned an apparition seen in St Sampson's, also on Guernsey.

A newcomer to the island purchased a house in the parish, not knowing that during the Occupation German soldiers were billeted there. After their daughter spent a holiday there and other English visitors stayed at the house, each of them said that occasionally they saw a soldier in German uniform about the place; the new residents made enquiries and discovered the history of the house. The house owner never saw the ghost herself or heard anything untoward, although one of the bedrooms had a sinister atmosphere that she could never fathom.

The German soldiers stationed in Guernsey were in great dread of being posted to the Russian front, as they frequently were, because of the high rate of casualties experienced by the German armies in that battle area and any such assignment was often looked upon by the troops as a sentence of death. It seems likely that a German soldier, billeted in that bedroom, not only left behind something of the stress and fear and terror that he felt, but did so in such quantity or quality or in such conditions that later his form was seen again watching and waiting in apprehension, restlessness and anxiety as to what might happen and perhaps did. It could be an ideal scenario for a time slip.

One evening in the early 1970s a young girl was cycling along the road between the Bourg and the airport on Guernsey when she came upon a platoon of soldiers in grey uniforms marching along.

When she arrived home she asked her mother and her neighbours if any soldiers were on the island. She was told that there were none and asked why she wanted to know. 'Well,' she replied. 'There are some now and I've just seen them.' She described the men and the uniforms they were wearing and the way they were marching, and the neighbour declared immediately, 'They are the German soldiers from the Occupation. I've seen them myself and so have other people.' Was this a cyclic replay of some traumatic episode in the eventful and often tragic history of the Channel Islands?

THE PHANTOM ARMY ON CRETE

On 17 May 1828 one of the fiercest and bloodiest battles of the Greek War of Independence was fought out on the south coast of Crete. Near the Venetian fortress of Frangocastello, 385 Greeks were attacked by a Turkish force 900 strong and the Greeks were slaughtered to the last man. There have been many reports over the years of these phantom armies materialising at dawn each anniversary of the battle, 17 May, but such reports have diminished in recent years and perhaps this 'recording' is at last beginning to run its course.

THE CYCLIC GHOST OF ROSYTH

A correspondent has informed me of what may well be a cyclic psychic phenomenon. Mrs E. McEvoy of Rosyth, Fife, tells me that during the 1914–18 war when she was 12 or perhaps 13 years of age, one night about 11 p.m. her brother, who had just come home from the cinema, and a younger sister, who should have been asleep, heard cups rattle in the kitchen. Thinking her brother or someone was still up she came out on to the landing, calling for a drink of water.

My informant and her brother were in the kitchen when they heard sounds from upstairs, on a higher landing than the one their sister was sleeping on, and not wanting her to be startled by anything of a ghostly nature – for it was *the* night of the year when the ghost was supposed to walk – my informant acted the older sister and told her brother to hold the lamp in the doorway at the end of the hall and she would then be able to see anything on the main staircase.

The unidentified ghostly form of a man in thick tweed jacket and trousers had, I was told, been seen in the upper portions of this house by all sorts of people, on this one night of the year. No one seemed to know who he was or why he appeared, but that such a figure had been seen by different people, some of whom had no idea that the form had been seen before, seems to be beyond argument.

Mrs McEvoy went on to say that she could dimly see a dark form starting to make its way down the upper stairs as she, heart in mouth, started to go upwards. Having almost reached the landing, she beckoned to her brother to come up to her but instead he turned tail and ran back into the kitchen, taking the lamp with him and leaving her to face the unknown in the dark!

Undecided what to do – for if she ran to the other side of the stairs or ran back down the stairs her younger sister would see her and be frightened – and in any case she had no intention of having her brother laugh at her, she made up her mind, held her breath and ran quickly up the last few steps with the result that she was now right in the path of the ghost!

She remembers stopping in full flight at the top step and with one foot poised in mid-air she saw the huge dark form coming towards her. She recalls thinking how big the buttons were on the jacket and then all went black. She awoke to find herself sprawled on the landing; of the dark form there was no sign and her little sister was bending over her. Later her sister said she had seen a man come down the upper stairs and when the two almost met, she had seen her sister drop in a faint to the floor. She had dashed across and then realised that the 'man' or whatever it was, was no longer there.

Subsequently, Mrs McEvoy and various members of her family sometimes sat up to see the ghost on the appointed night and sometimes they saw it or thought they did, while on other occasions it didn't appear, at least not when they were watching. Mrs McEvoy traced sightings of the figure, always on the one particular day, back more than 60 years and there was talk of a murder having been committed but nothing was every really established. At the time she saw the ghost the first time Mrs McEvoy had no clear idea about ghosts, although she had always seemed to know that a ghost walked that one day each year. She thought it was an isolated and individual instance of ghostly activity and was quite shocked to discover that such phenomena had been reported from all parts of the world for many centuries. Her brother, who had also seen the ghost that night, never referred to the matter if he could possibly help it, for the rest of his life. He never sat up for the ghost and whenever the subject came up he would get up and leave the room.

What is interesting, of course, apart from the fact that, knowing the ghost was due that night, they were half-way towards seeing it before seeing or hearing anything, is the fact that on this one occasion the ghostly form was seen from at least three different viewpoints. Mrs McEvoy saw it in front of her, her sister saw it from the side and her brother saw it from below. This suggests that, whatever it was, it was substantial enough to be seen from various angles, although it apparently made no sound whatever and no one who ever saw it mentioned any sound. Suggestion and auto-suggestion might well have played a part in some of the reported sightings of this 'apparition', but that it was seen over a number of years, on one particular day, by different people from different vantage points – if we are to accept human testimony – seems irrefutable.

DR SAMPSON'S
GHOSTS OF THE BROADS

One book, devoted almost exclusively to cyclical ghostly activity, is Charles Sampson's *Ghosts of the Broads*, published by The Yachtsman Publishing Company in 1931. The author detailed, described and elaborated stories of 25 of the Norfolk Broads, in each case recounting what purported to be personal experiences of ghostly activity on specific dates.

I have to say that intermittently during the last 50 years I have made a point of being in the right place at the right time in respect of the majority of the sites detailed by Charles Sampson and I have never seen, heard, detected or established in any way anything of a paranormal nature. On the other hand I have spoken to a number of people who claim to have been much more fortunate, or unfortunate, and they claim to have seen something of Sampson's cyclic manifestations.

All evidence, including evidence of psychic activity, is only as good as the person giving that evidence and so we need to know something about the author. Dr Charles Sampson is listed as residing at number 48 Harley Street, London, in 1931 (the year the book was published) and his name appears in *The Medical Directory* and in *The Medical Register* until 1940, so it can be assumed that he died around that year.

According to those respected annual publications his appointments included the prodigious Licentiate of the Society of Apothecaries (1905) and Licentiate in Medicine and Surgery of the Society of Apothecaries (1909). He is also credited with the authorship of several medical volumes including *Subconscious Activities, Célébration Retardie* (Paris, 1925) and *New Treatment for Rheumatism and Allied Disorders* (Aix-les-Bains, 1934). One is forced to ask oneself whether such a person with such a reputation would publish or permit to be published in his name a volume of fictitious happenings portrayed as fact. In his introduction to the original edition Sampson did say, 'how much of it is actually true must be left to the gentle reader's own discretion' but at the same time he refers to 'researches' of 'an almost incredible extent' and collecting the data 'during a period of 25 years' and finally presenting his work 'in the same good faith with which these chronicles are offered'.

Whatever the truth of the matter he produced a book that has been of wide interest and to date has run into five editions. Dr Sampson's book contributed to the evidence for cyclic phenomena and some of his statements and conclusions cannot but be interesting. He said, for example, that 'the periodicity of apparitions' coming around 'with extraordinary accuracy' on certain days was 'well known' and he especially mentioned St Mark's Day, 5 March, St Anthony's Day, 13 June and Hallowe'en, 31 October. He says that many of the appearances and happenings, following alterations in the calendar over the years, have accommodated themselves to the new order without changing their date and while I am not sure that this is always so it seems to me that if it is so it suggests quite strongly that the phenomena may well be subjective. Sampson appears to have foreseen this objection and hurriedly adds a reminder that 'all apparitions are not perceptible to everybody', as indeed they are not! He makes the point, made many times since but not often made before the 1930s, that light-rays, X-rays, Gamma rays, infra-red and ultra-violet rays are all invisible, but are present and can be photographically recorded.

One of the examples of cyclic phenomena recorded by Dr Sampson is the Potter Heigham manifestation. Legend has it that at midnight each 31 May a phantom coach and horses crashes into the bridge over the River Thurne and amid awful cries and the sound of splintering wood a tangled mass of bodies, coach, horses and debris is flung into the air and then falls into the river where it disappears and silence reigns again.

The story goes that in the eighteenth century one Sir Godfrey Haslitt married the beautiful Evelyn Lady Carew on 31 May 1741 at Norwich Cathedral and after a great feast the bridal procession, stretching over a mile, made its way back to Bastwick Place where a mysterious fire broke out and destroyed the great house, but the bride and groom escaped and drove at breakneck speed through the dark night until they reached Potter Heigham bridge where tragedy struck.

Dr Sampson seemingly traced a number of witnesses to this arresting spectacle: George Hallness in 1926, Matthew Denham in 1929 and John Fraser in 1930, the latter in the company of two friends. Sampson planned to see it himself in 1931 and to photograph the event but whether he ever went or what happened I have never discovered.

For myself I traced and talked with people who claimed to have experienced the remarkable scene including writer and broadcaster A.J. Alan who lived at Potter Heigham. He told me, swearing me to silence as long as he lived, that on 31 May 1937 he and three companions had, partly by chance and partly by purpose, been in the vicinity of the old bridge around midnight and they had all heard the sound of galloping horses' hooves, the grind of carriage wheels on gravel and faint screams before a shuddering crash from the direction of the deserted bridge, followed by a loud splash and then silence. None of the watchers saw anything untoward that bright starry night but the sounds remained to haunt them for years. Nothing would induce A.J. Alan to join me on another ghost watch at Potter Heigham bridge.

I did trace other good witnesses and I visited the area several times, with other investigators, photographers and sound recordists; but we never heard or saw or sensed anything unusual. Our photography and sound recordings showed no abnormality, only, as Dr Charles Sampson put it, in that still, almost expectant, brooding and poignant place, 'the silence of death'.

CASES FROM THE SOCIETY FOR PSYCHICAL RESEARCH FILES

Among the cases of apparent time slips I have always been intrigued by, I especially recall the case that involved the entrance hall of the old Grand Central Hotel, London.

One spring morning in 1915 a hotel chambermaid, Alice Bartlett, was working in Room 338. Her evidence states that she saw the hotel parcels boy suddenly appear in the doorway, only about five feet away from her. Thinking he was looking for her, she asked, 'Parcel for me, Charlie?' but the boy did not reply and when Alice began to approach the boy, he seemed to take a step back and then disappeared. Suddenly Alice recalled that the boy was no longer at the hotel and when she made enquiries she discovered that he had left the hotel two weeks earlier. Far from being friends, she had not noticed and did not know about his absence until after he had left. She never saw him again and often wondered whether he had been concentrating on the hotel at the time she had seen him. She never had a similar experience and never saw the boy, Charlie Howard, again.

Another historical case I recall from the SPR files occurred in January 1886 and concerned Mrs Augusta Gladstone of Shedfield Cottage, Botley, Oxford. As the weather was severe she went out of her way to visit an elderly sick neighbour, who lived about a mile away. This friend, Mrs Bedford, was ill in bed and Mrs Gladstone went upstairs to see her. While talking to her friend she noticed that the winter sun shone through the bedroom window, opposite the foot of the bed, and it occurred to her that it might interfere with the invalid's rest and she mentally made a note to see whether she could find some curtains. She said nothing about this in case she could not find anything suitable. She passed the odd word with her friend's husband, Mr Bedford, but said nothing about the window or the curtains.

Back home Mrs Gladstone, the following morning, took a piece of material from the cupboard in her bedroom and held it up in front of her with both hands to decide whether it would be suitable for her friend's bedroom window. She decided it was not long enough and did no more about the matter.

A few days later she again went to visit her sick friend and saw first Mr Bedford who said his wife was much better but had had a peculiar experience a couple of days previously. She had 'seen' Mrs Gladstone holding up a curtain with both hands; Mrs Gladstone had then said it was not long enough, had smiled and disappeared.

Both these instances, the latter in particular, were thoroughly investigated by SPR officials, and appear to illustrate the possibility of a time slip. The parcels boy is likely to have entered Room 338 with a parcel at some point in his duties at the Grand Central Hotel and Mrs Gladstone admitted to holding up material in front of her with both hands and deciding it was not suitable. Both these trivial incidents appear to have been repeated out of sequence and such activity seems to be happening from time to time all over the world for no apparent reason or purpose.

TIME SLIP IN VERSAILLES

One of the most famous time slips of all – if that is what it was – occurred in 1901 in the gardens of Versailles, nine miles from Paris, France. Two much respected Oxford academics were heading for the delightful Petit Trianon, a small mansion within the huge grounds of the luxurious royal palace built by King Louis XIV during the 1700s.

Unsure of which path to take the two ladies suddenly saw two men dressed in long coats and three-cornered hats, which they thought rather odd, but they asked for directions. Suddenly the entire atmosphere changed and everything became very quiet and seemed almost unreal. Feeling uncomfortable by this time the visitors noticed a scarred and ugly man wearing a cloak and a large hat.

When they arrived at the back of the Petit Trianon they both saw a woman sitting on the lawn wearing an old-fashioned dress, a white hat and a cape. She seemed to look at the ladies and then turned away. The puzzled visitors were then led away by another man.

For the rest of their lives the ladies, cultured and educated and distinguished, were convinced that they had somehow been back in time and seen Queen Marie Antoinette shortly before she was executed. They recognised the woman they had seen from portraits of the queen and spent years tracing to their satisfaction that the scenery, buildings and people they had encountered dated from days prior to the French Revolution of 1789, 112 years before. Nobody has ever completely succeeded in disproving their story which they detailed in a classic book entitled, *An Adventure*.

There are in existence many accounts of recent cases of apparent time slips, indeed some can be found in the archives of every psychical research society, and it is worth remembering that well-documented cases certainly exist that go back over a century, cases that were explored at the time in a scientific manner and remain inexplicable.

THE GHOST OF NAPOLEON

Sir George Joy, former Governor of St Helena, told me of what might have been a curious time slip nearly a century and a half ago.

On 5 May 1821, while Napoleon was in exile on St Helena, his mother Madame Bonaparte was sitting in the first floor drawing room of her house in the Palazzo Bonaparte in Rome, when a strange-looking man appeared at the door downstairs and requested an audience with Madame.

The hall servant was reluctant to admit him but when the stranger, who wore a large cloak and a broad-brimmed hat drawn low over his face, insisted that the matter was urgent as he had news of Madame's son, the servant took the man upstairs. There another servant asked the man his name and business, but by way of reply the visitor said his message was so important that he must speak at once with 'La Signora Madre'.

Madame Bonaparte was informed and she said she would see the stranger. Covering his face even more the man said to her, in a low voice, 'The Emperor is freed from his sufferings; today 5 May 1821, he died.' The mysterious stranger then retreated and quickly left the room. Madame Bonaparte was stunned ... her son dead! But how could the stranger know? It would take weeks for news to travel that distance – and the man himself; she felt sure she had seen him before. She rushed out of the drawing room to speak further with the man but he had vanished. She hurried into the anteroom and asked the servant there, whose business it was to sit all day in the room. He replied, 'Excellent Signora Madre, no one has passed through this room other than the servants and I have not left my post for a single moment.'

An immediate search of the house, of the vicinity, and indeed of Rome, failed to locate any trace of the mysterious stranger. In the days that followed Madame Bonaparte spent long hours in her chair in the drawing room, thinking about her son and the stranger with the bad news: whom could he have been and how could he have known what he said he knew? His whole bearing had been so familiar ...

Two and a half months later Madame Bonaparte received the news that her son had indeed died on St Helena on 5 May 1821 and always afterwards she believed that it was the ghost of her son who came to her: 'the same figure, the same voice, the same features, the same eyes, the same commanding presence,' she would say. Here, then, is a ghost that was seen by three people and not by others; a ghost that has been said to periodically return to the Palazzo Bonaparte and to appear at dusk in the drawing room; a ghost – if ghost it was – that might be regarded as a different kind of time slip.

TIME SLIP AT FOTHERINGAY CHURCH

The Revd John C. Dening, whom I have already mentioned, has brought to my attention an interesting and little-known recurring time slip or some such kind of haunting.

Fotheringay, a village a few miles west of Peterborough, was the scene of the death of Mary Queen of Scots at the long-since destroyed castle, and it is the church at Fotheringay that seems to have been the scene of an anniversary haunt.

In the year 1476, during the reign of Edward IV, it appears to have been decided that the body of his father, Richard Duke of York, should be brought from Pontefract Castle in Yorkshire and interred in the family mausoleum at Fotheringay. At length the solemn procession arrived in the early afternoon of 29 July (11 August according to our modern Gregorian calendar) with Edward and his queen waiting with a great retinue at the church gate. After a memorial service, between 2 and 3 in the afternoon, conducted with great pomp and ceremony befitting the occasion, the interment duly took place.

On a hot August day in 1976 a schoolmaster and his wife set out for Oundle to visit Fotheringay church. As they approached the church door, to their considerable surprise, they heard the clear sounds of a strange, rather primitive kind of martial music with trumpets and drums. Thinking that a rehearsal of some kind was taking place inside the church, they hesitated about entering but on gingerly opening the door and peering in they found, to their astonishment, that the church was deserted and there was no one whatsoever in the building. At the same time they realised they had ceased to be aware of the sound of music as they had opened the door. Retracing their steps to the churchyard gate, they were aware that they could again faintly hear the ancient music. As far as they could do so Mr and Mrs Priest established that their visit to Fotheringay church took place on 11 August 1976 or exactly 500 years after the interment there of Richard Duke of York which would undoubtedly have taken place to the accompaniment of some kind of martial music of the day, on 11 August 1476.

Subsequently a retired policeman revealed that 35 years earlier, on a hot summer day, he and a female cousin had visited Fotheringay church and as they approached the church door, they too heard music and singing, 'like monks chanting', coming from within the church. They, like the Priests, wondered whether they should disturb the proceedings but as they opened the door to find the church deserted, all sounds ceased. Other witnesses have since come forward with similar experiences to relate, always on a hot August day at Fotheringay church.

A SHORT-DISTANCE TIME SLIP

A correspondent from Auckland, New Zealand, wrote to tell me of an apparent time slip he and his wife had experienced in 1974, a time slip that appears to be only one year after the original event. He writes: '... We were coming home from the City at about 11.10 p.m. through Dominion Road to reach Mt Albert Road. All of a sudden we had company: a tall young man, I would say in his early twenties, was walking right behind us for quite a number of yards, and my wife said to me quietly that she thought he was going to attack us. I replied that if he had that in mind he would have done so before now. All right, I said to myself, this is where good will conquer evil, and I turned round quickly – but he had disappeared. He could not have gone in the front garden of any of the houses because there were long gardens and all the gates were shut; one of us must have seen him. Later we learned that the year before a tall young man was run over at that spot and killed; that was in August 1973.'

THE GHOST AT
MINSDEN CHAPEL

A recurring time slip ghost has long been reported to haunt the isolated ruins of Minsden Chapel in Hertfordshire. It was Elliott O'Donnell, whom Dan Farson has called 'the champion ghost hunter', who first told me about Minsden.

O'Donnell was a raconteur with an endless stock of remarkable ghost stories, many of them personal experiences, and a lot of famous ghost stories originate from his dozens of books.

Whereas Christina Hole, university lecturer and president of the Folklore Society, told me she believed that events sometimes 'imprinted themselves upon the surrounding atmosphere and can be seen by later generations as ghosts', Elliott O'Donnell was convinced that most ghosts were a form of thought and 'that the air was inhabited by multitudes of thought forms, radiated not only by the brains of the living but also by the brains of those who died long years past'. 'Thought,' he insisted, 'is quite possibly imperishable.'

Be that as it may O'Donnell was utterly convinced that the picturesque ruins of Minsden Chapel, which fell into decay as long ago as the seventeenth century, were haunted by a ghostly monk each and every Hallowe'en. He informed me that the event was signalled by the solemn tolling of the long-lost bells of Minsden at midnight. A cowled monk-like figure then materialised and walked or glided through the ruins to mount steps no longer visible and disappear to the sounds of 'sweet and plaintive music'. He told me that an alleged photograph of the ghost was a fake but that the ghost walked at Minsden he had no doubt for he and others had seen it on two successive Hallowe'ens. On one memorable occasion he had inadvertently been arrested as he was leaving the secluded and lonely ruins at some unearthly hour!

I went to see the Hertfordshire historian and solicitor Reginald Hine who had leased the fourteenth-century chapel of ease for his lifetime and knew all about the cyclic appearance of the ghost monk. He said he had unearthed stories of a murdered nun as well as a restless phantom monk and when I told him I might spend a Hallowe'en night at Minsden he replied: 'The last person who did was apprehended by the police – if you get arrested, I'll get out of bed and bail you out...'

One bright Sunday morning I visited Minsden accompanied by my brother and by Tom Brown. On reaching the secluded site of Minsden Chapel we eyed the fragmentary ruins and separated, Tom going away to the north and my brother following close behind me as I walked towards the east end of the ruins. Just as I turned the extreme east corner of the remaining east wall I heard faint but distinct music. Even as I stopped to listen, it ceased. Tom Brown, some 20 ft away at the time, hastened towards me and reported hearing identical sounds; my brother, only a couple of steps behind me, heard nothing. The ruins are extremely isolated and there seemed to be no question of any normal explanation for the music, which puzzles me to this day. After visiting literally hundreds of allegedly haunted houses, and spending nights in scores of allegedly haunted rooms, it does seem that the unexplained happens when least expected; perhaps it has something to do with the relaxed state of mind of the percipient.

On the first All Hallows' Eve that I spent at Minsden in the company of Tom Brown and Derek Clark we all saw, at 1.45 a.m., a white cross which seemed to glow with an unnatural brightness for a few seconds before fading, only to reappear a few seconds later. It continued fading and reappearing for some minutes. It was a *crux decussata* or Latin cross and appeared on what would have been part of the wall of the chancel. I suppose it could possibly have been a trick of the moonlight, as a full moon was shining down through the trees at the time. We also felt conscious of a presence occasionally, especially under one of the few remaining archways.

Time slips could certainly explain many reports of ghost sightings, especially those where the figure or figures are seen doing the same thing in the same place by different people on different occasions. Work is needed on these cases: is the weather the same or similar (it has been noticed that ghosts are rarely seen in a high wind)? Is the light similar? Is the witness in a similar frame of mind to previous witnesses (pensive, relaxed, dreamy perhaps)? Were any animals present and if so what was their reaction, if any? Was it very quiet? Were any birds or insects visible?

But from the possibility that some ghosts are nothing more than the replays of past events let us now explore the world of the poltergeist, that elusive, temporary, annoying and fascinating entity that has been with us since the beginning of time.

CHAPTER TWELVE

POLTERGEISTS

Poltergeist – what images the word conjures up! Strange sounds, strange happenings, strange people; almost a world apart and yet this extraordinary activity happens every day somewhere to some puzzled individuals. I have seen objects move when no human person has been near them; I have felt the heat of propelled objects that have suddenly appeared from nowhere; I have heard strange voices issue from children, even sleeping children; and I have seen the incredible results of so-called poltergeist activity.

THEORIES ABOUT POLTERGEISTS

Some years ago I thought we were beginning to know what made the poltergeist tick but now I am not so sure, although many of the disturbances seem to be attributable to the need for attention. In a famous North London case heavy furniture was hurled about and a teenage girl talked in the gruff voice of a previous resident, an old man who had died ten years previously. Under hypnosis the girl turned out to be deeply disturbed and may have been just trying to attract attention to herself.

In 1995 the Archbishop of York's adviser on occult disturbances, the Revd Tom Willis, revealed that he receives about 35 calls a year from people worried by 'supernatural phenomena' and he claims to have witnessed many instances of the poltergeist at work.

'I carried out an exorcism at a house in Hull, where I sat in the lounge with a woman, her two daughters and a policeman,' he recalled. 'On the mantelpiece were a clock, an ashtray, a candlestick, a dog ornament and a little copper kettle.

'Suddenly one of the family said: "Look, the dog ornament has gone again". A few moments later I heard a noise in the kitchen. No one had moved but there on the kitchen floor was the ornament. For a moment I thought someone was playing a joke and had come in through the back door with a replica, but the only outside door was locked on the inside.'

Poltergeist cases, in my experience – and I have such cases reported to me in the region of five or six a month – start gradually, build up, but are more of a nuisance than anything else and then continue for a period, sometimes a few hours, or a few days or weeks, occasionally a few months or even longer and then they cease as mysteriously as they began and nothing anyone can do, in our present knowledge, has any effect whatever. Often they are associated with an adolescent and when that adolescent reaches full adulthood the 'poltergeist' activity ceases; when it is associated with an elderly person, as it sometimes is, companionship can be helpful. Frustration and unhappiness are invariably to be found in poltergeist cases and it is perhaps a remarkable and natural example of mind over matter – the unconscious mind reacting in a way which the conscious mind cannot control.

During the course of an investigation into apparent poltergeist infestation at a house near Kew Bridge I became convinced that a young girl 'helped out' the happenings attributed to the poltergeist and this is not infrequently the case in my experience.

The family had contacted me because they were unable to account for the strange bangs and rapping sounds that emanated from one of the bedrooms and from the bathroom, and also the occasional disappearance of small objects from around the house.

In addition to a young baby the family had a bright girl of ten and I learned that the 'disturbances' had begun soon after the arrival of the new baby. Although obviously fond of her new brother whom she used to nurse and change and spend a lot of time with, I came to the conclusion, after a long chat with all the occupants, *en masse* and individually, that the girl might have been (consciously or unconsciously) jealous of the new arrival who was now the centre of attention in the household.

Certainly, on the evidence I collected, it would have been possible for the girl to have produced all the 'disturbances'; for she had been in the vicinity, unobserved, whenever knocks or raps sounded, and she appeared to have recently been in the precise locality whenever an object had 'moved'.

My suspicions were further aroused during the course of an attempted test. Having learned that the raps and taps sounded most frequently during the evening between 9 and 10 o'clock (when the girl was in bed), I arranged to be at the house at that time one evening and all the family co-operated by being confined to one back room downstairs, including the baby and the girl.

We set sound-recording apparatus upstairs and my assistants, in this instance Richard Howard and Tom Perrott, and I sat downstairs and waited. Time passed and there was not so much as a single tap. Then the girl came out of the room where she had been with the rest of the family, saying she needed to take her brother to the bathroom. I had no option but to agree, but my control of the family was broken and the girl disappeared upstairs with the baby.

A moment or two later several loud knocks sounded and within seconds the girl reappeared, her eyes wide: 'Did you hear that?' she asked. 'They came from my bedroom while I was in the bathroom'. Our sound recording apparatus showed that the knocks had come from the bathroom and not the bedroom.

During the course of this case I employed the use of Zener cards to draw interest away from the reported phenomena and to see how various members of the family responded to tests in telepathy; the girl was the only one showing a higher than average result. I also prepared a word-association test and again all the family agreed to try the psychological test individually. I had compiled a list of random words, with here and there a test word thrown in, to test reactions. The results showed me, without a shadow of doubt, that the girl was jealous of her little brother and all the attention he received.

I had a private word with the parents and suggested they should perhaps go out of their way to pay a little more attention to their daughter at this difficult time and to let me know if what I felt were subconscious calls for attention did not cease. I never heard from them again.

While there are many instances of well-attested cases that involve generally accepted ghost phenomena and generally accepted poltergeist activity, it is more usual to find these two psychic disturbances occurring independently; thus one usually expects to encounter either a haunting involving ghost sightings or odd happenings regarded as poltergeist activity. It does seem that ghost sightings in haunted houses involve apparitions or images of people, animals or other 'entities' being seen, frequently accompanied by impressions of emotion, voices, foot-steps and related sounds, whereas poltergeist phenomena usually in-volve objects, in the place of activity, being unaccountably moved or 'thrown', accompanied by the sound of banging doors and windows and other loud noises; inexplicable locking and unlocking of doors; unexplained smells; touchings; movement of objects including the appearance and disappearance of objects, often involving matter through matter.

Several interesting aspects of poltergeist phenomena have been noticed and verified over the years. For example, articles and objects that are moved invariably end up at a lower level than that at which they started, thereby using a minimum amount of energy. Articles seen in flight – and such objects have been seen and even photographed – invariably drop to the ground immediately, almost as though the human eye is a deterrent. Objects that have moved are, for a short while, warm to the touch. There is often a sudden and unaccountable feeling of coldness, although there may be no actual drop in temperature. Persons with injuries or problems find they experience more pain when in the area of poltergeist activity, suggesting a heightened condition of the nervous system. There are other poltergeist attributes but it is important not to assign to the poltergeist things for which it is not responsible.

By far the most widespread aspect of poltergeist activity is the belief that young people are involved and it may well be that poltergeist activity is some form of excessive adolescent energy, for time after time disturbances that have centred about an individual, be it a girl or a boy but more frequently a girl, cease completely after a while, often when the person concerned is no longer an adolescent or when circumstances surrounding that individual change completely for the better. When we investigate poltergeist phenomena and having isolated the nexus of the poltergeist we sometimes remove that person to a different environ-ment, whereupon the disturbances either take place there and no longer at the original locale or the phenomena cease entirely. A poltergeist infestation is a case of a haunted person as opposed to a haunted house. The interesting thing, of course, is where the geist stores the energy which has to be used in the movement of objects, etc. There is a possibility that there may be a connection here with the 'cold spots' and 'cold areas' almost invariably found in haunted houses, poltergeist cases included. There is also the puzzle as to why there are so comparatively few poltergeist infestations and what causes them to happen and affect some individuals and not others.

Young people are deeply interested in the paranormal, as I know from my enormous postbag, and many of them believe they have had personal experiences that have no rational explanation. In 1991 a questionnaire surveying belief in and experience of the paranormal was carried out among a group of young people and 54.4 per cent claimed personal experience of at least one paranormal event and 41.8 per cent reported experience of two or more different types of paranormal experience. The number accepting that paranormal happenings did occur was over three-quarters of those questioned.

THE FOCUS OF THE POLTERGEIST

Poltergeist disturbances are commonplace and practically ignored by scientists, yet there is no disputing the fact that such things do happen in the presence of certain people. A young person, or more rarely an elderly person, is the nexus or centre of the disturbances and objects do move, voices are heard, fires are started, strange smells are noticed and atmospheric changes have been scientifically recorded: four of the five senses being affected for I have yet to learn what a poltergeist tastes like!

Such happenings can, it seems, occur almost anywhere, in a council house or flat, in a mansion or a castle, even aboard ship or in an aeroplane – as long as the 'focus' of the poltergeist is present. When the affected person moves to another house, the disturbances follow him, or her, and on returning home, strange happenings follow again; until for some unknown reason the disturbances cease as mysteriously as they began.

Evidence extending back over hundreds of years and from every country in the world would seem to establish beyond any reasonable doubt that *some* people, especially young adolescents, exude a form of energy which builds up and then 'explodes'; where that energy is stored is a mystery. As I have said it may be that energy is sometimes withdrawn in some way from the atmosphere or it may be stored in 'cold spots' or cold areas which are so frequently found in poltergeist cases and also in hauntings proper.

No one knows what a poltergeist is and although the happenings rarely show any intelligence (rather they are mischievous and irritating), some people think they are elemental spirits, sub-human, a being evolved from the lower elemental nature of humans; others think they are a comparatively rare offshoot of an adolescent or a preoccupied mind.

Stones and other small objects are frequently thrown during poltergeist infestations and often, if they are handled immediately, they are warm to the touch – why is this so? Can it be the result of friction as the object has been projected through space at considerable speed? Articles have appeared unaccountably inside closed rooms on numerous occasions. Does this mean we are dealing with matter through matter? Raps and taps are also common, and they usually appear to originate in the vicinity of the affected person's bed. Does this mean that activity is easier and more powerful in the actual locality of the nexus? Why are beds and bedclothes so attractive to poltergeists? They appear to be fascinated by beds and bedrooms and bedclothes. Often the poltergeist subject will be particularly plagued while in bed; bedclothes will be interfered with, often being pulled off the bed by some strong force; not infrequently the bedstead itself will be rocked and even lifted clear of the floor. Is it relevant that activities often take place when the subject is asleep, unconscious to the world, and in a condition comparable to the mediumistic trance of the spiritualists? While the poltergeist *infests*, the ghost proper *haunts*; the ghost prefers solitude whereas the poltergeist likes company – what are we to make of all this? The only certain thing is that it does take place, not as commonly perhaps as most people think, but occasionally and rarely genuine poltergeist activity does occur.

INVESTIGATIONS INTO POLTERGEIST CASES

MARGARET'S MYSTERIOUS TAPPINGS

There was a case of mysterious tapping that was heard in the house of a young divorcée, Margaret, and her young child some years ago. Her man friend Ian always seemed to be present when the tapping occurred and by means of a simple code the raps appeared to impart messages relevant to the young lady and the young man who were convinced that a poltergeist was responsible.

The late Revd John Robbins contacted me after he had visited the house and talked at length with Margaret who seemed very distressed by the nocturnal disturbances. He considered the whole affair as an unfortunate poltergeist infestation. Margaret had been deeply attached to her grandmother who had recently died; she often dreamed of her grandmother and seemed to think that she could still obtain help and guidance from her, with the help of the poltergeist. She often felt the figure of her grandmother visited her in her bedroom and she was anxious for her blessing with regard to her becoming more attached to Ian, but she had divided loyalties.

When I visited the house in the company of the Revd John Robbins it soon occurred to me that it might be possible for Ian to be consciously responsible for the 'raps'. As we left the house I expressed my doubts but John Robbins did not feel such an explanation was viable in view of the answers obtained and in view of the favourable impression that Ian had made on him and of course John Robbins saw Margaret when she was deeply distressed, which I did not.

What was manifestly evident was the fact that for the raps to occur it was necessary for Ian to be present and for him to stand up (although we were told that on rare occasions the raps had been heard when he was sitting down) and invariably there was a waiting period before they were heard; they were heralded by Ian who always knew when the 'communicating entity' was present by the fact that the right side of his body and right arm went 'goose-pimply' and afterwards his right leg muscles would continually twitch.

On the occasion of our second visit, after we had been at the house chatting for over an hour, Ian eventually agreed to stand up in an endeavour to encourage the 'spirit' or the 'poltergeist' to manifest. After nearly 40 minutes he said 'she' was present and that his arm and right side were telling him so. His leg muscles (right leg) were certainly twitching involuntarily and this was established when I held the back of his leg at the top of the muscle below the knee. The twitching continued and Ian appeared to be completely unable to control it. The tapping, when it eventually came, appeared to originate from the centre of the sole of his right foot. I stood very close to him while the 'tapping' was taking place and certainly the floor seemed to vibrate slightly and it always seemed to be centred on the sole of his right foot, although his foot was not vibrating and there was no question that he was tapping his foot on the floor; once it seemed to me that the sound originated a few feet away from him but this may have been an auditory illusion.

I asked him to move to the other side of the room and to stand on the carpet as opposed to linoleum and again I stood close beside him. The 'taps' came, exactly as before, and even when I led him outside and we stood on the concrete in the back yard, the 'taps', still seeming to originate from his right foot, sounded *exactly* the same. I think it is significant that the sound was identical whether on lino, carpet or concrete, and this suggested to me that the sounds might be made consciously by Ian 'cracking' his foot or toes in some way and the more I thought about it, the more I felt that this might be the answer. The fact that the sound was always associated with his right foot, that the 'raps' were only heard when Ian was present, that he always had to stand for some little time before they came, thereby inducing a twitching in his leg (a sign of tension) and apparently a kind of light cramp – all this suggested to me that the 'taps' might not be of paranormal origin.

I had a slight accident with my right thumb many years ago when a cricket ball landed on the end of it and ever since this thumb has the habit of quickly going 'numb' if it is in one position for a little while and when I then bend it, to 'wake it up', it causes quite a loud 'crack'. It may be significant that the alleged entity we were investigating invariably sided with Ian in condoning his friendship with Margaret and I think it is possible that Ian began making those 'raps' as an entertainment or for amusement, only to find that the 'messages' were taken seriously, whereupon he continued to produce them. Certainly he seemed oddly embarrassed when producing them. On at least one other occasion Ian's feet had been the centre of apparent paranormal activity: when he was lying on a bed it was noticed that his toes were being bent about, backwards and forwards, backwards and forwards, and I suggest that this too points to the fact that he may have had unusual ability in his feet and been able to move his toes more than most people and that he moves them when he can to offset a tendency to slight cramp.

The fact that correct answers were obtained to leading questions does not unduly impress me, for talking to both the people concerned it seemed that just as many questions had been answered incorrectly; but, as with other apparent contact with psychic entities with many people, the incorrect elements of the contact were forgotten and only the hits were remembered. The only other apparently inexplicable happenings were the vague 'touchings and brushings' and 'slurred footsteps' heard by the occupant while she was alone in bed and I cannot help feeling that they may have been subjective and have a psychological origin, but further investigation might have established this one way or the other. By the same token practical investigation of the 'raps', such as a hand beneath Ian's bare foot when the 'raps' were occurring, ought to have established whether or not he was responsible but the opportunity for further investigation did not present itself and the case remains an interesting exercise, but perhaps one of the less puzzling cases that have confronted me.

FIRE-RAISING IN PECKHAM

What must have been a more vicious and dangerous entity seemingly manifested itself at the home of a young family in Trafalgar Avenue, Peckham some 20 years ago but a very typical example and an illustration of another of the poltergeist's favourite pranks: fire-raising. Graham and Vera Stringer were in their early thirties at the time and they had a young son, Steven, aged three. Before she was married Vera Stringer lived with her sister at New Cross and she told me that there a number of inexplicable happenings took place, usually around Easter each year.

One particular incident concerned the displacement of the lids from large china ornaments which stood on the mantlepiece; time and time again these were found removed from the vases and the lids, which had deep lips, were placed in the centre of the mantlepiece. For some time Vera and her sister took no notice, each thinking the other had been looking for something in the vases and had not replaced the lids. Eventually it transpired that in fact neither had removed the lids.

I was told that this happened scores of times for several weeks around Easter although the lids were never seen in movement. Then one night, just before Easter it was noticed, Vera and her sister decided to try and find out exactly what was happening and they sat up the whole of one night determined to watch the vases the whole time, but of course they dozed off and when they awakened, there the lids were in the middle of the mantlepiece! On this occasion Vera immediately attempted to replace the lids but found that she could not do so, even with the combined strength of both hands – 'something' seemed to be pushing up out of the vase and preventing the lid from going on; nor was her sister any more successful. After about five minutes they tried again and found no difficulty in replacing the lids.

At this time Vera's sister, who had always been rather afraid of the dark anyway, became distinctly frightened of the curious happenings that were continually taking place and she was really frightened when 'something' switched off her bedroom light just before one Easter, while she was undressing; not while she was removing her shoes or stockings but while she was pulling her dress over her head. Mrs Vera Stringer told me her sister was nowhere near the switch at the time and it was an enormous bedroom. It was not unusual for her sister to wake up in the middle of the night screaming out that she was certain that someone was standing beside her bed.

Soon after the Stringers married and moved into their combined first-and-second floor flat in Trafalgar Avenue, at 11 o'clock one night, three weeks before Easter, some toys belonging to their small son were found alight on a chair by the window in the living room. Mrs Stringer had gone up to bed ahead of her husband and Mr Stringer, after seeing that all was well, followed his wife up the curved stairs to their bedroom. He was no sooner out of the living room than his wife called out that she could smell smoke and he returned to find the room full of smoke and the toys ablaze. He was only out of the room for a moment and is convinced that a normal fire (though how any fire could have started is a mystery) would not have taken hold so quickly.

Just before the Easter holiday the same year Mr Stringer's mother brought some woollies for Steven and some stockings for Mrs Stringer. These were left on the table in the living room and on the Good Friday, first thing in the morning before a fire or stove or anything had been lit – before Mr Stringer even had time to light a cigarette – while Mrs Stringer and Steven popped out to get some hot cross buns, the woollies were found alight! They were burned right through the middle down to the bottom, although the stockings, which were under the woollies, were unharmed. On the Easter Monday there was another unexplained fire, this time in Steven's bedroom when woollen articles were again destroyed.

A grey transparent column was seen in several rooms by Mr Stringer, by his mother and, it is thought, by Steven who was too young at the time to say what it was that he saw when he continually pointed to one corner of his room and kept saying, 'Go away – go away'. This column was seen in Mr Stringer's dark room (he is a photographer) by himself and by his mother, at different times, and also in the hallway-cum-stairs by Mr Stringer.

Mrs Stringer had a book thrown at her in her husband's dark room; again it was not seen in movement but landed beside her when no one else was in the room. Also in the dark room Mr Stringer once had a box of photographic plates thrown to the ground. Again they were not seen in flight but they did not simply fall, they had to jump over a small ledge to get off the shelf they were kept on and they did not splay all over the floor when they landed but rested gently and neatly in a pile.

Once too, the milk disappeared from a milk bottle in the kitchen and once the front door was found open at 3 o'clock in the morning. On this occasion the Stringers' dog howled and showed every sign of being terrified. As Mr Stringer descended from the first floor, he found the dog backing away from the wide open door – howling as it backed up the stairs. Mrs Stringer added that it was a very friendly dog (which I can personally vouch for!) and had there been anyone at the door, she is certain the dog would have welcomed them!

Several times, after Mr Stringer had departed for work, Mrs Stringer heard distinct sounds as if the front door was being opened; of footsteps walking along the passageway, up the stairs and into the living room. Each time Mrs Stringer, having a little extra time in bed, thought that it must be her husband returning for something, and when she did not hear the footsteps go out again she got up, fully expecting to see her husband there, but no one was ever there and she never found anything to explain the sounds.

Once too at Trafalgar Avenue a pair of shoes were 'snatched' (Mr Stringer's own word) out of Mr Stringer's hands as he came downstairs one morning. He was half-way round the bend in the stairs when he dropped the shoes, he picked them up and as he did so they were snatched from his hands and went forward away from him, broke a window and fell back on the floor.

A Catholic priest visited the house to bless Steven and the whole property but this does not appear to have had any lasting effect, for on the following Tuesday an armchair was found ablaze in the living room. I examined the resulting fire stain on the floor and found it to be a yard in diameter. The carpet was also severely damaged and the linoleum burnt. Mrs Stringer smelt the burning after her husband had left for work and again the room was full of smoke in an incredibly short time.

The fire brigade was called and went to the wrong room, the main bedroom, which was also full of smoke, although the door of the living room had been closed. Eventually the source of the fire was found and it was put out, but the firemen were unable to ascertain the cause of the fire.

Called home from his business Mr Stringer was cutting the damaged carpet in his garden in an endeavour to salvage some of it while his wife took the curtains from the damaged room to the launderette, taking Steven with her, when Mr Stringer chanced to look up at the window of his dark room and saw the curtains alight!

He raced up and threw a couple of basins of water on the blaze but quickly saw that he was not going to be able to cope with it and again the fire brigade was called, and again they and the police were unable to discover any cause for the fire.

The Stringers were not insured against fire when I saw them for the simple reason they could not find a company who would insure them; they had been told they were too great a risk.

I examined the child's bedstead which was severely damaged in the most recent fire and it was obvious that the blaze had got a good hold before being extinguished; the bedding was severely burnt, and the curtains and parts of the window frame, since the bed was positioned directly beneath the window.

Summing up immediately after my visits I decided that it would have been possible for one of the occupants to have been responsible for practically all the incidents. The fires had either started in a room that person had recently left after being in there alone or while that person was completely alone in the house. On the other hand curious incidents for which the person was certainly not responsible had occurred and it seemed difficult to suggest how a transparent column was achieved, a phenomenon seen by only one witness. The column was seen to move and on one occasion Mr Stringer put his hand through the column and it remained there while he did so and afterwards. If, as seems most likely, this was a natural phenomenon, perhaps some trick of reflected light, this explanation could hardly apply when the column was seen in the dark room where there was no access for any kind of light, assuming that the door was securely closed at the time. It is perhaps curious that Mrs Stringer never managed to glimpse this 'phenomenon'; on two occasions she had been called when it was visible but each time it had disappeared before she could see it.

I found Mr Stringer anxious to impress with details of the incidents and several times his wife pulled him up by suggesting that such and such an incident could well have a normal explanation. I also found he quickly absorbed any poltergeist peculiarity that I discussed with him, after hearing the full story of the case, and such peculiarities would be included in recounting incidents later. I asked Mrs Stringer whether she was frightened of the happenings and she said she was because she didn't know when they were going to occur, the fires especially, and then she added rather oddly I thought and surprisingly, turning to her husband: 'Although it seems to affect Graham more, really'.

I felt Steven was too young at three to have been responsible for the fire incidents and there were no reports of movement of single objects such as one might expect if a child was responsible. He could, I suppose, have been responsible for the 'disappearance' of the milk but it is perhaps significant that the occupant of the ground floor flat of the house was entirely sceptical of any supernormal explanation for any of the incidents.

My considered opinion at the time and I have no reason to alter it since, is that the incidents attributed to poltergeist activity at the Trafalgar Avenue house were a combination of natural accidents which became coloured in the light of being possible poltergeist activity, and conscious and unconscious fraud.

INVESTIGATIONS IN WEST CROYDON

In the company of four reliable friends I spent eight hours of darkness at a reputedly haunted house in West Croydon several years ago, following reports of the frequent movement of objects, including heavy furniture, interference with beds and bedclothes, strange sweeping and dragging sounds from a rear downstairs room, doors opening and closing by themselves, inexplicable footsteps and screams and voices in each room of the house.

At the top of the stairs the figure of 'an old woman dressed in black' was reportedly seen by Janet, the ten-year-old daughter of the divorced tenant, who had waited nearly six years for a home of her own – they stayed one night! We were told that Janet had been thrown out of bed, bedclothes had been stripped off beds, footsteps had been heard from empty rooms, there had been the sound of someone dragging a sack, the ticking of an invisible clock, vases had been turned upside down and red marks had appeared on Janet's throat while she had slept. The tenant's sister confirmed to us that footsteps had sounded from empty rooms and she told us, 'Whatever is here, it doesn't sound like children'.

On arrival at the house in Waddon New Road, Croydon, we examined the whole house including the cupboard in the living room with its newly cemented floor where, we had been told, there used to be a cellar – but we discovered that there are no cellars to these properties; the house being a terraced cottage: two up and two down, and apparently almost identical with its neighbours. Although there is talk of the site once forming part of a burial pit for victims of the Great Plague, excavations in the roadway some years ago only brought to light bones of extinct mammals, nothing of human origin.

We visited each room in the house singly and collectively, and could only comment on the pleasant atmosphere throughout the house, although the vicinity of the bathroom did have a somewhat ominous air.

Having heard that a candle had flown across one of the rooms we arranged for lit and unlit candles to be in all rooms of the house at different periods; none of them showed any abnormality, although during the course of a number of seances which were held in the front room, the candle there dimmed and spluttered rather curiously at significant times during the impromptu attempts at communication and once or twice we heard slight noises we could not readily explain and one candle which had been left alight in the living room was found unlit although there was plenty of candle left and the wick was upright and relit without difficulty. We placed a clock in one of the bedrooms and rapped from time to time hoping for answering raps but without success.

Some of us took part in planchette and table-turning seances but practically nothing of significance occurred, although a couple of times the name 'Janet' seemed to come through, but the most puzzling incident during the seances took place after we had been asking numerous questions without getting any replies and then, quite suddenly, without anyone asking anything, we received the message: Y AR U HERE? Our replies to this and further attempts at communication proved abortive.

We found that most of the doors were ill-fitting which could account for them opening, closing or jamming, but we could offer no explanation for the alleged movement of furniture or the apparently paranormal removal of the bed-covers from two beds. Poltergeist activity is notoriously attracted to beds and bedrooms and stairways: in this respect the present case ran true to form; and there was the presence of the child. Often a young child or one in his or her teens is found to be associated with these curious happenings and it is not impossible that the 'geist' draws energy in some way from the child or that the child unconsciously exudes excess energy that can be used.

We had been told that a sweeping sound had been reported from the empty house, at other times described as a dragging sound, and we thought that a possible explanation for this noise, providing of course that no living person was in the house at the time, lay in the fact that the back door was a particularly bad fit at the base where the gap was wide enough to admit a good number of dry leaves which had collected inside the locked door. Wind playing through this gap upon the dry leaves could conceivably have produced a 'sweeping' noise. We discovered that the walls between adjoining houses were not sound-proofed, and the reported screams and other noises could have originated in a neighbour's house, either from some of the occupants or from the radio or television.

It was a cold night when we were there and it was certainly cold in the house, but not abnormally so. It has frequently been found that haunted houses are particularly cold – and this has been established scientifically. It has been suggested that the haunting entities draw the necessary energy for manifestations (such as the movement of furniture which obviously must use energy of some kind) from the atmosphere, leaving a cold spot, or cold room, or cold house. We did hear noises we could not explain, mostly from the vicinity of the top of the stairway where two of my party caught a brief glimpse of a dark human-like shape or form.

Although a railway runs nearby we found no undue vibration; there was some but it was slight. Our photographic and sound recording apparatus picked up no abnormality of any kind and while grateful for the opportunity of spending a night at the house we had to conclude that nothing in the nature of spontaneous psychic activity was in evidence during our visit; although I can still recall spending 30 minutes alone in the dark at the top of the stairs, with the feeling that 'something' might be behind me, something that might propel me head-first down the steep stairway at any minute, for it was here that the frightening form of the haunting entity reportedly manifested. I have long ago lost count of the haunted houses where I have spent hours and hours in darkness but that half-hour still brings a shudder to my mind.

THE ENFIELD CASE

The remarkable Enfield case in 1977–8 was expertly investigated by Maurice Grosse and Guy Lyon Playfair. Typical for a poltergeist the first recorded incidents were slight and they did not seem to be difficult to explain such as bangings on walls; but then furniture began to move, to turn over and to levitate without anyone being near it. Soon marbles zoomed around rooms like hornets, raps were seemingly answered, objects hurled across rooms and once a box hit Maurice Grosse on the head. Janet, the 12-year-old nexus of the disturbance, was levitated in full view and captured on film. Stones were thrown, pipes wrenched from walls, words scribbled in excrement, curtains swished off their rails and some whipped round Janet like a lasso; a goldfish and a budgie died inexplicably.

After the house was searched by the police the press got hold of the story and soon the case became one of the most exhaustively investigated and varied poltergeist infestations in the annals of psychical research and still, as with most poltergeist cases, the evidence is inconclusive.

The council house was occupied by a single parent and her four children, two girls and two boys, and the two girls seemed to be especially targeted: time after time they were tipped out of their beds and a remote control camera showed the sleeping girls having their bedclothes suddenly peeled back and the girls were 'spun' off their beds, waking up to find themselves on the floor. Sometimes this sort of thing happened as many as ten times in a single night. Soon apparitions were reported: a grey-haired lady, an old man and a child. In all 1500 apparently paranormal events were carefully logged and it may be significant that Janet was experiencing menstruation for the first time when the disturbances were at their height. In common with many poltergeist infestations the Enfield case seems to have been genuine at the beginning, but probably descended into conscious trickery later on.

THE BLACK MONK OF PONTEFRACT

Another classic poltergeist case has been investigated and documented by Colin Wilson, vice-president of the Ghost Club Society. Dating from 1966 it involved clouds of a grey-white powder, inexplicable pools of water, taps being turned on, toilets flooded, the materialisation of a green foam, kitchen utensils being interfered with, crashing sounds being heard, furniture and heavy objects being moved and the temperature dropping.

There were even physical attacks, bedclothes were pulled off beds, mattresses shot up into the air, unexplained perfumes pervaded the house and shadowy forms were seen, including a tall figure dressed in a black monk's habit with a cowl over the head. It looked solid enough but then suddenly disappeared.

One member of the family involved had just passed the age of puberty. It was all so typical and it typically ceased as mysteriously as it began, but the case of the Black Monk of Pontefract is a truly fascinating one and Colin Wilson wrote about it fully in his book *Poltergeist!*

OTHER POLTERGEIST EXAMPLES

Interestingly enough the activity is almost always mischievous and individually irritating to the family concerned. I recall investigating an outbreak of poltergeist activity that affected a rambling vicarage on Ham Common in London, where the vicar, a bachelor, always tried to be methodical and regulated, planning each hour of each day as far as he could. He used to set his alarm clock to awaken him an hour before he needed to rise in the morning and, on the pad he always had beside his bed, he would plan his day. When this was done he would turn over and have another half-an-hour in bed before getting up. But since the poltergeist had put in an appearance (so to speak) he could not have a clock in his bedroom because if he did he was kept awake all night by moans and whisperings, yet when there was no clock in the bedroom he slept soundly and was undisturbed. The only thing was of course that this meant he did not get to prepare his list of events for the day and so he was disorganised which he found very irritating and annoying.

I have personally come across a number of unhappy and frustrated young people in whose presence poltergeist activity occurred and I especially recall a case in 1991 in Hampshire where a fostered teenager resented the attentions showered on the daughter of the family and there was a case as recently as 1994 where an elderly widower felt he was unwanted and on the point of being put into a home by the rest of the family. In both cases the resentment, the unhappiness, the frustration of the position these people found themselves in resulted in an outbreak of uncontrolled and irrelevant activity that we call 'poltergeistic'.

In recent years the Rosenheim poltergeist case created considerable interest among psychic researchers. At a lawyer's office in Bavaria the epicentre was a teenage clerk, Anne-Marie Schaberl, who was tense, aggressive and unhappy with a tangled love life. Light bulbs exploded in her presence, lampshades fell to the floor, four telephone bells rang repeatedly at the same time, pictures rotated on the walls, drawers slid open by themselves, documents were moved and loud banging sounds were heard all over the building. On film Anne-Marie was seen walking along a corridor with the lights swinging and gyrating as she passed.

Professor Hans Bender of Freiberg University, an accepted authority on poltergeists, told me the phenomena only occurred when the girl was under stress and then the power supply in the building seemed to drain – quite inexplicably. Many of the Rosenheim disturbances were recorded on video-camera and among the expert investigators was Colin Wilson, vice-president of the Ghost Club Society. When Anne-Marie left the office the phenomena ceased, but ten years later she was still the subject of interest among her contemporaries and she still claimed she could not understand what had happened. Hans Bender's team concluded that the disturbances were caused by 'intelligently controlled forces that have a tendency to evade investigation' – which is an excellent description of poltergeist activity.

AUSTRALIAN EXAMPLES

There were two interesting and typical outbursts of poltergeist activity in Australia some years ago. In March 1957 farmer Alan Donaldson reported a mysterious gentle plopping of stones that seemed to come from nowhere, falling on his land at Pumphrey, Western Australia. For weeks the stones rained down and once, in front of their eyes, Donaldson's two sons claimed that stones fell on the floor of their tent, which did not have a tear or gap or any possible entrance for the stones. The pebbles were just ordinary stones, sometimes seeming warm to the touch. Scientists suggested at the time that the stones may have been swept into the air by freak gusts of wind.

Seven months later a more severe outbreak occurred on the farm of George Dickson at Boyup Brook, 180 miles from Perth, also in Western Australia. Heavy milk churns were flung considerable distances; a pair of rubber boots, missing for two days, were found at the top of a lemon tree; stones fell on open fields while ploughing was taking place; and other showers of stones fell while the farmer was feeding his pigs and milking his cows; he was also pelted with bones, tins and pieces of bark. Once, travelling at 40 miles an hour in his car with all the windows shut, stones fell inside the car and especially around Harvey, the 11-year-old son of the family. At the height of the disturbances Richie Ham, a TV cameraman and a feature writer from the *Melbourne Sunday Times*, spent a night at the farm and compiled a piece for television viewers in Australia which showed apparent poltergeist activity actually taking place.

Twenty-five years ago Ghost Club Society member Dr A.R. George Owen asked, in his monumental volume, *Can We Explain the Poltergeist?* (Helix, New York, 1964), 'Does the poltergeist originate in the conscious, the subconscious or the unconscious mind? Or is it a purely physiological function?' Sadly, a quarter of a century later we still don't know the answers to those pertinent questions. That poltergeist activity occurs cannot be denied, why it occurs is still largely unexplained, how it occurs still baffles us. Shall we be any the wiser 25 years hence, I wonder?

SELECT BIBLIOGRAPHY

Adams, Norman *Haunted Neuk: Ghosts of Aberdeen & Beyond* Tolbooth, 1994

Bardens, Dennis *Ghosts and Hauntings* Zeus Press, 1965

Bouchier, Chili *Shooting Star* Atlantis, 1996

Brooks, J.A. *Ghosts of London* Jarrold, 1982

Brown, Raymond L. *Phantoms of the Theatre* Satellite, 1978

Coran, Michael *Conan Doyle* Bloomsbury, 1995

Douglas, Alfred *Extra Sensory Powers* Gollancz, 1976

Hauck, William D. *National Directory of Haunted Places* Athanor, 1994

Higham, Charles *Kate: The Life of Katharine Hepburn* Norton, 1975

Kenward, Trevor *Sedgemoor and its Ghosts* Private, 1994

McAll, Kenneth *Healing the Haunted* Darley Anderson, 1989

McCarthy, Christine *Some Ghostly Tales of Shropshire* Shropshire Libraries, 1988

Norman, Michael & Beth Scott *Haunted America* Doherty, 1994

O'Donnell, Elliott *Trees of Ghostly Dread* Rider, 1958

Owen, George & Victor Sims *Science and the Spook* Dobson, 1971

Pennick, Nigel *Secrets of East Anglian Magic* Hale, 1995

Playfair, G.L. *This House is Haunted (the Enfield Poltergeist)* Souvenir, 1980

Senate, Richard *The Haunted Southland* Charon, 1994

Underwood, Peter *Gazetteer of British Ghosts* Souvenir, 1971
> *Gazetteer of Scottish & Irish Ghosts* Souvenir, 1973
> *The Ghost Hunters* Hale, 1985
> *Ghosts of Somerset* Bossiney, 1985
> *Haunted London* Harrap, 1973
> *Hauntings* Dent, 1977
> *Nights in Haunted Houses* Headline, 1994
> *No Common Task* Harrap, 1983
> *Queen Victoria's Other World* Harrap, 1986
> *This Haunted Isle* Dobby, 1993

Wilson, Colin *Poltergeist!* New English Lib., 1981

INDEX

A–Z of British Ghosts 75
Abbeville, Louisiana, USA 63
Aboriginals 65
Abyssinia, NE Africa 118–9
Adams, Matthew 102
Adelphi Theatre, London 41–2
Admiralty, British 161–2
Africa 38, 50, 101–2, 118–9, 151
Ahnstrom, Doris 164
Ainsworth, Harrison 110
Airship L8 148
Alamo, San Antonio, Texas, USA 124
Alan, AJ 185
Albany Evening Times 147
Albert Embankment, London 55–9
Albery Theatre, London 42
Alda, Frances 50
Aldershot, Hampshire 54–5
Alderton Hall, Loughton, Essex 81–2
Alexander, Hope 87
Alfieri, Count Vittoria 113
Alice Springs, Australia 19
Ambrose, Ernest 37
An Adventure 187
American Civil War 94–5, 168
American Indians 48, 95–6
Angel Hotel, Guildford, Surrey 52
Anglo-Zulu War 101–2
Angus, Scotland 20
Animals and ghosts 3, 26, 27, 30, 45,
    51, 52, 54, 68, 70, 71–2, 76, 77, 78,
    82, 86, 87, 107, 110, 111, 112, 114,
    128, 130, 131, 165–76, 192
Annan, Scotland 63
Antoinette, Queen Marie 187
Anton-Stevens, Revd Hugh 38–9
Anwyl-Davis, Dr 57
Arctic Ocean 158
Arthur, Lieutenant Desmond 152–3
Asgar the Steller 28
Aspley Guise, Bedfordshire 8–9
Astronomer Royal 178
Athenodorus (philosopher) 1
Athens, Greece 1
Atlantic Ocean 158, 162
Auckland, New Zealand 190
Australia 19, 50, 59–60, 65–6, 120,
    142, 148, 159–60, 166–8, 210–11
Avon 175
Avro Lancaster aeroplane 150
Avro Lincoln aeroplane 150–1
Ayers Rock, Alice Springs,
    Australia 19

Bacon, Terry 37
Baden Baden, Germany 63
Bainbrigge, Revd 37
Baker, Frederick 50
Balfour, Arthur 2
Ball, Captain Albert 148
Banbury, Oxfordshire 102
Bardens, Dennis 139

Baring-Gould, Revd Sabine 73
Barlow, Ambrose 143
Barnoldswick, Lancashire 37
Barnes, David 60
Bartlett, Alice 186
Barton, Jake 171
Basingstoke Canal, Hampshire 21
Bastwick Place, Norfolk 185
Bath 44, 154–6
Bath, Earl of 113
Battersea, London 8, 74, 88–93
Battle Farm, Edgehill,
    Warwickshire 106
Battle of Britain 150
Battle of Cedar Creek, Virginia,
    USA 94–5
Battle of Edgehill 102–6
Battle of San Pasqual, California,
    USA 97
Battle of Sedgemore 106–8, 118
Bavaria 19, 210
Bayham Abbey, Sussex 19
Bear Hotel, Woodstock,
    Oxfordshire 52
Beaumont Manor, Hertfordshire 112
Becket 46
Becket, Thomas à 55
Bedford, Duke and Duchess of 29–30
Bedford, 'Flying' Duchess of 148
Bedford, Mr and Mrs 186
Bedfordshire 8–9, 29–31
Beloff, Professor John 178
Belstead, Essex 52
Bender, Professor Hans 210
Benedictine order 143
Benson, Edward White 2
Bentine, Michael 37
Berkshire 110–111
Berry Pomeroy, Devon 19, 121–2
Bettiscombe Manor, Dorset 143–4
Betjeman, Sir John 38
Beverly Hills, Los Angeles, California,
    USA 128–9
Bickford, Gwyneth 79–81
Bide, Mr and Mrs Charles 56
Biggin Hill, Kent 150
Biggin Hill Flying Club 150
Bildeston, Suffolk 52
Binbrook, Lincolnshire 154
Bircham Newton, Norfolk 154
Bird Cage Inn, Thame,
    Oxfordshire 51
Black Death 55
Black Sally's Tree, Hyde Park,
    London 112–3
Black Shuck 169–70
Blackwood, Algernon 6
Blandy, Mary 116–7
Blickling Hall, Norfolk 33
Blood River, South Africa 102
Blue Posts Inn, Portsmouth,
    Hampshire 52

Bluebird 138–9
Bodmin Jail, Cornwall 53–4
Bodmin Moor, Cornwall 54
Boleyn, Anne 22, 30
Bolingbroke, Viscount Henry St
    John 91
Bolingbroke House, London 91
Bonaparte, Madame 188–9
'Bonnie Dundee'
    see Graham, Viscount John
'Bonnie' Prince Charlie
    see Stewart, Prince Charles Edward
Booth, John Wilkes 50
Bontida Castle, Translyvania 19
Borley Rectory and Church case 5,
    15, 37–8
Boscastle, Cornwall 51
Boswell, Nancy 173
Botley, Oxfordshire 186
Bouchier, Chili 44–51
Boulia, Queensland, Australia 142
Bourg, Guernsey, Channel Islands 98,
    180
Bowth, Sergeant Lyah 142
Boyup Brook, Western
    Australia 210–11
Bradford, Yorkshire 46
Bradshaw, Revd Arnold and Mrs
    Irene 67–73
Bramber, Sussex 19
Bramshill House, Hampshire 33
Bramshott, Hampshire 130
Brecon Beacons, Wales 156
Brede Place, Sussex 32–3
Brentwood, Los Angeles, USA 126–8
Bridgewater House, London 113
Bristol 25, 44, 45
Britannia Trophy 159
British Broadcasting Corporation 5,
    51, 87, 139, 162
British Museum, London 103
Broadstairs, Kent 133
Broadway, New York, USA 50
Brockenhurst, New Forest 85–87
Bromley-Davenport, Lt Col Sir
    Walter 23–4
Bromley-Davenport, William 23
Brooklands Racing Track 138
Broome, Theophilus 143
Brown, Tom 5, 8–9, 50–1, 170, 192
Buckeridge, Mrs Dennise 73
Buckingham Street, London 78–81
Buckinghamshire 74
Buckstone, John Baldwin 42
Bull, Sister Jacqueline 60
Bull Hotel, Long Melford,
    Suffolk 50–1
Bullet Hill, Edgehill,
    Warwickshire 106
Bungay, Essex 170
Burke, Norah 37
Burley, Idaho, USA 173

Burton, Lord 111
Burton Agnes Hall, Yorkshire 143
Bury St Edmunds, Suffolk 19, 37
Bush Hotel, Farnham, Surrey 51
Butler, Adele 79–81
Butler, Elizabeth 130
Buxton, Derbyshire 37

Caiden, Martin 145
Cairo Museum, Cairo, Egypt 136–8
Calgarth Hall, Cumbria 143
California, USA 88, 95–6, 97, 126–9
Calypso 123
Cambridge Military Hospital,
　Aldershot, Hampshire 54–5
Cambridge University 2
Cambridgeshire 52, 67–73, 189–90
Cameron, Sue 42
Camfield Place, Hertfordshire 131
Campbell, Catherine M 25
Campbell, Commander AB 162
Campbell, Donald and Tonia 138–9
Campbell, Sir Malcolm 138–9
Campbelltown, Australia 120
Can We Explain the Poltergeist? 211
Canada 109, 144, 154, 179
Canterbury, Archbishop of 2, 55
Cape Cod, USA 149
Cape of Good Hope, South
　Africa 161–3
Capesthorne, near Macclesfield,
　Cheshire 23–4
Caravan Rug Corporation 128
Carew, Lady Evelyn 185
Cartland, Dame Barbara 130–1
Cartman, Fred 140
Castle Hill, Edinburgh 20
Castle Theatre, Farnham, Surrey 42–3
Cecil, Winconson, USA 173
Cedar Creek, Virginia, USA 94–5
Cetewayo, King 102
Channel Islands 97–8, 179–81
Channel Islands Occupation
　Society 98, 179
Chaplin, Charles 47
Charles I, King 28, 102, 104
Charles II, King 28
Chateau Gratot, France 19
Cheales, Revd HS 37
Chelmsford, Essex 37
Cheltenham, Gloucestershire 25–7
Cheshire 23, 31–2, 85
Cheshunt, Hertfordshire 112
Chilton, Charles 37
Chilton Cantelo, Somerset 143
Chislehurst, Kent 138
Churchill, Lady 90–1
Churchill, Sir Winston 28, 32, 90,
　145–6
Civil War (English) 83, 102–6, 131
Clarence, Prince 162
Clarion, Hippolyte 48
Clark, Derek 192
Clarke, Arthur C 27
Cleopatra (ship) 162
Clevedon, Avon 175
Cleveland, Duchess of 113
Clift, Montgomery 127
Clifton, Bristol 25
Cochran, Washington County,
　USA 146
Cody and Adams 148
Coldness 15, 17, 30, 44, 48, 52, 53,
　56, 61, 78, 90, 127, 132, 146, 161,
　171, 196, 197–8, 207
Coldwater Canyon, Los Angeles,
　California, USA 128–9
Coleby Grange, Lincolnshire 154

Coleman, Dr Michael H 178
Coliseum Theatre, London 42
College of Psychic Studies, The 2, 5
Collins, Arthur 41
Collins Music Hall, London 42
Colorado, USA 139
Colt, Sir Henry 113
Comédie Française, Paris, France 48
Coniston Water, Cumbria 139
Cookson, Dame Catherine 165
Cooper, Jilly 172
Cook's Lane, Testwood,
　Southampton 77
Copenhagen, Denmark 19
Corfe Castle, Dorset 19
Cornell, Tony 17, 178
Cornwall 51, 53–4, 73–4
Cornwallis-West, George 28
Cosford RAF Museum,
　Shropshire 150–1
Courtney, Roger 118–9
Cousteau, Jacques 123
Coutances, France 19
Coward, Noël 47
Crawford, Earl Alexander of 20
Crete, Greece 181
Cromarty, Scotland 19
Cromer, Norfolk 170
Cromwell, Oliver 83
Croom-Hollingsworth, Geoffrey 37
Crowe, Catherine 3
Crown Hotel, Bildeston, Suffolk 52
Croydon, London 205–8
Cruickshank, George 110
Culloden Moor, Scotland 100–1
Cumberland, William Augustus, Duke
　of 101
Cumbria 74, 139, 143
Cutten, John 17

Dancing Years, The 40
Danmark Tree 109
Darracq racing car 138
Dartford, Kent 67
Dartmouth, Devon 154, 170
David, King of Scotland 21
Day, James Wentworth 41, 107, 169,
　171
de Manderville, Geoffrey 28
de Montfort, Earl Simon 21
De Morgan Collection 89
de Vos, Paul 37
Death in Hollywood 126
Denham, Matthew 185
Dening, Revd John 104, 189
Denmark 19
Dent, Anthony 175–6
Denver, Colorado, USA 139
der Decken, Captain Hendrikvan 161
Der fliegende Holländer 163
Derbyshire 37, 144
Despard, Captain and Mrs 25–7
Despard, Rosina 25–7
Devon 19, 52, 66, 121–2, 154, 170
Dickson, George 210–11
Dieppe, France 94
Dockacre House, Launceston,
　Cornwall 73–4, 75
Doenitz, Admiral Karl 162
Dolphin Hotel, Penzance,
　Cornwall 51
Dominion Road, Auckland, New
　Zealand 190
Donaldson, Alan 210
Dorset 19, 74, 143–4, 170
Dowding, Lord 3
Doyle, Sir Arthur Conan 96, 170
Drury Lane, London 38–42

Dublin 47
Duchy of Lancaster 60
Dudley, Captain 103
Dudley, Susanna 37
Dumfries, Scotland 63
Dundee, Scotland 99
Duns, Scotland 74
Duse, Eleanor 28
Dyfed, Wales 156–7
Dymond, Charlotte 54

Earhart, Amelia 148
'Earl Beardie' 20
Early, General 95
East Acton, London 38–9
Eastern Airlines 163–4
Eastwood, Flight Lieutenant
　Derek 151
Eclipse Inn, Winchester 51–2
Edgehill, Warwickshire 102–6, 163
Edinburgh, Scotland 20
Edward II, King 22
Edward III, King 22, 32
Edward IV, King 189
Edward VII, King 28, 110
Edward VIII, King 111
Egypt 134–8, 162
Egyptian State Broadcasting 136–8
Eleanor, Princess 21
Elizabeth I, Queen 73, 83, 87, 90,
　112, 113, 130
Ellison, Professor AJ 178
Elm Vicarage, Cambridgeshire 67–73
Emily's Bridge, New England,
　USA 63–5
Elizabeth Bay, Australia 60
Enfield haunted house 208
Engelback, Keeper of Cairo
　Museum 137
ENSA 41
Epping Forest, Essex 81
Essex 5, 15, 37–8, 51, 62, 81–2, 170,
　171
Ethie Castle, Tayside 74
Etty, William 79
Europe 108, 147, 157
Evans, Dame Edith 48
Everglades, Florida, USA 163
'Everlasting bloodstains' 73–4, 75
Evitt, Father 37

Fairfield, Dr Letitia 35, 87
Farnham, Surrey 42–3, 51, 74
Farnham Castle, Farnham, Surrey 43,
　74
Farouk, King of Egypt 137
Farson, Dan 191
Fatal Cherry Tree 109
Fell, William 171
Ferguson brothers 63
Ferry Boat Inn, Cambridgeshire 52
Fielding, Beau 113
Fife, Scotland 181–3
Fifth Helena Drive, Brentwood, Los
　Angeles, California, USA 126–8
Finley, Foster 48
First World War 37, 42, 53, 78, 103,
　111, 140, 144–5, 148, 150, 152–4,
　181–3
Fisher, Fred 120
Fisher's Ghost Creek, Campbelltown,
　Australia 120
Fitton family 31
Fleming, Revd Kingsley R 59
Florida, USA 48–9, 163
Flying Dutchman 161–3
Foggin, Major Cyril 152
Folklore Society 191

Forbes, Malcolm and family 8, 88, 89
Ford's Theatre, Washington, USA 50
Forest of Illusion 118–9
Fotheringay, Cambridgeshire 189–90
Foundation for Research on the Nature
  of Man 16
Four Sisters Crossroads, Suffolk 61–2
Fox sisters 2
France 19, 29, 48, 94, 102, 133, 148,
  187–8
Frangocastello, Crete 181
Frankfurt, Germany 63
Fraser, John 185
Fraser, Simon, Lord Lovat 101
Frederici (Frederick Baker) 50
Freiberg University, Germany 210
French, Mr 56–7
French Revolution 187
Frewen, Roger Moreton 32–3
Frewer, Edwin 56–7
Fu Manchu 107
Fuller, John 163–4
Fuller, Robert, Joseph, Harold and
  Tom 170
Futter, Elaine 45

Gaddis, Vincent 95
Gallipoli campaign 140
Gamma rays 184
Garlick Hill, London 38
Garrick, David 40
Gatti-Casazza, Guilio 50
Gatwick, Surrey 160–1
Gauld, Dr Alan 17, 178
Gaulden Manor, Tolland,
  Somerset 82–85
Gawsworth Hall, Cheshire 31–2
Gawsworth Old Rectory, Cheshire 31
Gedi, NE Africa 118–9
George V, King 162
Germany 63, 97, 102, 103, 109,
  144–5, 148, 150, 154, 179–81, 210
Getty, Paul 3, 87–8
Ghost Club Society, The 2, 5, 81,
  107, 108, 151, 170, 208, 210, 211
Ghost of Flight 401 163–4
Ghost photographs 147
Ghost Society, The 2
Ghosts of the Air 145
Ghosts of the Broads 183–5
Gielgud, Sir John 47
Gladstone, Mrs Augusta 186, 187
Glamis, Lady 20
Glamis Castle, Scotland 20–1, 33
Glasgow, Scotland 47, 101, 160
Gloucestershire 25–7, 37, 74, 172
Godfrey, Sir Theodore 112
Godl, John 65–6
Goff's Oak, Theobalds,
  Hertfordshire 112
Gold Brook Bridge, Stowe,
  USA 63–5
Gold Brook Road, Stowe, USA 63–5
Goldberg, Dr Oskar 39
Goldney, Mrs KM 'Mollie' 35
Goldsmith family 28–9
Goldston, Will 140–1
Goodman Field airbase, USA 149
Goodwin, Cliff 165
Gordon, Peter 43
Graham, Viscount John 99
Grand Central Hotel, London 185–7
Grant, Major 112
Granville, Dowager Countess 20
Graves, Robert 3, 121
Grayson, Lieutenant 145
Great Fire of London 55

Great Leighs, Essex 51
Great Missenden Abbey,
  Buckinghamshire 74
Great Plague 55
Greece 102, 181
Greek War of Independence 181
Green, Martin 156
Green Park, London 113–5
Greenwich, London 74
Gregorian calendar 189
Grenadier, Hyde Park Corner,
  London 51
Gresley, Sir Nigel 28
Griffith, Anne 143
Grimaldi, Joey 41, 42
Grosse, Maurice 208
Guernsey, Channel Islands 98,
  179–81
Guildford, Surrey 52, 87–8
Guinness, Sir Alec 47
Gurre Castle, Denmark 19
Gwynne, Nell 28–9

Haldeman, Dr and Mrs JN 159–60
Halifax, Lord 20
Hallness, George 185
Hallowe'en 184, 191–2
Ham, Richie 211
Ham Common, Greater London 209
Hamilton, General Sir Ian 140
Hamlet 2
Hampshire 19, 21, 22–3, 33, 42,
  51–2, 54–5, 130, 209
Hampstead, London 52, 74
Hampton Court Palace 33
Hanging Tree, The 116–7
Harding, Laura 129
Hardy, Thomas 82
Harlaxton Manor, Lincolnshire 33
Harley Street, London 183
Harlow, Essex 37
Harman Trophy 159
Harrison, Dr Vernon 89, 178
Harrison, Miss 165
Haslitt, Sir Godfrey 185
Hastings acroplane 155
Haunted House', 'The, (poem) 2
Haunted London 114
Haunting of Toby Jug, The 133
Hawaii 102
Haymarket Theatre, London 42
Heath, Mrs Irene 61–2
Heddon Oak, Somerset 118
Hendon RAF museum 150, 156
Hendry, Alexander 153
Henley-on-Thames,
  Oxfordshire 116–7
Henley Town Hall, Oxfordshire 117
Henning, Revd AC 37
Henry, Marquess of Tavistock 29
Henry I, King 21, 22, 38
Henry VIII, King 30
Hepburn, Katharine 129
Herle, Nicholas and Elizabeth 73–4
Herne the Hunter 110–1
Herne's Oak, Windsor Great
  Park 110–1
Hertfordshire 3, 19, 28–9, 46, 74,
  111, 112, 131, 191–2
Higham, Charles 129
Hine, Reginald 191
Hislett, Miss 141–2
Hitler, Adolf 162
Holden, Jim 63–4
Hole, Christina 191
Hollywood, USA 122, 126–9

Hollywood Boulevard, Los Angeles,
  California, USA 127
Holmes, Major PL 153
Holmsley South Airfield 154
Holy Trinity Church, York 38
Holzer, Hans 127
Home Office 53
Homes and Gardens 166
Honington, East Anglia 154
Hood, Thomas 2
Hopkins, Thurston 143
Hound of the Baskervilles 170
Howard, Charlie 186
Howard, Richard 195
Hull, Yorkshire 193–4
Hunter, Mrs 84–5
Hurricane aeroplane 150, 152
Hurton, Julie 173
Hutchins, Lynn 123–6
Hyde Park, London 112–3
Hyde Park Corner, London 51

Idaho, USA 173
'Ignatius the Bell Ringer' 70–73
Illinois, USA 147
India 109
International Ghost Society, The 2
Ipswich, Suffolk 61
Ireland 102
Irving, Sir Henry 46
Isabella, Queen 22
Isandlwana, Eastern Zululand, South
  Africa 101–2
Island Observer Corps 63
Isle of Man 168–9
Isle of Skye, Scotland 63
Italy 113, 131

Jacobites 99–100
James II of Scotland, King 20
Japan 148
Jeans, Sir James 178
'John, Father' 33
John, King 21, 22
Johnson, Amy 148
Jones, Betty Jo 41
Joy, Sir George 188
Julius Caesar 2

Karloff, Boris 128–30
Kean, Charles 41
Keating, Rex 136–7
Keble College, Oxford 67
Kelstern, Lincolnshire 154
Kemp, James 20
Kenneth, George 9
Kensington, London 79, 130
Kent 44, 67, 133, 138, 150
Kent, Robert H 111
Kenton Theatre, Henley-on-
  Thames 116–7
Kentucky, USA 149
Kenward, Trevor J 107–8
Kettles, Alex 153
Kew Bridge, Surrey 194–5
Kiely, John 179
Kiernander, Steuart 37
Killiecrankie, Battle of 99–100
Killiecrankie Pass, Scotland 99–100
Kimbolton 154
Kineton, Warwickshire 103, 104
Kingsford-Smith, Sir Charles
  Edward 148
Kingsmill, Captain 104
Kingston Seymour, Avon 175
Kipling, Revd Stanley C 37
Kipling, Rudyard 143
Kirke, Colonel Lewis 102
Knightsbridge, London 130

La Vassalerie, Channel Islands 98
Lafayette, Louisiana, USA 63
Lake Oswego, Oregon, USA 146
Lake Superior, USA 149
Lamb, Michael 45
Lambeth, London 55–9
Lancashire 37, 143, 144
Langenhoe, Essex 36, 104
Lanzarote, Spain 160
Lauder, Harry 47
Lauceston, Cornwall 73–4
Laurbruch, Germany 154
Laurel and Hardy 47
Lavater, Lewes 1
Lazenby, Kenneth BH 89
Le Fevre, Sheila 45
Le Gendre Starkie, Mr and Mrs
    James 82–5
Legge, Mrs Walter, JP 111
Leinster, The 103–4
Leno, Dan 39, 41, 47
Les Rouvets Farm, Guernsey, Channel
    Islands 98, 179
Leslie, Sir Shane 20
L'Estrange, Guy, JP 37
Levens Hall, Cumbria 74
Lincoln, President Abraham 2, 50,
    147
Lincolnshire 33, 42, 154
Lindbergh, Charles 157–8
Lisle, Lady Alice 51–2
Little Baldwin Creek, Washington
    County, USA 146
'Little Gatton', near Reigate,
    Surrey 138
Llandeilo, Wales 156–7
Llandovery, Wales 156–7
Lloyd, Marie 46, 47
Lock, Lt. Gen. Sir Kenneth 87
Loft, Captain Bob 164
London 8, 15, 28, 33, 36–7, 38–42,
    45, 51, 52, 55–9, 74, 78–81, 88–93,
    103, 105, 107, 112–5, 122–3,
    131–3, 148, 150, 156, 172, 183,
    185–7, 193, 201–8
London Bridge, London 103
London Palladium 42
London University 15, 37
Long Beach, Los Angeles,
    USA 145–6
Long Melford, Suffolk 37, 50–1
Longleat, Wiltshire 74
Los Angeles, USA 145–6
Louda, JC 112
Loughton, Essex 81–2
Louis XIV, King 187
Louisiana, USA 63
Lowry, Dan 47
Lupino, Ida 41, 122–3
Lupino, Stanley 41, 122–3
Luton Area Assessment Board 9
Lyme Regis, Dorset 170
Lyndhurst, New Forest 133
Lyric Theatre, Wellingborough,
    Northants 45–6

McAll, Revd Dr Kenneth 95–6, 98,
    171–2
Macbeth 2
McCaldin, Patricia 88, 91–3
Macclesfield, Cheshire 23
McEvoy, Mrs E 181–3
MacGregor, Alasdair Alpin 21, 60,
    89–90, 120
McIntosh, Ian G 153
Mackay, General 99
Macklin, Charles 41
MacLiammor, Michael 48
McQuary, Laurie 146–7

Magicians' Circle 140
Magna Carta 21
Maiden Lane, London 42
Mallaig, Scotland 101
Manderston House, Duns,
    Scotland 74
Mannheim Forest, Germany 109
Mansfield, Barbara 45
Mansfield, Sir Peter 152
Mantell, Captain Thomas 149
Maple, Eric 81–2, 144
Marceau, Marcel 47
March, Eve 129
Margate, Kent 44
Marlborough, Wiltshire 101
Marlborough, Duke of 91
Marlborough Theatre, London 42
Marshall, Samuel 103
Marston Moor, Yorkshire 106
Martin, Harry 42
Mary Blandy's Tree, Henley-on-
    Thames, Oxfordshire 116–7
Mary Queen of Scots 52, 189
Mason, Kenneth 39
Matthews, Jessie 48
Matthews, Maria 37
Maude, FR 87
Mauretania 138
May, John 37
May, Prebendary Clarence 36–7
Medical Directory, The 183
Medical Register, The 183
Mee, Arthur 21
Melba, Dame Nellie 28
Melborough Camp,
    Warwickshire 104
Melbourne, Australia 50
Melbourne Sunday Times 211
Memphis, Tennessee, USA 49–50
Merlin aeroplane engine 150, 154
Merry Wives of Windsor 110
Messerschmitt aeroplane 150
Metaphysical Society 2
Metropolitan Opera House, New York,
    USA 50
Metropolitan Theatre, London 42
Mexico 97, 102
'Michaeli' see Romney-Woollard,
    Michael
Midland Hotel, Bradford 46
Mill Hotel, Sudbury, Suffolk 174
Miller, Glenn 148
Miller, William 173
Millvale Church, Pittsburgh, USA 39
Min Min Lights 142
Ministry of Civil Aviation 152
Ministry of Defence 155
Minsden Chapel (ruins)
    Hertfordshire 19, 191–2
Minshall, Bert 124
Mirus gun site, Guernsey, Channel
    Islands 98, 179
Monmouth, Duke of 107, 118
Monroe, Marilyn 126–8
Montagu, Sir John 28
Montrose, Scotland 152–4
Montrose Aeroplane Museum
    Society 152–4
Moore, Philip 89, 151
Morar Loch, Scotland 101
Morgan, Joan 116
Morning Glory 129
Morris, David 42
'Morton' ghost 25–7
Mosquito aeroplane 150
Mt Albert Road, Auckland, New
    Zealand 190
Moyses, Dennis 89

Murphy, Andrew and Dorothy 160–1
Myers, Arthur 64, 125
Myers, John 127

NAFFI (services canteen) 152
Napoleon 23, 46, 51, 188–9
National Army Museum 102
Nativity Wood, Scotland 109
New College, Oxford 12
New Cross, London 201
New England, USA 63
New Forest 85–7, 96, 133
New Orleans, USA 129
New Park Manor, Brockenhurst, New
    Forest 85–7
*New Treatment for Rheumatism and
    Allied Disorders* 184
New York, USA 49, 50, 157, 172
New York Times 115
New Zealand 190
Newark Park, Gloucestershire 74
Newport, Shropshire 115–6
Newport Harbour, Rhode Island,
    USA 123–6
Night Side of Nature 3
Nightingale, Florence 55
Nights in Haunted Houses 121–2
Norfolk 33, 74, 154, 170, 171,
    183–5
Norfolk Broads 183–5
Norman, Michael 48
Norman Conquest 28
North American Space Agency 158–9
North Korea 142
North Pole 158
Northamptonshire 45, 52
Northcote, Cornwall 73
Norwich Cathedral, Norwich,
    Norfolk 185

Odiham, Hampshire 19, 21
O'Donnell, Elliott 191
O'Farrell, Charles 50
Old Battersea House, London 8, 74,
    88–93
Old Inn, Widecombe-in-the-Moor 52
'Old Jimmy Garlick' 38
Old Shires, The, Elm,
    Cambridgeshire 67–73
Old Silent Inn, Stanbury,
    Yorkshire 52
Old Talbot Hotel, Worcester 173
Old Vic Theatre, London 42
'Old Willie' (aeroplane) 144
Olympia Theatre, Dublin 47
*On Ghosts and Spirites Walking by
    Night* 1
Oregon, USA 146
Orpheum Theatre, Memphis,
    USA 49–50
Osborne, Mrs AM 171
Otis Air Base, Cape Cod, USA 149
Oundle, Northamptonshire 52
Owen, Dr George 24, 31, 211
Oxenbridge family 32
Oxfordshire 12, 51, 52, 67, 116–7,
    186, 187

Pacific Islands 108
Palace Theatre, Watford,
    Hertfordshire 46–7
Palazzo Bonaparte, Rome 188–9
Panorama 139
Panton, Colonel 168
Paramount Studios, Los Angeles,
    USA 126
Paris, France 48, 187

Patricia Hayes School of Inner Sense Development 125
Peckham, London 201–5
Peel, Sir Robert 113
Peel Castle, Isle of Man 168–9
Penzance, Cornwall 51
Pepys, Samuel 79–81
Perrott, Tom 195
Perth, Provost of 20
Perth, Western Australia 210
Perthshire, Scotland 99–100
Petit Trianon, Versailles, France 187
'Phantom music' 10
'Pigg, Margaret' 92
Pigott, Madame 115–6
Pinney, Mr and Mrs Michael 144
Pittsburgh, USA 39
Pittville Circus Road, Cheltenham 25–7
Playfair, Guy Lyon 208
Pliny the Younger 1
Plymouth University 66
Pocock, Tom 79
Poe, Edgar Allan 2
Pontefract, Yorkshire 208–9
Pontefract Castle, Yorkshire 189
Polly 176
Poltergeist! 209
Poltergeist activity 11, 17, 193–211
Pontius Pilate 22
Pope, WJ Macqueen ('Popie') 39–41
Port Elizabeth, South Africa 38
Portchester Castle, Hampshire 19, 22–3
Portsmouth, Hampshire 52
Potter Heigham, Norfolk 184–5
Pretoria, South Africa 159
Price, Harry 41
Price, Professor Henry Habberley 12
Priest, Bill 104
Priest, Mr and Mrs 190
Prince Alfred Hospital, Sydney, Australia 59–60
Princess Theatre, Melbourne, Australia 50
Psychic Research Organisation, The 2, 5
Public Records Office 106
Pumphrey, Western Australia 210
Pungsan, North Korea 142
Putney Common, London 172

Quarantine Station, Sydney Harbour, Australia 65–6
Queen Alexandra Imperial Nursing Service 55
Queen Mary 145–6
Queen Mother 20
Queen's House, Greenwich, London 74
Queensland, Australia 142

Raegan, Ronald 125
RAF Colerne, Bath 154
Rahere 38
Randall, Miss 118–9
Ray, Laurence 43
Raynham Hall, Norfolk 74
Regensberg, Bavaria 19
Reigate, Surrey 138
Rendlesham, Lady 171
Repo, Don 163–4
Rhode Island, USA 123–6
Rhodes, Edward 63–5
Rice, Ann 117–8
Richard Duke of York 189–90
Richard II, King 22, 110
Richards, HW 9
Richards, Raymond and Monica 31

Richmond, Surrey 19
Richthofen, Baron von 148
Ricketts, Mrs JM 76
Robbins, Revd John 199
Robert the Bruce 21
Robinson, Mr and Mrs Horace 107
Rohmer, Sax and Elizabeth 107, 138
Roll, William G 125
Rome, Italy 188–9
Romney-Woollard, Michael 105
Roosevelt, Franklin D 6
Roosevelt Hotel, Hollywood Boulevard, Los Angeles, USA 127
Rorke's Drift, South Africa 102
Rose, Charles Hugh 107
Rose Hall, Sarratt, Hertfordshire 3–4
Rosenheim, Bavaria 210
Rosyth, Fife, Scotland 181–183
Roughtor, Bodmin Moor, Cornwall 54
Roundabout, Bramshott, Hampshire 130
Roy, Professor AE 178
Royal Air Force 67, 144, 150, 152–4, 156
Royal Flying Corps 152
Royal Maritime Auxilliary Service 154–6
Royal Photographic Society 89
Rumasa, (formerly Testwood House) 75–8
Runnymead, near Egham, Surrey 21
Rupert, Prince 104
Russell family 29
Russia 97, 180
Rutley, Henry 42

Sadler's Wells Theatre, London 42
St Albans, Duke of 28
St Albans, Hertfordshire 28
St Anne's Castle Inn, Great Leighs, Essex 51
St Anthony's Day 184
St Bartholomew's the Great, London 38
St Dunstan's Church, East Acton, London 38–9
St Helena, S. Atlantic Ocean 188–9
St James's Church, Garlick Hill, London 38
St James's Park, London 113
St James's Theatre, London 42
St Mark's Day 184
St Martin's Lane, London 42
St Mary Overy's Priory 55
St Mary's Collegiate Church, Port Elizabeth, South Africa 38
St Sampson's, Guernsey, Channel Islands 179
St Thomas's Church, Regent Street, London 36–7
St Thomas's Hospital, London 55–9
Salisbury Hall, St Albans, Hertfordshire 28–9, 74
Sampson, Dr Charles 183–5
San Antonio, Texas, USA 124
San Diego County, California, USA 97
San Francisco, USA 148
San Pasqual, San Diego County, USA 97
San Pasqual Battlefield Park, USA 97
Sarratt, Hertfordshire 3
Saunders, St John 37
Screaming Phantom of Mannheim Forest 109
Schaberl, Anne-Marie 210
Schwarzenberg Fortress, Bavaria 19

Scotland 20–1, 47, 63, 74, 99–101, 109, 141, 152–4, 160, 181–3
Scott, James Duke of Monmouth 107
Scott, Sheila 158–9
Scott, Sir Walter 147
Scottish Television 47
Second World War 33, 41, 53, 55, 56, 76, 94, 97–8, 111, 136, 144, 146, 150–1, 152–4, 156, 158, 162
Security Council, United Nations 39
Sedgemoor, Battle of (site), Somerset 106–8, 118
Sellers, Peter 98
Senate, Richard 97
Seymour, Dr Percy 66, 178
Shakespeare, William 1, 2, 31, 110
Sharpe, Becky 44
Shaw, Sebastian 22
Shaw, Shirley 89
Shedfield Cottage, Botley, Oxford 186
Shepherd, Lieutenant 150
Shepton Mallet Prison, Somerset 52–3
Sheridan (American commander) 94–5
Sheridan, Clare 33
Sheridan, Dick 33
Shields, Mary 140
Shooting Stars 44
Shropshire 115–6
Siddons, Sarah 45
Simons, Jon 37
Skull House, Lancashire 144
Skulls, haunted 143–4
Sligachan, Isle of Skye, Scotland 63
Smith, John 63
Society for Psychical Research 2, 5, 9, 16, 17, 37, 89, 94, 185–7
Society of Apothecaries 184
Somerset 52–3, 82–5, 106–8, 117–8, 131, 144, 170
South Africa 38, 50, 101–2, 159, 161–3
Southampton, Hampshire 75–78
Southern Pacific Railway 146–7
Southgate, Mrs E 62
Spaniards Inn, Hampstead Heath 52
Spain 95–6, 160–1
Spelman, Charles 140
Spelman, Emerson 140
Spelman, RJ 140
Spinney Abbey, Cambridgeshire 170–1
Spirit of Oregon (train) 146–7
Spirit of St Louis (aeroplane) 158
Spitfire aeroplane 150
Squiers, Glanville 87
Stamford Theatre, Lincolnshire 42
Stanbury, Yorkshire 52
Steele, Vickie and Bob 146
Stevens, William Oliver 172
Stewart, Prince Charles Edward, 'Bonnie Prince Charlie' 100-1
Stirling, Wilhelmena 89–93
Stone-tape theory 12, 19–20
Stour, River 174
Stowe, Vermont, USA 63–5
Stowe Historical Society 63
Stradishall Manor, Suffolk 37
Strand, London 41–2
Stratford St Mary, Suffolk 61–2
Strathmore, Lord 20
Stringer, Graham and Vera 201–5
Strubby, Lincolnshire 154
Subconscious Activities 184
Sudbury, Suffolk 174
'Sudbury Cat' (mummified) 174

Suez, Egypt 162
Suffolk 19, 37, 50–1, 52, 61–2, 67, 105, 174
Summer Hill, Sydney, Australia 65
Surrey 19, 21, 42–3, 51, 52, 87–8, 138, 160, 194–5
Sussex 19, 32–3, 107, 140, 143
Sutton Place, Surrey 87–8
Swinhoe, Mr and Mrs Henry 25–7
Sydney, Australia 59–60, 65–6, 120

Talana, South Africa 102
Talbot Hotel, Oundle, Northamptonshire 52
Tampa Theatre, Florida, USA 48–9
Tauber, Richard 115
Taunton Priory, Somerset 83
Taylor, Professor John 15, 37
Taylor, Sir Charles MP 23
Tayside, Scotland 74
Tempest aeroplane 150
Tennessee, USA 49–50
Terriss, Ellaline (Lady Hicks) 41
Terriss, William 41
Testwood House, Totton, Hampshire 75–8
Texas, USA 124
Thackeray, William Makepeace 44
Thame, Oxfordshire 51
Theatre Royal, Bath 44
Theatre Royal, Bradford, W.Yorkshire 46
Theatre Royal, Bristol 44
Theatre Royal, Drury Lane, London 39–41
Theatre Royal, Glasgow 47
Theatre Royal, Margate, Kent 44
Theatre Royal, Portsmouth 42
Theobalds, Hertfordshire 112
Thompson, Florence 9
Thorne, Sarah 44
Tich, Little 47
Tilley, Vesta 47
Timbs, John 103
Tolland, Somerset 82–5
Tollesbury, Essex 171
Totton, Southampton, Hampshire 75–8
Tourmaline (ship) 162
Tower of London 83
Tower Hill, London 107
Towy Valley, Wales 156–7
Trafalgar Avenue, Peckham, London 201–5
Translyvania 19
TriStar jet airliner 163–4
Tunstead Farm, Derbyshire 144
Turberville family and phantom coach 82–4
Turberville, James, Bishop of Exeter 83
Turkey, Europe/Asia 181

Turner, James 37
Turpin, Dick 52, 82
Tutankhamun, King 134–8
Typhoon aeroplane 150

UFOs 149
Unitarian Society for Psychic Studies 2
United States of America 8, 16, 39, 41, 42, 48–50, 53, 63–5, 88, 89, 92, 94–7, 108, 123–9, 139–40, 145–7, 148, 149, 154, 157, 158–9, 163–4, 168, 173

Vallender, Grant 37
Valley of the Kings, Egypt 136
Vanity Fair 44–5
Vaughan family 170
Veidt, Conrad and Lily 131–3
Veiller, Mr and Mrs Bayard 172
Verba, Helen 139–40
Vermont, USA 63–5
Verney, Sir Edmund 103
Versailles, France 187–8
Victoria, Queen 42, 79, 110, 141–2
Virginia, USA 94–5

Waddon New Road, Croydon 205–8
Wagner, Richard 163
Wainsman, Captain 103
Wales 156–7
Walford, John 117–8
Walford's Gibbet, Somerset 117–8
Walker, Stuart 99–100
Warbleton Priory, Sussex 143
Wardley Hall, Lancashire 143
Warwick Recording Society 104
Warwickshire 102–6, 154
Warwickshire Regiment 102
Washington, USA 50, 124–5, 146, 147
Washington Post, The 64
Watford, Hertfordshire 46
Watling, Jack, Deborah, Nicola and Giles 81–2
Wayne, John 123–6
Wazny, Nancy 145
Webster, Norrie 153
Weeks, Matthew 53–4
Wellesbourne Mountford, Warwickshire 154
Wellingborough, Northants 45
Wellington aeroplane 150, 156–7
Wellington Hotel, Boscastle, Cornwall 51
Weston Manor Hotel, Weston on the Green, Oxfordshire 52
Weston on the Green, Oxfordshire 52
West, Dame Rebecca 35
West, Dr Donald J 9

West, Violet 45
Wheatley, Dennis 3, 133–4
Whitby, Yorkshire 75–6
Whitchurch 154
White House, The, Washington, USA 124–5
White House Road, Edgehill, Warwickshire 104
Whitney, Bill 170
Whyle, JW 101
Wicken Fen, Cambridgeshire 170–1
Wickham St Paul, Suffolk 174
Widecombe-in-the-Moor, Devon 152
Wild Goose, The 123–6
Wild Hunt 169–70
Will, Mrs IE 166–8
William III, King 99
William the Conqueror 28, 112
Willis, Revd Tom 193–4
Wilshire Boulevard, Los Angeles, USA 128
Wilson, Colin 208–9, 210
Wilson, Mr and Mrs and Vivienne 37
Wiltshire 74, 101
Winchester 51–2
Winconson, USA 173
Windsor, Berkshire 110–1
Windsor Great Park, Berkshire 110–1
Windy Oaks, Shropshire 115–6
Wisbech, Cambridgeshire 67
Woburn Abbey, Bedfordshire 29–31
Wolfeton House, Dorset 74
Women's Auxiliary Air Force 154
Wood, William, JP 103
Woodfield, Aspley Guise, Bedfordshire 8–9
Woodstock, Oxfordshire 52
Wookey, Eric E 87
Wootton, Lt. Col. Patrick A 179–80
Worcester 173
Worrall, George 120
Wright, Basil 154–6
Wrotham, Kent 67
Wyatt, Sir Thomas 113
Wyck Rissington, Gloucestershire 37
Wyndham, Sir Charles 42

Yachtsman Publishing Company 183–5
York 38, 193
York, Archbishop of 193
Yorkshire 52, 106, 143, 175–6, 189, 193–4, 208–9

Zeals House, Wiltshire 74
Zener or ESP cards 9, 16, 195
Zulu 102
Zululand, Eastern South Africa 101–2